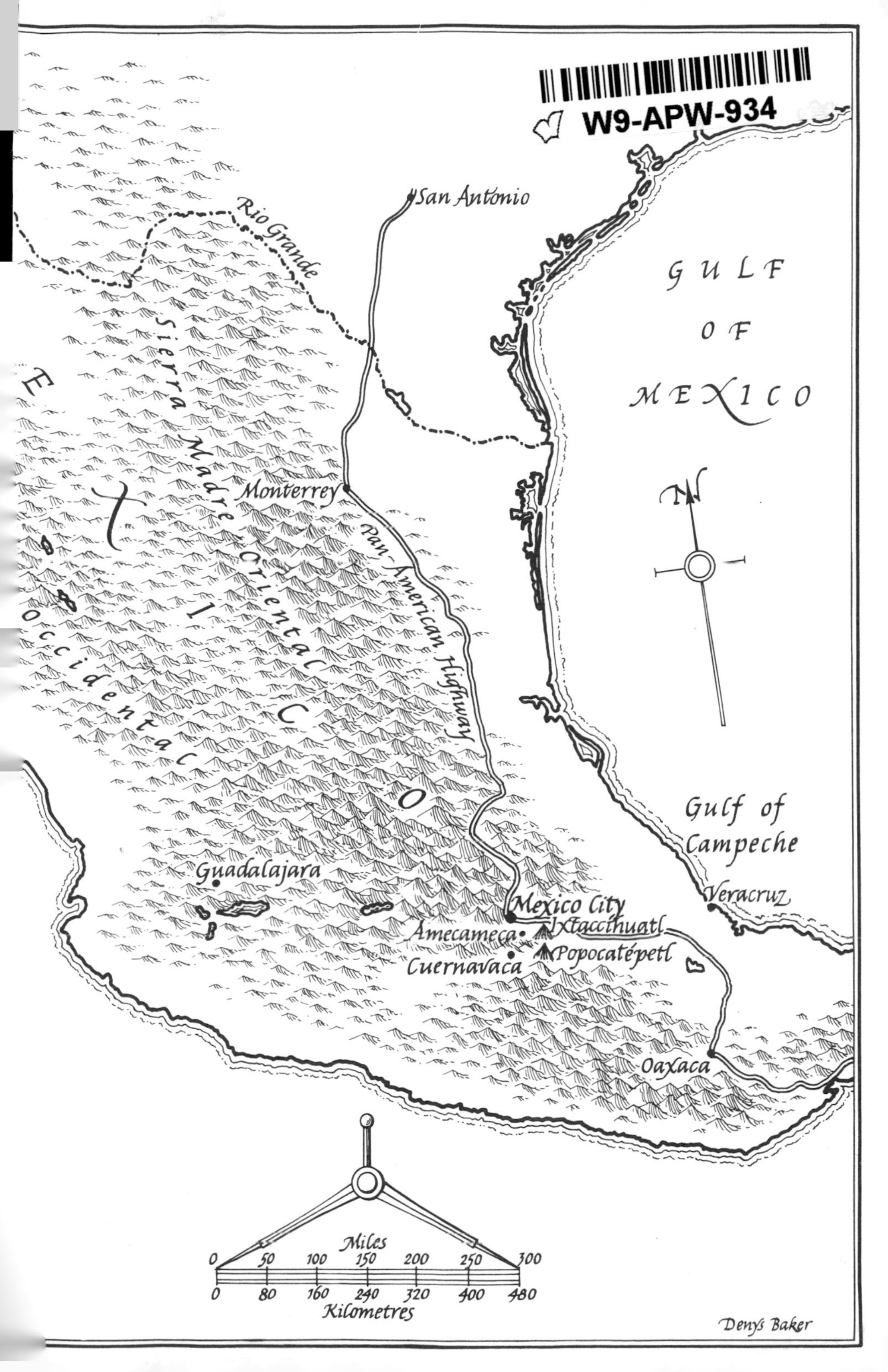

W9-APW-934
San Antonio
Rio Grande
GULF OF MEXICO
Sierra Madre Oriental
Sierra Madre Occidental
MEXICO
Monterrey
Pan-American Highway
Gulf of Campeche
Guadalajara
Veracruz
Mexico City
Amecameca
Ixtaccihuatl
Popocatépetl
Cuernavaca
Oaxaca
Miles
0
50
100
150
200
250
300
0
80
160
240
320
400
480
Kilometres
Denys Baker

So Far from God

by the same author
Road to Katmandu
Fantastic Invasion: Dispatches from Africa
Lourdes: A Modern Pilgrimage

So Far from God

A Journey to Central America

Patrick Marnham

ELISABETH SIFTON BOOKS
VIKING

ELISABETH SIFTON BOOKS • VIKING
Viking Penguin Inc.,
40 West 23rd Street,
New York, New York 10010, U.S.A.

First American edition published in 1985

LIBRARY OF CONGRESS CATALOGING IN PUBLICATION DATA
Marnham, Patrick.
So far from God.
"Elisabeth Sifton books."
1. Central America—Politics and government—
1979- . I. Title.
F1439.5.M36 1985 972.8'053 85-40026
ISBN 0-670-80449-5

Printed in the United States of America by
R. R. Donnelley & Sons Company, Harrisonburg, Virginia
Set in Garamond

To
Ralph Marnham

'Poor Mexico! So far from God,
so close to the United States.'

(Traditional)

Acknowledgments

I acknowledge the assistance of Andrew Osmond, who first turned my thoughts towards Latin America, and I am grateful for the hospitality of Susanna and Alexander Chancellor while writing this book.

An earlier version of certain passages first appeared in *Granta* or the *Spectator*. For some of the information in chapter twelve about the background to the Salvadoran revolution I am indebted to an article in *Dissent* by Gabriel Zaid. *The South American Handbook*, which must be one of the best guidebooks ever published, was of frequent assistance in my travels.

I would also like to pay tribute to Susan Morgan, foreign correspondent, whose adventurous spirit led her into danger and whose courage enabled her to triumph over the consequences.

London, February 1985

Contents

Introduction

This is the story of a journey that started and finished in Granada. It was a journey that took me from Spain to Central America, and from California – the capital of the twenty-first century – through the ruined countries to the south where the word 'America' was coined.

The first time I arrived in Latin America, in 1982, it was midnight at San José airport in Costa Rica. I had taken the regular evening flight from Miami, a connection arranged in more optimistic days when it was believed that Costa Rica had a future as a cheap playground in the tropical sun for those who had retired from life's struggle in the United States. How old they seemed, my fellow passengers from Miami, how subdued, how few. Central America no longer beckons the senior citizens of the United States. Politics have intervened, and too many people have discovered that in Costa Rica it rains heavily for ten months of the year. It was raining heavily that night. I was electrified by the Latin American immigration officials; female and armed. Then I was carried by taxi through a haze of rain and exhaustion to a dimly-lit hotel, and shown to a room without a view. It had curtains but there were no windows behind them.

I was excited to be in Costa Rica. Latin America was the land of stained white suits and cheap dance music. I half-expected to see Carmen Miranda at the airport. This was the place where life was lived to a natural rhythm, where birds were devoured by spiders and men fought over women, with knives. They had always indulged this habit. It said so in Bernal Diaz's history of the conquest of New Spain. Before he became the first conquistador, Hernando Cortés lived in the Spanish colony of Cuba. He concealed his ability, made some money and enjoyed himself as a young man should. 'Every morning he recited prayers from a Book of Hours and heard Mass with devoutness. He was fond of cards and dice and excessively fond of women.' There was a knife scar under his lip. Then, at the age of thirty-three, something changed this Cuban Don Juan into a soldier, one of the greatest of Christian soldiers. On 15 August 1519, the feast of the Assumption into Heaven of the Mother of God, Cortés marched from the coast of Mexico towards the fairy city in the interior, the city of lakes and flowers and gold and human sacrifices, the capital of the Aztecs. He burnt his boats before he left, disobeyed his orders, and attacked this extensive empire with 500 swordsmen, ten horses, ten brass cannon, and a relic of the True Cross. He came down on Montezuma like a doom. The story of 'Central America' starts with that wild adventure.

Waking next morning in my windowless room and paddling out into the flooded city, I found little sign of the adventurous spirit. Today the people of Costa Rica are known for their placidity. They are placid because they lack Indians. This is the most European of the countries of the Isthmus. The original Indian people of the highlands perished not from European conquest but from European disease. The Hispanic people who have replaced them are strikingly handsome, mostly descendants of the original colonists from Estremadura, the Spanish province in which Cortés was born. In Costa Rica there is an election every four years without fail. The opposition always wins. The outgoing government is justly reviled for its greed and jobbery. Then the whole process is repeated four years later. This is what is known as 'genuine democracy' in Latin America. It is a vast improvement on the systems favoured by neighbouring countries, but it calls to mind the words of the humorist, Finley Peter Dunne: 'A man that'd expect to train lobsters to fly in a year is called a lunatic. But a man that thinks men can be turned into angels by an election is called a reformer, and remains at large.' Of course, if Dunne had lived in Costa Rica rather than the United States, that observation would never have occurred to him.

A new political administration had begun work in San José a few weeks before I arrived, under somewhat difficult circumstances. On their first day at work the incoming ministers were unable to get into their offices because the previous office holders had locked the doors and thrown away the keys. And when the new president finally burst into his suite it was to find that all the furniture, including the presidential lavatory, had been removed by his predecessor and donated to a favoured charity.

Unfortunately this carefree anarchy seems to be restricted to the country's ruling class. For a week I searched the bars of San José for that mythical world of white suits and cheap music. I found instead a decorous tedium. One small boy had discovered a fine jet of water squirting from between the paving stones of a busy street. The boy put his foot over the spray, waited for a pedestrian then, at the right moment, removed his foot. The jet was high enough to hit you in the face. This solitary *farceur* seemed to have monopolised all that was left of the national frivolity. It was to be many months before I discovered the place of white suits and cheap music.

I had been interested in New Spain for several years. One sunny winter morning in Seville I got up early and walked through the stone-flagged streets of the *barrio* to visit the *Archivo General de Indias*. The building is still named after the continent which Columbus was under the impression he had discovered. There, studying the maps and street plans and architectural elevations of the first fortresses and towns of the New World, Spanish America, my interest in Spain became concentrated on its past and on this extraordinarily wealthy and utterly destroyed empire. Having travelled for ten years in India, the Near East and Africa I was used to stumbling at every turn upon the wreckage of British empire. Here was a reminder that Seville was the city where the Spanish conquest of 'America' was planned. Amerigo Vespucci and Magellan both embarked from the quay near the *Archivo General* and set sail down the Guadalquivir. I was intrigued by the ruins of an earlier empire which had died as the British empire gathered strength and which had given birth to a monstrous child, a world power whose character could hardly be less Spanish.

This conflict between the national characteristics of the United States and its Latin American neighbours was also interesting. Much of the present United States – Texas, California, parts of New Mexico and Arizona, Nevada and Utah – was first Spanish then Mexican territory. There is no immediate prospect of Mexico regaining its lost territory, instead the Spanish-speaking people of the American continent migrate to the north in increasing numbers, sometimes legally sometimes not. The Hispanic immigrants to the United States are the largest cultural group who have refused to learn English. White Anglo-Saxon Protestant America finds this worrying. The city of Miami has had to resist new laws which would have made Spanish an official language. The Hispanic threat is muddled in the north American imagination with the Communist menace. Washington believes that Cuba and Nicaragua pose a military threat. I wanted to see for myself the defiance offered to the most powerful country in the world by these tiny ancestors, and to find out whether the Hispanic immigration could make any impression on the most impervious of all modern cultures.

I was also intrigued by the political activity of the Catholic Church. The Vatican claims, still proudly, that there are over seven hundred and ninety-four million Catholics in the world. Until recently this vast Christian army marched in step. The Catholic Church was effectively defined by its certainty and its authority. Other Churches were more in touch with the times, other Churches provided a welcoming haven for the innumerable oddities of the individual conscience or allowed a less tortuous relationship with scientific rationalism. Across the range of Christianity there was a rich choice. But Rome, the touchstone and the unifying factor, remained constant. The ecumenical movement changed all that. In the name of bureaucratic 'unification', the unifying certainty was abandoned. The consequent disorganisation into which one of the most powerful institutions in the world was thrown is most vividly apparent in the countries of Latin America. I was interested to observe that too. In *The Power and the Glory* the whisky priest despairs of his Mexican-Indian flock. Faced with the fanatical hostility of a Marxist persecution they were beginning to drop away. The priest became 'aware of faith dying out . . . the Mass would soon mean no more to anyone than a black cat crossing the path'. It did not occur to me when I first read Graham Greene's novel that it would be the priests who reduced spirituality to superstition: perhaps it did not occur to the novelist either.

But all that came later, and was remote from the documents displayed in the *Archivo General*. While still in Seville I had driven out along the valley of the Guadalquivir to visit friends. Their house stood on a village street in a line of similar houses, a line of glaring white walls and heavy wooden doors. From the street one had little idea of the splendours within. Once inside, past the hall with its grilled peep-hole, we walked through several rooms to reach the only one that was heated; it was December and bitterly cold in Andalusia. In this one room were the television and the *camilla*, the round table with a pan of charcoal set into its base. Over the table a heavy cloth reached down to the floor and trapped all the heat from the fire. To warm yourself in that icy house you simply took a seat at the table and draped the cloth around your legs.

Outside the house, on the far side from the street, completely enclosed by the village and the river, was a large garden. It contained tall palms, ornamental fruit trees, a sweet lemon, cypresses, roses, jasmine, lawns, a vegetable patch and an irrigation tank large enough to swim in. The land all around was irrigated by the Guadalquivir and was more productive than ever, but the family who owned this house were discussing ways to sell it. Though the garden was still beautiful they said that it was only a shadow of its former glory. The man who made it, and who filled the house with his treasures, died in the last days of Franco. His wife had preferred Seville. He had preferred his garden, and his terrace overlooking the Guadalquivir and his music. He had an antique English machine for playing cylinders which operated a keyboard. He had a library of theological works. He had made a family shrine to the Virgin in one of the cooler corridors and cut niches into the walls of other rooms to hold statues of the saints. He had set aside a room by the garden for his spiritual director who made regular visits. Slowly he filled the house with furniture and paintings and lived for much of the time in a world of his own creation, waiting patiently to satisfy his curiosity about the world to come. With his departure accomplished and his curiosity satisfied, the house and the garden lingered on. But the trees grew ragged, the books gathered dust, the furniture faded. His heirs slowly came to accept that though they loved the house they could not give it life. It had died when he died. It had been too private, too completely his alone.

It seemed when I visited that house that its fate was an image of the country as a whole. All over Spain people were facing this decision. A country which had avoided much of the nineteenth century and accepted the first seventy years of the twentieth on a very selective basis, was now determined to catch up all at once. The superficial changes which had taken place in a short period of time were remarkable. Public manners had lost much of their formality. Women could be insulted and pushed around in the streets of a city while the crowd passed unheedingly by. Private and public property were regularly destroyed by children as well as adults. The *tapas* bars were suddenly in competition with 'burger bars' and had been forced to install computer games in self-defence. Spanish football supporters had learned the international code of grunts and moans. Fifteen years of fundamental change behind the heavy, closed doors of the Spanish family home had abruptly marched out on to the street.

In 1970, convent schools in Seville inculcated discipline and self-denial by methods that would have interested Dickens. The girls were not allowed to drink water, even during the height of summer, except with meals. Every Christmas a play was performed, one of the social occasions of the school year. During the performance the nuns sat at the back of the hall watching it. The girls stood before them, with their backs to the stage, watching the nuns. They were told that this was more polite. Today they look back on it all with amazement but agree that it was not an unhappy period in their lives. When they left school they threw themselves into the struggle to change Spanish society. Without warning the opposition posed by tradition collapsed. They found they had won. Almost at once they began to notice some of the disadvantages of their victory.

Wherever one travelled in Spain in the years immediately following the death of El Caudillo one could sense this anxious desire for European normality. 'Are we modern enough?' people seemed to enquire of the foreigner. 'Are we considerate enough, predictable enough, trivial enough, *boring* enough, to count as one of you?' The answer was, 'No, you are not.' There remains far too much evidence of a higher culture in Spain. Quite unimportant people are unable to lose the habit of thinking for themselves. The country is still deeply marked with a living religious faith and by potentially violent disagreements over ideas. Many people solve the problem of low wages by working seriously at two jobs. Family life flourishes. They derive their sense of dignity from their character and behaviour rather than from their income or professional standing. Above all, it is a country that dwells on its past and honours its own history. In Spain one can see Chesterton's epigram come to life: tradition as the democracy of the dead.

A common sight by the roadside are the memorials to the Civil War. These stones are usually simple in appearance but savagely partisan in their wording. I stopped to read one outside the village of Cobrisa, near Toledo. It was a gravestone standing under an olive tree. The farmer had ploughed round it carefully for forty-five years. The stone listed the names of four men called Redondo who had died on 6 September 1936. Then, in one line, the dry recital sprang to life. 'Murdered by the Marxist gang': *La horda marxista* was the only title allowed to the legitimate forces of the elected Republican government by those in the Nationalist uprising.

Most of these wayside monuments are Nationalist in sympathy, they were erected during the years of Franco. The graves of the Republican dead are generally unmarked, a lack of emphasis that does nothing to diminish their mythic value. One of the most celebrated of the Republican martyrs was the poet and playwright, Federico García Lorca. He was among the 4,000 citizens of Granada who were shot by the Nationalists during the first months of the war. It is an appalling story, one repeated all over Spain on both sides of the line.

The Granadan executions took place at various sites. Thousands were shot beneath the high walls of the city's cemetery. Others were taken to the *barranca*, a ravine, near the little village of Víznar where the 'Black Squads' of the Falange had a barracks. In shooting Lorca the Nationalists made a mistake. Precisely because his grave was unknown, hundreds of the poet's admirers travelled to Granada, and then to Víznar in the years after the Civil War to make enquiries. Among them two Englishmen, first Gerald Brenan then Ian Gibson, did more than most to establish the exact details of Lorca's end. The Nationalists could not have drawn more attention to their crime if they had erected one of their hideous, hilltop Winged Victorys in Lorca's name.

After my visit to Seville I went to Granada, and while in Granada I drove up to Víznar along the well-beaten track. The village is in the foothills of an outcrop of the Sierra Nevada and in December, however bright the sun, the wind cuts you to the quick. The village has changed much less since Lorca's day than has Granada. There are new summer villas up there but no private water supply, the communal wash-house is still in use. I bought a beer from a shop without electricity, but since the bottle had been sitting on the counter it was nicely chilled. Even the old lady in the shop complained of the cold. Her only heat came from a pan of glowing charcoal. When I asked her the way to the village cemetery she smiled. 'You are looking for García Lorca,' she said, 'but he is not in the cemetery and the place where he lies is unmarked.' It was far too cold and at least thirty years too late to suggest that she might like to show me exactly where that was. She seemed a cheerful character. She would have been a girl during the Civil War. Life in Víznar had got better since those days when the Black Squads lounged outside the big house and waited for the lorries to drive up from Granada. Those lorries made a lot of noise as they climbed the hill. People living by the road would be woken by them in the night, and would wait in fear until they had carried their coffles of silent prisoners out of earshot.

I went out to the *barranca* and climbed up above its steep edge. From there you can look over the plains below Granada, rich country as far as the next mountain range. Had Lorca looked that way in the chill early light he might have made out the settlement of Fuente Vaqueros, where he was born. The Falange and Catholic Action singled Lorca out for death that morning not because he was a Communist, which he was not, but because he symbolised the world of secular intelligence which was already taken for granted in the rest of Europe. When they shot Lorca, they thought they were shooting the future.

Later that day in Granada I found a pamphlet in a bookshop which suggested that Lorca was not quite such an appropriate symbol of liberal anti-clericalism as his murderers had supposed. In 1929, seven years before his death, when he was thirty-one, he volunteered to act as one of the masked bearers of the Confraternity of Our Lady of the Alhambra. With his fellow penitents he carried the statue of the Virgin down from the Alhambra and through the streets of Granada. As an additional punishment he chose to undertake this honourable humiliation barefoot. Once the procession was over he slipped away, leaving on his folded robes a note which read, 'What was owed to God has been paid.' Perhaps of all the sights in Spain the penitential processions with their hooded and robed figures are the most alarming or incomprehensible to the secular mind. But for Lorca, for the Spanish secular mind, they had a use. It is an ambivalence towards the modern world which one finds again and again in Spain and in Spanish life. One finds its origin in the church where Lorca's procession started from, The Church of Our Lady of the Alhambra, a Christian shrine surrounded by a Moorish palace, the character of neither being compromised. It was in the fall of the Alhambra, and the end of the Muslim kingdom in Spain, that the country, unified at last, found the wealth and energy to begin its conquest of 'the Indies'. And the Spaniards who sailed down the Guadalquivir for New Spain took that sinister ambivalence with them.

I suppose that when I first travelled to Central America my knowledge of the Isthmus was about that of the average European newspaper reader, supplemented by the *South American Handbook 1982* and the Penguin Latin American Library. I knew that there had been a terrible earthquake in Nicaragua but had forgotten that there had been a more terrible one in Guatemala. I was aware of the civil war in Nicaragua which had caused the downfall of the dictator Anastasio Somoza. I knew that Guatemala had territorial claims on the former British colony of Belize. I knew that Honduras produced bananas and that Costa Rica produced coffee, but not that Costa Rica produced bananas and Honduras coffee. I had heard of the United Fruit Company of Boston which, after some notably bad behaviour, succeeded in reducing Honduras to a condition where it earned the original title of 'banana republic'. Above all, like most newspaper readers, I had followed events in El Salvador. There was a small war there between an unsatisfactory right-wing government backed by the United States and a romantic guerrilla movement backed by Cuba and Nicaragua. Journalists occasionally got shot in El Salvador, which always ensures heavy press coverage. Priests and nuns and social workers got shot more frequently. The Catholic Church in that part of the world was widely identified with communism. I vaguely remembered an old cutting from *The Times*, in 1977 possibly, describing the death of a Jesuit missionary. He was an advocate of land reform and had been murdered by supporters of the government, that is by one of the early 'death squads'. He had been strung up in a tree, and then a fire had been lit beneath him, then he had been shot. I only kept the cutting because of his name, Father Pedro Alas. When I first read that story I was under the impression that El Salvador was a small island in the Caribbean.

On the day before I left England on this journey the newspapers reported that the Welsh Nationalists had denounced a new car because its computerised voice did not issue instructions to the driver in Welsh. Here was a story from the *Noddyland Chronicle*. Perhaps that is the usual impression England makes on those who view it from foreign parts. English jokes, self-deprecation, the relentlessly frivolous attitude to ideas, and what the English choose to quarrel about, all the national qualities, are pared away by the harsher reality of more turbulent regions; and one starts to think of one's country as an eternal kindergarten for squabbling children who – deprived of their toys – are reduced to undoing each other's shoelaces.

With such churlish thoughts I boarded a plane for San Francisco. I intended to travel from there to Nicaragua, mostly overland. I had satisfied my curiosity about the southern part of the Isthmus in 1982; Costa Rica and Panama seemed too settled to call on again. Between them and Mexico stood the three small countries where all the trouble occurs. Guatemala, El Salvador and Nicaragua. These three had not disappointed me; I wanted to go back. They recalled the old Spanish curse, 'May you live in interesting times'; three insignificant little places posing problems which not even the United States could solve.

I decided to start in California, that part of America which is so far into the future that it is practically detached from the continent. But it started life as an outpost of New Spain. It was named after Calafia, a female character in an epic popular among sixteenth-century Spanish sailors. And the Franciscan friars who first ventured into it came not from the east but from the south; they took their orders from Mexico City. To travel from California, south, suggested a journey from an existing future into a living past.

PART ONE

Gringolandia

1

The Greatest Country in God's Universe

'Time itself has got to wait on the greatest country in God's Universe. We shall be giving the word for everything: industry, trade, law, journalism, art, politics and religion, from Cape Horn . . . to the North Pole . . . We shall run the world's business whether the world likes it or not.'

The Boston banker in Conrad's *Nostromo* (1904)

The first group of Mexican citizens I saw were stumbling up the slope from the border, trying to keep their feet in the glutinous mud of southern California and hoping to avoid the United States Border Patrol. It was a moonless night and raining heavily. They chose a track which led directly towards the Patrol Supervisor's pick-up. He had been watching them through his night-glasses for some minutes, enjoying the contrast between the warmth of his seat and the weather they were struggling with. He flicked on his headlights and the Mexicans just walked quietly up the beam. There were four of them, men of three generations, from Sinaloa, a state of Mexico 650 miles to the south. They were farm labourers looking for work. They were true wetbacks, soaked to the skin.

Despite the distance they had travelled they carried very little, a shoulder bag, a pack of *Barrio* cigarettes, a safety razor. Each wore two sets of clothes. Supervisor Larry Laudner carried a gun on his belt but said that he rarely had to draw. The meeting was courteous, both sides seeming familiar with the procedure. Most of the thousands of Mexicans who cross illegally into the United States have been turned back once or more. Eventually they find a way past the Patrol and are able to continue northwards, to work. This is an unexpected fact about the United States, accepted as the most powerful country in the world; it is apparently unable to defend its own borders against the incursions of an illiterate peasantry.

Waiting in the truck for the group from Sinaloa, Mr Laudner and I watched the lights of Tijuana twinkling across the river. Like all the Mexican border towns it is larger than its opposite number to the north, in this case San Diego. My companion, stung by this reflection – San Diego is after all the seventh largest city in the United States – pointed out that the size of Tijuana was an illusion since about half its population tried to leave every night. It was his task to send them back.

Much of the U.S. border patrolman's professional pride comes from the idea that he is all that stands between the most privileged country in the world and barbarism. By ancient reputation the border patrol is a brutal and corrupt body of men. Allegations of murder against its agents used to be commonplace. The only person I know who grew up on the United States – Mexican border remembers as a small child seeing a border patrolman shoot dead a Mexican in her grandmother's orchard. She remembers it because the explanation given was that 'the Mexican was full of dope'. But something must have happened to the border patrol in recent years. The youthful group of agents who burbled to each other on Mr Laudner's radio about 'working traffic' (rounding up wetbacks) seemed more accustomed to hide and seek than to homicide.

My day with Mr Laudner had started at the Travel Lodge Motel, just north of the San Isidro border crossing. One moment we were sitting high up in the cab, finishing a hamburger and talking about the cost of living in London, the next he was out in the street, chasing round the corner of the motel, his pistol flapping on his belt, yelling at me to follow him and not to lock us out of the truck. By the time I caught up, his unseen quarry had gone, not back to Mexico but deeper into the United States. His calls for assistance on the radio met with no response at all. The woman who ran the Travel Lodge, and whose day was punctuated by illegal immigrants scrambling through her backyard, laughed at his failure and said that this lot had been carrying chickens.

The border between the United States and Mexico has been

described as a separate country rather than a line on the map. Within an unmarked area on each side of that line people share a complicated way of life which is dependent on their neighbours opposite. That is a natural state of affairs. But further back from the border, North Americans start to believe in the line on the map. They regard illegal immigrants whether from Mexico, Cuba or places still more remote, as a serious threat to their way of life. Among the younger members of the border patrol this thin-grey-line mentality was commonplace. After the three men from Sinaloa had been driven away to overnight detention Mr Laudner drove a few miles down the road to the point where the rest of his section were at work. 'There's Norma, getting cutesy on the radio again,' he muttered. 'If I've told her once . . .'

Norma turned out to be a junior agent raised in New York, born in Puerto Rico, fluent in Spanish and English, about 5 feet tall and ferociously efficient in action. When Mr Laudner joined the patrol, women agents were unheard of. Now quite a few women were recruited but they seldom stayed for long. Mr Laudner didn't know why. Possibly they didn't appreciate the masculine comradeship of the patrol. Their only drawback, he said, was that other agents tended to worry about them. If Norma went down into the *barranca* alone her colleagues always worried until she reappeared. The *barranca*, the ravine by the river, was a dangerous place. Armed gangs preyed on the wetbacks down there, drug smugglers fell out with each other in the *barranca*, it was a place of bodies, as it had been outside Granada. I remembered the hideous collection of blades, some home-made, all lethal, all removed from wetbacks, which I had seen displayed in Mr Laudner's office.

We reached the point where Norma was at work. She emerged from the mud and darkness at the head of a long line of Mexicans, about nine of them, all young men. Several uniformed Anglo-Saxon males brought up the rear. Norma was in charge. She ordered her captives to sit down in the mud with their hands on their heads, barking instructions in Spanish at the bemused group of agriculturalists. They were bemused by the puddles they were invited to sit in, by the lights shining in their faces, perhaps most of all by her Puerto Rican accent. Eventually Mr Laudner intervened with the comment that in his day they had tried to get everyone out of the rain and into the trucks. His relaxed air dissolved the growing tension. Later I asked him about Norma. It seemed rather inappropriate for this zealous Puerto Rican to be spending her time enforcing the immigration regulations. But he declined to speculate. 'Yeah,' he said. 'Well . . . she's one of those Noo *York* Pooerto Ricans.'

I asked Mr Laudner if he spent much time in Mexico on vacation. He spoke pretty good Spanish and he seemed to like talking to the men he captured. He said he never went into Mexico at all if he could help it; once or twice on official business, that was about it. Wasn't he tempted by the cheap goods over there, or by the empty beauty of Baja California, the perfect place for a resourceful man like himself to take his family on a camping trip? Mr Laudner gave me a dry look. No, he wasn't tempted by that at all. He didn't like going into Mexico. He did not feel safe there. He did not understand Mexican laws, he preferred his own government. He was not a stay-at-home, he was a veteran of Vietnam. I wondered why he avoided Mexico, whether it was just the paranoia of a disarmed policeman or whether there was something else which made him wary. But I did not press him, he was getting restless. My time was up.

The following day was St Patrick's Day. The waitresses at the coffee shop – who looked pretty silly anyway in their Mabel Lucy Atwell gingham smocks and bonnets – looked even sillier with green plastic tiaras plonked on top of the rest of it. But they served the usual, excellent coffee of the United States. Fifty per cent of it is imported from Latin America, 10 per cent from Guatemala and El Salvador alone. On St Patrick's Day, at lunchtime, they insisted on serving vivid green beer. Enough was enough and I took the bus to Tijuana.

Traditionally the Mexican border towns provide everything you can get north of the border but at half the price and twice the risk. In San Diego I had eaten at a smorgasbord parlour with a sign on the counter saying that if I returned to help myself to more food 'federal health regulations' ordained that I would have to take a 'fresh' plate. You take the twenty-minute bus ride to Tijuana and step out of the bus and try not to fall into the deep holes along the city pavements and realise, with heartfelt relief, that you have left the land of fresh plates and green beer. In Tijuana there was no sign of St Patrick's Day at all. I found a whole block of *optica-dentals*; dentists' offices behind plate glass windows which advertised 'Crowns, Dentures, Partials, Estimates'. They all took credit cards and worked in partnership with opticians. They were a rebuke to the cost of illness in the United States. The only professionals reputed to be more expensive than U.S. doctors are U.S. lawyers and they too had their shadows in Tijuana. One of the most prominent signs was situated above a lawyer's office; three-foot-high neon capital letters flashed on and off, DIVORCE-OPEN-24 HOURS. The lawyer inside handed me a card which announced his whereabouts for all hours except those between 3 and 4 a.m. He said that under Mexican law he could dissolve any marriage contracted anywhere in the world in less than six weeks, after which he could arrange for a Mexican marriage ceremony. His professional manner was that of a solicitous Cupid. I spent a couple of happy hours in Tijuana, wandering around in the rain. These people's behaviour frequently seemed absurd; their manner was frivolous and their life was a pose but all the same they seemed to know what was important. Most of them possessed very little and had very few prospects of improvement; how did they manage then to complain about so little and to keep so much hope alive? After a week in California I felt in Tijuana that I was surrounded by grown-ups. The bus back to San Diego jumped the long queue of cars by zigzagging through the line of shacks crowded close to the frontier wire. Inside these houses guides were making up parties for the night crossing, money was changing hands, men were being bled dry on the distant promise of a new life in the United States, mothers were drugging their children to keep them quiet. But in Tijuana people even made a joke of this, their best chance. A view of the town, sold as a postcard, showed the traffic jams, backed up from the border post, all trying to leave.

Behind one shack which stood right on the curve two Mexican police cars were parked. One car was empty, doors hanging open; the other contained two occupants, a dishevelled police officer and a girl. Another quiet afternoon for the Mexican border patrol.

I never hit it off with California. I had started from San Francisco a week before my day with Mr Laudner. The day after

I arrived there the newspapers published an opinion poll which claimed that 95 per cent of the U.S. population believed in God. The headline to the story was 'The Godliest People in the World.' It was a Sunday so I went to mass at St Boniface, the headquarters of the Franciscan Friars, the founders of San Francisco. Outside the church stood a long line of drunks, down-and-outs and mental cases waiting not for mass but for the free lunch which the friars provide. Here was the unpublicised side of Californian life; these people were laid back so far they were practically horizontal. I hope that the meal they were given was better than the spiritual dog's dinner served up inside the church.

It was one of the advantages of the old Tridentine Catholic Mass that, however obscure its Latin may have been, the congregation did at least know which way to face at the beginning of the service. '*Introibo ad altare Dei*', the first words, explained it all. 'I will go in unto the altar of God. Unto God, who giveth joy to my youth.' We knew what we were in for at St Boniface when the priest said, 'Now all turn to the back of the church,' where we were faced by a crowd of what seemed to be clerics. On closer inspection they turned out to be women togged up to look like Catholic priests in flowing cassocks and short haircuts. Lost somewhere in the middle was the Franciscan priest supposedly officiating at this sacrifice. Here was the alternative Catholic Church of the United States in full cry.

Throughout the mass the dominant figure on the altar was one particularly bitter person in spotless cassock who gave out a prayer of her own invention. It was for 'those hurt by the institution of the Church, those called to the lay ministry', and judging by the expression of controlled fury on her face we were being invited to pray for her career prospects. She followed this with the 'Litany of the Alienated', for 'those living in sin, homosexuals, women and meths drinkers'. She did not make it clear whether these unfortunate people were supposed to be alienated through their own fault or through that of the Church, but since the first two categories are still regarded as sinners, the third as people and the fourth as desperate it did not seem to matter.

At one point a living alien, a meths drinker, stumbled noisily in and then relapsed into a more or less respectful silence.

Perched high above his head, entangled in a prominent range of his Afro-hair, there was a little woollen cap. The church beadle wanted this removed. He approached the black man silently from behind and tapped him smartly on the shoulder with a hooked umbrella handle. More than slightly startled, the meths drinker snatched the long-forgotten woolly bobble from its perch, then some minutes later, in a belated attempt to restore his own dignity, left the church. Somewhere on the distant altar a thin, self-absorbed voice continued to give out the Litany of the Alienated.

In the course of several years spent travelling round Africa and Central America, and writing a book on the pilgrimage to Lourdes, I have attended many infinitely depressing, deadening and useless versions of the modern mass, but there was something about the service in San Francisco which took the biscuit. At one point the priest plucked up the courage to preach a sermon in which he prayed for peace in Central America and then rebuked the memory of the Crusaders and the Inquisitors. This, for an American Franciscan, was pretty cool since it is most unlikely that there would have been a Franciscan friary in California, or even a California, without those two maligned institutions. Columbus would never have raised the money for his voyage to the Indies if the Benedictines of Huelva had not persuaded the King of Spain that the expedition was a crusade against the infidels of the East. And the Franciscans were the first Inquisitors. Enough of their original spirit survived for this parish priest to call down the ancient public curse of 'anathema' on President Reagan and his administration for their belligerent attitude towards 'blacks, Indians, most elderly citizens, the sick and the urban underclass'.

But it was neither the undermined, apologetic priest nor the do-it-yourself liturgy that was so depressing; what drove one to despair at this mass was the sight of the poorest members of the congregation, the Spanish people, periodically leaving the service to pass down a side aisle and light a candle before some favoured image. Here, among these illiterate, unassuming and unnoticed people some quite different end was in view. These Spanish people were undoubtedly members of 'the urban underclass', but they were not interested in cursing Mr Reagan. Slipping away from the organised mayhem of the service to their private devotions, they reminded one of the Indian adherents of the old religion who practised image-worship in the secret parts of the forest, centuries after they had submitted to the compulsory baptism of the Franciscan Inquisitors.

I had lunch at a fish restaurant by the sea and was advised by the waiter to take a coach tour of the city. He recommended his friend, Teddy. I failed to ask for Teddy, the driver I got instead was a look-alike for Jack Nicholson in *Five Easy Pieces*. He was a good guide. He pointed out the beauties of San Francisco Bay but mentioned the area's importance as a military and naval base. A report had just been published which listed forty-five wars going on in the world in twenty of which the United States was the major arms supplier. Much of the wealth of California comes from its arms trade. Then he took us out to Seal Rock to watch the seals in the grey Pacific surf, and then to 'Gay town' to view the city's famous homosexuals. San Francisco must be the only place in the world where the homosexuals have become an attraction for coach tours. We rubber-necked the gay bars and leather boys from the safety of our coach; they didn't look as human as the seals.

After a few days I left San Francisco. I took a train south called the 'Spirit of California' and slept well. For the price of a medium hotel room one got nine hours in bed and woke in Los Angeles. Early in the morning the steward said that we were passing through Dog Town, a suburb of Los Angeles where the inhabitants were in the habit of chucking rocks through the windows of the train. Outside, the graffiti beside the tracks read 'Viva Dog Town', 'Barrio Dog Town' and 'Dog Town Diabolos'. No rocks were thrown. The only figure in sight was a bearded bum, asleep in the sun, his hat pulled low over his eyes and one leg stretched in provocative nonchalance across the nearest rail, ready to be severed at the ankle. In Los Angeles I paused long enough to interview the editor of a Spanish-language newspaper. Then I took the Greyhound bus to the border city of San Diego, arriving the same evening in time to check into the Vacation Village Hotel.

San Diego has long claimed the finest weather in the United States. For that reason it is also said to be the most expensive city in the United States. Its climate attracts the wealthiest stock pensioners, determined to enjoy fine weather at the end of their days. For the few days of my visit the weather in San Diego was atrocious – cold, stormy and very wet. The men who had designed the Vacation Village Hotel had not taken this possibility into account. Much thought had gone into the palm trees, none to the possibility of rainy weather. As I climbed out of my taxi I had the uneasy feeling that someone wanted me to think that I was in an Hawaiian hutted village. The hotel was spread out across an extensive park, and my hut was at the furthest corner of the compound. The young man who took my case led me outside and ushered me to a seat at the rear of an electric golf cart. As we set out across the settlement, the first drops of rain began to fall. The golf cart with its forlorn passenger disappeared into a forlorn palm thicket to re-emerge, after a considerable interval, on the far side of the ornamental water-fowl pool and well beyond the observation tower, thrown up perhaps to aid the search for missing guests. The ornamental water-fowl were having the time of their lives. I was less happy. My tropical hut turned out to be a forlorn bed-sitter with kitchenette, barette and restroomette. Consulting the map of the settlement I discovered that the dining hut had been sited about half a mile away on the shore of the lagoon. By now there was an entirely authentic tropical downpour emptying itself into the semi-tropical jungle that grew just outside the ceiling-to-floor picture windows. Not a single drop of rain could escape the observation of an attentive guest. The golf cart had gone, and I realised that if I was to reach the dining room without getting soaked to the skin it would be necessary for me to return to the centre of the city in order to rent a car. Two hours later, and for $16 a day, Rent-a-Car-Cheep had provided me with a Pontiac Catalina that was twenty feet long and painted in military camouflage. Since this was the same price as I had been charged for the taxi to their office I was quite pleased with the deal.

After a few days in San Diego, and my meeting with Border Patrolman Larry Laudner, I was ready to set out; on the morning of my departure I witnessed one more vignette of West Coast life. I had moved out of the Vacation Village Hotel after one night. The Hotel San Diego's air of faded prosperity was out of sorts with the rowdy young naval ratings and marines who were its chief customers, but on that last morning all the noise was made not by the military but by an elderly man whose room was just down the corridor from mine, and whose wife had locked herself into it by mistake. The key was jammed into the lock and she could not move it. Her husband, out alone on some hazardous breakfast-time mission, had apparently instructed her to lock herself in, in his absence. Now he was in the corridor and she was in the room and no power in the hotel could instantly reunite them. The bell boy had given up trying and had left the old fellow to deal with the situation by himself. His method of proceeding could be heard through much of the hotel.

'Move it up, or move it down,' he shouted. 'Move it now. Move it with two hands.' If I stood in the corridor and watched him I could just hear the muffled responses from the other side of the door; not the words, just the occasion of them. The question of offering to help did not arise. The man was far too irascible.

After listening to a few more mumbles, he started again.

'Get it OUT. If your life depended on it you would get it OUT.'

This seemed a strange way for him to talk to his wife, trapped as she was in this awkward situation, uneasy about being confined to her room, prone perhaps to panic, the future from her side of the obstruction offering many fewer opportunities than it did from his; and yet harried by this short, bald, furious, noisy man on the free side of the door. Inconvenienced no doubt he was, but he could walk to Rio de Janeiro if he so chose – look on the bright side, perhaps he would – there was not a single locked door in his path.

But not at all. 'Where is it NOW?' he was shouting at her again. 'Where is it NOW?'

One might have thought that was one question he did not have to ask. It was clearly still stuck in the door lock, but he repeated his enquiry on a rising note, all self-control abandoned, his rage and panic long since having overcome any notions he might once have possessed of dignity or privacy. He paused between sentences but it was not in order to absorb her views. This was not a reflective passage in this elderly person's life. The serenity associated with age had momentarily evaded him. Here he was in a state of bellowing terror and it had taken so little to bring this about. This was not supposed to be part of the Californian experience. He on one side of the door, his wife on the other, and no way of parting the three-quarters of an inch of wood between them. For forty years he had been led to expect a greater degree of intimacy than this. The sun filtered down the corridor, my friend the maid cleaned another room. She smiled and enquired about my health. '*Gracias a dios*,' she said when I told her I was going to Mexico. Somewhere a radio was playing dance music. And he continued, out of control. His enraged instructions, alternating with the odd moan from within, rang out for some time. Then – silence. His wife had turned the key. The door had opened. The Third World could breathe again. He made no comment about this. He just walked into the room. The door closed behind him. They were together again, locked into their dance of death. The rights of this individual American were no longer being violated. It was no longer a moral issue.

2

The Mexican Hairless

'Drop the cursed pettiness that belongs to men that live their lives as if death will never tap them.'

Carlos Castaneda, *Journey to Ixtlan*

The West Coast ended in the Greyhound bus station in San Diego, just across the street from my hotel. Here I was out of kookie-land and into middle-America. Waiting for the bus to Mexicali I bought a shoeshine. It was run by two white men instead of the usual black man and they made a big fuss about doing a good job. I asked one of them if San Diego was his home town. He said no, home was Connecticut. Then he said he'd lived in San Diego for thirty years. I was surprised at that so I said, 'After thirty years home is still Connecticut?', and he shut up like a clam. He did not want to think about it. Inside the bus station a very old lady, travelling with a similar, tried to extract a cream bun from a vending machine. She lost both her bun and her money. When I went to the machine for a cold drink I received instead her bun. I presented this to her and as her painted and powdered lips closed around the flour and sugar and paste she thanked me. 'You're a doll', she said, I think.

At the front of every Greyhound bus there is a notice prohibiting 'intoxicants', and another which gives the name of the driver under the heading 'Safe, reliable, courteous'. That morning it was safe, reliable, courteous Bob Cole. He managed the first two but gave the impression that he had to answer too many dumb questions to qualify for the third. He warned one young Hawaiian drunk, whom he had picked out way down the line, 'You don't look too straight. Any trouble and that's where you get off.' Since this was the service to New York City and our first stage was across the Californian desert, it was no empty threat.

Buses are the cheapest form of public transport in the United States. In a country whose size allows travel to promise a fresh start on a new frontier the buses have inherited the tradition of the stage-coach. They are still run in stages and frequently between the old stage-coach towns. Drivers are changed instead of horses, but the bus goes on. Ours was due to arrive in New York in three days' time.

The road from San Diego to Phoenix, Arizona, is called Interstate 8. We passed turnings to Kitchen Creek Road and Live Oak Springs. The succession of boulders, brush and sand, so familiar from so many films, also contained scattered ranch houses surrounded by palings and the only trees in sight. Cattle grazed beyond the palings, seeming to cling to the houses for company. The unfulfilled horizons on all sides gave a vivid impression of how empty the country still is. Then the road started to climb. At 4,181 feet there was a sign by the road announcing the fact and to the east the mountains towered still higher. Another sign warned that strong winds were possible for the next twenty-eight miles. At El Cajon we stopped by a small parking-lot. The town seemed little more than a collection of fragile houses and a gas station. Here a family had gathered to say goodbye to their son. The boy was about fifteen, tall and very slight with red hair. His mother, a handsome young woman, was in tears by his side. He flung his arms around her and kissed her twice. Then he turned to his sister, also red-haired, about thirteen, who just punched him on the shoulder and did not cry. His father shook his hand. The boy put a baseball cap on his head and followed the other passengers to a seat at the back of the bus. He looked rather quiet. His family did not wait for the bus to leave. They walked back to their car. Before they drove away the girl was already laughing at her mother's tears. One wondered, watching this family separation, what it was that El Cajon could not provide which had made this painful parting a necessity.

We crossed the mountains, then plunged back into the desert brush. From 4,000 feet we reached down to sea level in about forty-five minutes. In the wilderness there were goats herded into paddocks and then the first signs of intensive irrigation and crops just outside the next stop, El Centro. Here Bob Cole called 'Fifteen Minutes' and everyone got out.

El Centro is a desert town laid out in blocks on the flat ground. It must once have been an oasis on a hard journey. I was expecting to find a thriving little drugstore at this bus station, with its daily stream of 'fifteen minute' customers, but the only refreshment to be had was from a vending-machine. Almost the only people I saw in my fifteen minutes in El Centro were my fellow passengers. Opposite was the 'Roberta Hotel 1927', one of the few two-storey buildings in sight, but its windows remained dead. No one left and no one came. Where were they all, the El Centrists? And why, once again the desolation and fragility of the settlement raised the question, why when surrounded by all the wealth and the ease of the United States, did they choose to live *here* – with the flies? Who stayed in these places, and who left? For the temptation to leave was presented daily by the gleaming blue and grey 'Americruiser 2' with the three words of its destination prominently displayed above its smoked glass windshield, about as unsettling as any three words you might read in El Centro. Stepping a few paces down the street I came to another sign, erected apparently by one of those who had stayed, B. F. Goodrich. He had painted above his large garage, 'B. F. Goodrich – We are the other guys'. His business seemed adequate to serve the entire desert and I could not imagine what the first guys found to do. I thought about B. F. Goodrich frequently in the weeks that followed, wondered about his strange mixture of ambition and stick-in-the-mudness, concocted quite a saga about his life history, until stuck in a traffic jam in Mexico City my gaze wandered out of the cab window and came to rest on the bus tyre motionless about four inches away and read the name 'B. F. Goodrich' and even then thought for a moment that this megalomaniac garage proprietor was supplying the bus companies of Mexico City from his hometown, until click, click Goodyear, Goodrich, we are the other guys, and I realised that I had not even read the name of an inhabitant of El Centro.

Then I did finally see them, the El Centrists. Just as we were finishing our warm-Coke and stale-cookie breakfast, two or three forlorn little family groups assembled to effect their separation. They stood around in their bright clothes, their jeans and T-shirts and baseball hats, just like regular city Americans, and saw whoever it was on to the bus and looked a bit at a loss, hopped from foot to foot, wondered whether to wait, and then walked back to their outsize cars, and drove out into the emptiness and resumed doing whatever it was they did which kept them pinned to this human margin. And again one wondered, why did they stay? As the town filled up with new citizens from south of the border and fell in on itself instead of growing, and their neighbours left, the harder it must have been for them to answer that question. There were sunsets, after all, on the West Coast.

As we left El Centro we could see where they had painted the sea-level mark on the town's gas tank. It was about thirty feet up in the air.

At Calexico Bob Cole continued on his way to Phoenix and I switched to safe, reliable, courteous M. M. Ramirez for the cross-border bus to Mexicali, which must be one of the shortest routes Greyhound run since Calexico and Mexicali are the same town. M. M. Ramirez was a very neat number, a U.S. Mexican who wore an identical two-tone blue uniform to those worn by male drivers, but in her case fitting very close. She handled the twelve tons as though she had just got her commercial pilot's licence and she was flying it. She also showed an unembarrassed excitement about her job. She was as thrilled to be wearing these clothes and driving this bus as some people are thrilled to be on the footplate of a steam engine.

As we crossed the border the resigned but cheerful chorus of Mexican matrons started to discuss how much the customs officers were going to steal from them. Their apprehension increased when a rogue in uniform, who spoke no English, boarded our bus. Afterwards the matrons compared losses and then asked me how much I had been taken for. M.M. explained to them that the customs officials generally confined their attentions to their fellow Mexicans. The matrons pondered this information, and I could feel the magical, despised aura of the protected gringo forming around me. I said goodbye to M. M. Ramirez at the bus station. In her crisp clothes, with her lovingly-tended bus, which arrived to the minute on a timetable set in San Diego six hours earlier, she symbolised everything Mexico was not and never would be.

In the booking hall at the railway station I noticed, way behind me in the very long, very slow queue, a girl. There was something about her, not exactly an intelligence but an alertness of expression, an anxiety, that betrayed her, despite her Mexican appearance, as a U.S. citizen. Finding myself close to her I asked her something in English without any preliminaries and her immediate response was, 'How could you tell we spoke English? We stand out, don't we?' She had her parents with her, and her twin daughters, and this was her first visit to Mexico, although both her parents had been born and brought up south of the border. They had chosen to travel to Guadalajara overland because it was cheap, but her father, after six hours in the land of his birth, was in a state of mild shock. He had forgotten what it was like. The queue was in any case a waste of time. We were eventually told that the next train south, the night train, had no sleepers on it. For sleepers you had to take the day train and queuing for that did not start until the middle of the night. Since this was a two-day journey none of us wanted to go without a sleeper so we all postponed our departure. I said goodbye to the girl who was from Santa Cruz and went to the station buffet to enquire about a hotel.

In the buffet three young children sat solemnly watching television as though it were the first time they had ever seen it. They were very poor. Their mother, anxious and exhausted, was with them. She had come up the Pacific coastline on the previous night's train and was waiting for a friend to join her. She had no money left, her friend had that. When this person eventually arrived they would join forces and try to cross the border. Both their husbands were on the other side. She was a pretty woman who avoided everyone's glance. She was embarrassed by the recent increase in her poverty. The children were watching a pop show. A group of Puerto Rican boys were singing a cute, lisping song of the sort which was having a huge success all over Latin America. Boys could sing in these kiddie pop bands commercially and make a fortune until their voices broke. After that they were commercially dead. A man sitting in the buffet picking his teeth ordered tortillas for the children without asking her permission. Their mother thanked him gravely, almost without raising her eyes, while the children fell on to the food and the fizzy drinks. He had ordered nothing for her. That would have changed an act of courtesy into a gift and a gift might have imposed a sense of obligation and an obligation one could not fulfil might have to be rejected. The man watched the children eat, then left the buffet.

I spent an uneasy night in my hotel. I did not want to miss the train. I was impatient for the uncertainties of life in Mexico. But it was precisely these that were preventing me from enjoying them. There was *supposed* to be a sleeper on both the day and night trains. You were not *supposed* to have to start queuing at 3.30 a.m. in order to catch a train that did not leave until 8.30. Then I remembered the first rule of Mexican life. '*No hay reglas fixtas, señor*'. The first rule of Mexican life: there are no fixed rules. When Flandrau noted this in 1908, he added: 'A well-regulated, systematic and precise person always detests Mexico and can rarely bring himself to say a kind word about anything in it.' Could it be as bad as that?

Next morning at 4.30 I made my way back to the booking office and found that the queue was already over an hour long. Somewhere way ahead of me stood the girl from Santa Cruz. A single window was open for the sale of tickets to the south. The booking office was not clean. There were numerous puddles on the floor through which we had to drag our luggage. The line doubled and redoubled on itself from end to end of the booking hall. The few gringos visible were dotted around in it at random intervals but as time passed we tended to draw closer together and closer to the end of the queue. The Mexicans had a skilful ability to transfer themselves from one loop of the queue to the next without bothering to move to the outer edge of the loops. The children, who ran everywhere, were the usual excuses for these moves, it being impossible to establish exactly where their proper place was in the queue. The girl from Santa Cruz had been joined by a Mexican aunt, and her party was the first to discover that there were no sleepers left. The entire section had been booked. Faced with a forty-four-hour journey, this was not good news. The next rumour was that there were a few sleepers but the clerk was not so stupid that he was selling them. A certain inducement had to be offered first. This suggestion drove the father of the girl from Santa Cruz into a deeper silent rage than yesterday's. The dirt, the inefficiency, and now, name of God, the corruption! and they not yet out of sight of the U.S. of A. Everything he had shed on that illegal crossing forty years back mocked him now, from the puddles on the floor to the ingratiating smile on the villainous face in the ticket office window. I told his daughter that her twins were lovely and she said 'Thank you' with a surprise and pride that were somehow more Mexican than gringo. She explained the silence of her parents by saying that both 'preferred' to speak Spanish. The truth was that, like so many first-generation Latin immigrants, neither of them had bothered to learn much English, even after forty years in California. Her mother knew hardly any, her father spoke it badly. He looked as though he did not trust himself to speak Spanish either at that moment, but just then the entire party were ushered through the barrier. The aunt had entered into negotiations and saved the day. They had their sleeper. The porters grinned at the father as he passed through. They seemed well-accustomed to the enlarged ideas of Mexicans returning from the States.

By the time I reached the ticket window it was not possible to buy a sleeper on any terms at all, so, with a sinking heart, I prepared myself for two days and nights in the first class. I noticed as I climbed into my carriage that the lavatory was already blocked. A committee of six señoritas formed up outside to wave our train goodbye. One had a flower in her hair and very charming she looked but they got little response from me. I was under the impression that they were waving goodbye to the family seated behind. Too late I realised that they knew no one on the train, they were just practising a sentimental farewell. At 8.30 a.m. on the dot the *rapido* started up, moved about two hundred yards out of the station and then stopped. Exasperated I made my way down towards the *coche comedor* and tried to take stock of my immediate prospects.

Later that morning we began to wind our way across Baja California Norte. In the *coche comedor* there were limp white table-cloths and food-stained walls. Beyond the encrusted window lay the encrusted land; 'Baja California Norte', it had a ring to its name, the land Agent Laudner did not choose to tread. It was sandy soil out there, flat as far as the distant mountains of the Baja peninsula. I had originally intended to travel through Baja California; I was intrigued to know why it had never become part of the United States. Then I learned that it was as long as Italy, almost uninhabited and possessed only one road, and decided to get on with my journey instead. Somewhere between those mountains and the tracks, invisible from my window, lay the Gulf of California, breeding ground of the Pacific whales. Only a month previously one of these had surfaced beside the small boat of an enthusiastic ecologist set on filming this awesome coupling and, with an idle swish of its tail, reduced the voyeur's skull to matchwood, a statement of moral absolutes intelligible even to a Californian.

By the side of the track lay the traces of everything which rail passengers carry. Not the heavy accumulation you would see by the track of an English train – you have to go to a developed country for the full piggery – but impressive none the less because in a dry climate packages take so long to deteriorate. I resumed my book. I was reading *Las Muertas*, 'The Dead Girls', by Jorge Ibargüengoitia the Mexican novelist. It describes how the well-intentioned madame of a brothel gets on the wrong side of the authorities, loses her licence and ends by murdering her staff. When everything goes wrong for the madame she tries for the traditional solution, she takes a bus for the border and is eventually arrested heading for Nogales. Later she reflects on the fate of the girls she had arranged to kill and on the immortality of the soul. It was her opinion that when you died your soul remained floating in the atmosphere. As long as people who had a bad memory of you lived, your soul suffered. Good memories of you gave it joy. When nobody living thought of the dead person the soul disappeared. If so original a theory of immortality could be produced by a procuress I began to wonder whether it was correct to describe Mexico as a Christian country. Then the *carrotero* entered the *coche comedor* and settled down to read at the table next to me. I knew he was the *carrotero*, apparently some sort of senior conductor, by the brass letters on his képi. He was a man of advanced age, one of the many working pensioners of the Mexican railways, which are run on humane principles as a social service for the elderly, and he took no further interest in the proceedings. As he sank back into his armchair I saw the title of his book, *Esclavos Blancos*, and realised that Mexico was a Christian country after all. You can tell a country's religion by its sense of sin. The *carrotero* read of the white slave trade with the gravity of a man making up the day's accounts, nothing broke his concentration and when the matter of my ticket was broached it was not by him but by the head waiter. This wonderful man offered to find me a sleeping berth for 748 pesos, that is for the correct price and offered against receipt. No more of the plastic, superannuated Japanese first-class carriage with its stinking toilet and knobbly Japanese seat; instead the far more battered and far more comfortable surroundings of the superannuated U.S. Pullman car, very similar in design to the 'Spirit of California' but more spacious because this one was built in the 1930s. Sitting behind the cracked pane of my *dormitorio* window the simple pleasure of travel reached me for the first time since I had left England.

At lunch-time, as at breakfast, the only other customers in the dining car were the entire team of *comedor* stewards, all eating. It is wonderful, the devaluation of the peso. Any traveller with a few dollars in his pocket can purchase the solitude, albeit faded, of a misanthropic millionaire. *El Carrotero* was still reading *Esclavos Blancos*. He had not moved. Ibargüengoitia is illuminating on the nature of Mexican uniformed authority, and *El Carrotero* had become for me a character in the book I was reading. My first impression of this country and its people was formed by the imaginary cast of *Las Muertas* who accompanied me at a sedate pace across the northern desert. The procuress in *The Dead Girls* wanted to learn how to fire a revolver. She wanted to murder the man who had jilted her. So she persuaded a subsequent admirer, an army captain, to teach her. To do this he invited her round to the barracks. Teaching a procuress to fire revolvers is rather irregular, it seems, even in the Army of Mexico, so he sent the entire garrison on a route march in order to empty the barracks. There was a magnificent triviality about this route march, this garrison, this army, this country. All over the world unthinking people might suppose that men joined the Army of Mexico in order to defend the Republic of Mexico at the cost, if necessary, of their blood, their honour, their guts. Not so if the captain had to teach a procuress how to fire a revolver. If that happened they were not training in order to defend the Republic. They were training in order to allow this stout, middle-aged female to blaze away in the empty barracks unobserved. Anyway the entire operation was a waste of time. The revolver in question was a heavy ·45. When Serafina eventually pointed it at her former admirer and pulled the trigger she managed to shoot up most of a bakery but missed her target. As she herself put it 'the gun did not obey her'.

So with *El Carrotero*. Since 1927 Mexico has been ruled by the same party, the Revolutionary Institutional Party (P.R.I.). The P.R.I. has never ignored the interests of organised labour. Whereas it might appear that the public railway system is run as a form of public transport, it is actually run in order to enable elderly and respectable Mexicans such as *El Carrotero* to get out of his home, away from the wife, earn a decent whack, enjoy a change of scenery and find somewhere comfortable to pursue his interest in the white slave trade.

Outside the windows the desert was no longer encrusted. It had sprung to life. South of Puerto Penesco we had branched inland from the Gulf of California. The clocks had gone forward one hour. We were now in the state of Sonora which keeps Mountain Time, not Pacific Time. I left the *comedor* and went outside to the open observation platform which joined the Pullman cars. There were red, yellow, white and purple flowers clustered in the grass. Doves swooped past a distant circle of mountains walled in this wilderness like some vast forsaken garden. Only the occasional salt-pan reminded one that it was also a desert. Flowers or not, this place remained a refuge. In the last century rogues from the north who could cross this desert and live might find in Mexico a new life. The fugitive traffic was in the opposite direction now. For several hours, while the sun sank slowly to one side or other of the train, I stood outside, happily drunk on the desert, the wind and the noise. The ancient observation platforms crashed and bucked along the ancient line. Only once was there sign of human life. A man on a horse, an Indian in a cowboy hat, reined in beside the tracks and gazed the length of the passing train without purpose or gesture.

In the late afternoon I was joined by two train bums from the United States. For $125 each had purchased a ticket which allowed unlimited travel on Amtrak's western division. They had started up on the Canadian border in Washington State, had crossed the Rockies twice and, with only one bus link, had transferred to the Mexican system. They shouted all this information above the extraordinary racket made by our centipede-slow train.

'Old trains never die,' they shouted, 'they just go to Mexico.'

'Well, they seem to stay on the tracks,' I shouted, resenting this gringo obsession with new rolling stock.

'Generally, yes,' they shouted in reply. 'But last month there was a derailment on the Chihuahua-Pacifico. About fifteen killed.' I remembered that Jorge Ibargüengoitia had advised me to try the Chihuahua-Pacifico and decided that I did not wish to hear any more about this. And so we trundled into Benjamin Hill.

Look where I might all over Mexico, I never found another town or village with an English name, and the syllables 'Ben-ghameen-ill' do not roll off the Hispanic tongue. All around stand San Miguel, Santa Ana, Magdalena, La Union; but there it is, Benjamin Hill, eight and a half hours down the line from Mexicali, a rail junction, and defiantly Protestant on the ear. At Benjamin Hill I saw again the girl from Santa Cruz, well through the second day in the land of her fathers and by now the ambivalence was getting deep. It was the aunt from Mexicali who appeared to be keeping the show on the road, evidently happy with her task of supervising the twins despite the language barrier. The mother had disappeared into a sleeper and failed to reappear, even for this extensive opportunity to stroll on the platform. The father came to the door of the carriage, but only to search worriedly for his daughter. The best news she had to give him was that I had spent some time in Africa and was therefore 'accustomed to all this'. By the wave of the hand around her I took it she meant normal life in Benjamin Hill. Her father was still suffering from a serious case of embarrassment at the state of his former homeland. So much so that she offered him the news about my African experience eagerly, as though he needed it. She needed it too. Normality had suddenly become the dirt, the harshness, the droopy pace, the obvious poverty of Benjamin Hill, a state of affairs she could hardly see as anything but desperate. The realisation that a potential source of embarrassment, a gringo who might even associate her with 'all this', was in fact enjoying the surroundings was too important to keep to herself.

Just then, as we talked on the platform, as if in conspiracy to brighten her day, the modern world re-entered in the shape of three powerful locomotives pulling a train of low wagons loaded with the rear halves of articulated lorries. The curved steel bases, each bearing so easily their massive cargoes, looked wonderfully efficient; an obvious improvement on any known road system, just the place to store all articulated lorries in the future. This train took several minutes to pass, the unyielding movement of the machinery saying to her that even in Mexico there was hope. Then all was spoiled by the last wagons in the train, for there, humped in the shade between the locked tyres of the lorries, were entire families, women, babies, exhausted men, enjoying a free ride south towards the hopeless part of the country; those too poor to afford even a train ticket, torn by the wind, soaked by the rain, proceeding away from Eldorado for some insufficient reason of their own, their scattered and fragile human scale washing away all the confidence induced by the brutal modernity of the steel rigs they misused. What were these people, crazy?, to be risking their lives on this journey, a truck could shift, a tyre roll, a wagon lurch, and it would be a crushed skull or a broken back or a dead baby. Some of them were actually picnicking up there. *El Carrotero* watched them pass. He stood in a group of brass-studded railway officials. They were as unconcerned as anyone at this irregularity. The benevolent arm of the Revolutionary Institutional Party did not only extend to officials who wished to be carried up and down the system reading pulp literature, the poor too had their less comfortable place on the gravy train. The train slowed to walking pace as it ran between the crowded platforms of Benjamin Hill, the silhouetted families glanced up, indisposed to leave. No one moved, no one waved. Then it speeded up again and the girl from Santa Cruz revealed that not only was she shocked and ashamed of this country, she was also proud of it.

She resolved her shame over Mexico by attacking the United States. *Her* culture shock she said had occurred when she went to live in Minnesota. After California she felt like the only Hispanic in town. Everyone else was white she said, then changed the word to 'anglo'. In fact everyone else was *Swedish*. She described their blonde hair and blue eyes and succeeded in making them sound like albinos. When she took her little girls to the hospital the Swedish mothers of Minnesota saw her brown hair and brown eyes and asked if her sleeping babies had brown eyes too. The Minnesotan doctor had looked at her and asked if she spoke English. She was doing her M.A. at the time and her husband was teaching at the University of California. She told me all this very quickly, like someone who had very little time left. Actually we spent two hours at Benjamin Hill, but her father wanted her back on board. Before she left she asked where I was going and did not wish me luck. 'Have a good trip,' she said; no doubt El Salvador would be very like Benjamin Hill. Ahead of *her* lay Guadalajara and gobbledegook. I never saw her again but the day after she was due to arrive in Guadalajara the newspapers reported that there had been a huge explosion in that town. Five streets had been blown up, cars had been tossed around like matchboxes, much of a *barrio* had subsided by several feet. Three million citizens had been thrown into panic. They were still wondering what had happened. There was a theory that something inflammable might have got into the town drains.

Darkness fell in Benjamin Hill as we waited to link up with the train from Nogales, the connection from Tucson, Arizona. I fell asleep and woke with a jolt to find we had reached Empalme. I remembered Jorge Ibargüengoitia and his advice about the Chihuahua-Pacifico. As the train began to move I realised that this would be the junction. Fortunately my cases were all packed up and there was no one blocking the corridor. Leaving only my slippers behind I managed to throw my baggage down and reach the platform safely. It was midnight. The sixteen-hour ride in a private compartment had cost £8 (800 pesos). As the lights of the train disappeared slowly into the darkness I consulted my map and discovered that I had got out at the wrong stop. And Empalme is a railway station without a hotel.

I waited in the warm, still night for nearly an hour until some rumour reached the nearby town of Guaymas and a taxi came up to the station. The driver charged me 400 pesos for a ride to a hotel. I reproached him with the information that for that amount of money one could travel on the train all the way to the U.S. border. He had a friend beside him in the front seat and as they drove off I heard them discussing how very reasonable the rail fares were nowadays.

Next morning I looked around the town. Guaymas is a small port on the Gulf of California, a rather grubby place I judged it. The main annual event is the deep-sea fishing competition. That was not taking place. I set out to look for somewhere to breakfast. On the way I found a bookstore which stocked a few tattered volumes in English. One of them was a memoir of the student revolution at Berkeley University in 1968. There was a picture of the students. They were dressed up in their best clothes for a demonstration, to emphasise the purity of their arguments. One girl was marching in a cocktail dress, high heels, long white gloves and a new perm.

After breakfast I decided to take the bus down the coast to Los Mochis, the town where I should have left the train to change to the Chihuahua-Pacifico. The bus ride was 220 miles and would take most of the day. In Mexico the train is the cheapest way to travel. It is only in the developed world that buses cost less. None the less the bus station in Guaymas had attracted a crowd of drunken layabouts. One of them was sober enough to tell me, in atrocious English, that unlike the rest of the idlers he was not actually hanging around with no work and no home and nothing to do. He was just sitting in the sun for a few days while he waited for the U.S. consul to issue him with his visa. Then he would return to California to rejoin his family. He derived some self-respect from this story, but his eyes strayed towards my unguarded luggage as eagerly as the next man's. The bus for Los Mochis left with very little warning, bringing some relief from the flies which had accumulated in the sticky shade of its interior. It was an old Greyhound bus. Mexican transport seemed to rely largely on the abandoned machinery of the North. The most noticeable difference from the last Greyhound bus was that the various notices about the safe, reliable, courteous operator and federal smoking regulations had been removed. In their place was just one sign – '*En caso de Mareo pida su bolsa*', in case of sickness ask for a bag.

I received little more impression of Los Mochis than I had of Guaymas. As I drove towards the Hotel Santa Anita that evening the traffic was halted at a green light but nobody was hooting. As we approached the lights three armed policemen leapt from a Jeep and started to haul the occupants from a car with a shattered windscreen. The senior policeman, an elderly gentleman, was holding two revolvers of different sizes, one in each hand. This made it difficult for him to grip his miserable-looking quarry. Apart from that incident I recall only a group of cheeringly flirtatious schoolgirls watching a street raffle, a restaurant menu whose English translation offered 'chicken bosoms', the sugar cane factory which poured its treacly black smoke all over the most expensive offices and shops in the town centre, the street noises that started up at 4.30 a.m. and the early morning taxi-driver who took me to the railway station. When he complained of the weight of my suitcases I told him they were full of books. 'You must be *el jefe*,' he said, '*el profesor*,' which made me think of Carlos, my Spanish teacher.

The Chihuahua-Pacifico must be one of the last railways to be built which opened up remote country. It cuts through a previously impenetrable mountain range, the Sierra Madre Occidental, and was completed by Mexican engineers after gringo experts had abandoned the project. Efforts have been made to turn the route into a tourist attraction, but although the looping gradients are occasionally impressive it is impossible to appreciate the engineers' achievement from within the train. At a halt called Naczari, high up in the Sierra, a small Indian community was engaged in the sale of oranges. It was sunny but terribly cold. The Indians wore thick jackets and straw cowboy hats or peaked baseball caps. A girl aged about thirteen, in a jacket marked 'Houston Oilers', was shredding uncooked cabbage on to a wooden board with a vicious looking knife. The men made a meal out of the oranges and cabbage. A lorry arrived, originally it must have come up on the train because no road crosses the Sierra Madre at this point, and the Indians jostled to unload more sacks of oranges. None of the Indians, men or women, smiled. On the steep hillside behind the station, a two-roomed shack was marked 'Hotel Batopilas', another 'Clinica San Rafael'. A few weeping willow trees, incongruous in these bleak surroundings, forced their way out of the stone and baked mud terracing. The railway committee of Naczari had attached a notice, now yellowing, to the station wall. The word CORRUPTOS had been scrawled across it. Even here? In the past the Indians of north Mexico were famous for the speed at which they could run. They could outrun the deer they hunted. Now that the country had been opened up they sucked cans of Coca-Cola and watched the trains go by. As ours drew out I noticed that the unsmiling girl had finished with the cabbage and was now using the long blade to carve up an orange, very slowly. On her chipped fingernails there was still a trace of pink varnish.

In Mexico the women like to paint themselves. One woman on our train was exquisitely painted, in the style of an Aztec. Her over-tended appearance made some of her fellow passengers look all the stranger. They were a group of two women, with scrubbed, leathery faces, two men and two boys. The men were identical, old and blond with wrinkled, sunburnt necks; so were the women, old and grey, wearing black shawls and embroidered smocks like Swiss peasants. If you looked at them directly their hands moved to their shawls as though they were about to cover their faces. The boys were remote, solemn, very blond and rather lumpy, not deer runners. The only time I saw these women laugh was when the Aztec woman emerged from the train's lavatory, even more highly-painted, scented and dimpled than before, to see her little son shitting in the gangway. She stepped over the results and summoned the steward.

I asked the man next to me who the embroidered people were. Were they German? They spoke a guttural tongue. He glanced at them and said that they were either German or Dutch but in any case Mexican. They lived here. Then he reinserted his scholarly nose into the book which had absorbed him since our departure, *La Doctrina Secreta* by Madame Blavatsky. I was not to solve the mystery until I visited the museum in Chihuahua and saw a room devoted to the Mennonites. They had first come to Mexico in 1921 from the United States. They spoke a German dialect. They were not quite so extreme as their American relations, the Amish, who forswore buttons on their clothes in favour of hooks and eyes. Some of the Mennonite children were now taught Spanish. And sure enough when the ticket collector came round on the train it was the two boys who dealt with him. These boys wore the same dungarees and check shirts as their fathers, but in place of the straw hats they too wore the peaked baseball caps found everywhere else on the American continent. I learned in the museum that their sisters were given scaled down but usable enamel kitchenware as toys, in contrast to the toys given to the neighbouring Tarahumara Indians who gave *their* children crudely-carved wooden monoplanes and helicopters with the windows drawn in with biro.

The Mennonites got off the train at Creel, a logging station trying to turn itself into a tourist centre. The two boys, despite their baseball caps, looked wistfully back. They faced a life apart. I wondered what they would have to do to make themselves unacceptable to the rest of their community: wear zips on their trousers perhaps.

At Divisadero Barrancas, the central point of the Sierra Madre, we were allowed half an hour off the train. This is the head of the Urique Canyon, 'Mexico's Grand Canyon' as someone has dubbed it, and here the Indians were lined up again. But these people were so poor they weren't even drinking Coke. The women just sat in a resigned line on the steps leading down to the tourist viewing platform, too despondent to bang the drums or wave the baskets which they wanted to sell. From the viewing platform one could look down into a forest of orange trees, avocado trees, and banana trees, one could accept that it concealed pumas, parrots and monkeys but splendid though it was, it was not the Grand Canyon, and it was hard to believe that many Indians still chose to live in it. None of us troubled the exhausted Indians with our custom as we made our way back to the impatiently whistling train.

Later on the way there was a graveyard, somehow hacked out of the stony soil and the wire rooted grass. Its wooden crosses were painted gay shades of pastel blue and green and garlanded with flowers, as though for a wedding. A grave is a luxury for the Indians. It costs 500 pesos, twice the price of a shelf-space in the local mausoleum. This cemetery stood on the kind of mountain plateau that, however parched the ground, however harsh the sun, looks cold. Around the cemetery wall grazed the woolly-coated, half-grown longhorns, shrunken cousins of the famous Texas breed. Small though they were it seemed remarkable that they reached even that size given the sparse grazing. The iron ground, the clear air, the graveyard at this altitude, all these combined to question the possibility of life. The colours denied it most emphatically; the land went grey where it was parched, not brown, as though it had been blanched by snow rather than burnt by sun.

There was only one delay, at San Juanito, while we waited for a goods train to pass on its way down to the Pacific. Then, as the day drew to a close, I realised that I had spent fourteen hours in the crowded carriage of a Mexican train and what a painless experience this had been. Fourteen hours in one seat, no dining car, two sandwiches, one beer, one fizzy orange, between 7 a.m. and 9.30 p.m., and compared to the horrors of fourteen hours on a British Rail Inter-City Express the whole experience had been rather enjoyable. The difference lay in the behaviour of the Mexican passengers and crew. They included no louts, no transistor radio bores, no squalling kids, no sulky and resentful waiters anxious to impress their customers with the hardship of their lot. Children who started to cry were immediately drowned in female attention. The atmosphere was one of patience, humour and courtesy.

As darkness fell I struck up a conversation with Teresa, a student of engineering at the University of Chihuahua, who had been acting as guide on the train. It was her eighteenth birthday, and she was returning home with her fiancé, José Luis, a twenty-four-year-old dentist. Teresa was a rich Mexican mixture of childishness and maturity. While she was working one would have taken her for twenty-four years old. But when she stopped discussing heights, distances, dates and turned to the things that really mattered, her family and her fiancé, she was much younger in her manner than any English eighteen-year-old. The elegant hostess suddenly became a person who wrinkled her nose, stuck out her tongue and refused to address José Luis in anything but baby talk. The subjects she chiefly teased him about were his advanced age and the frightful possibility that he might one day have to marry her.

José Luis was the first Mexican with whom I risked a political conversation, and the first Mexican to produce for me the political catchphrase – 'Poor Mexico. So far from God, so close to the United States.' At the time I thought he was a rather cynical young man. He said that the only hope for Mexico was to take a United States governor-general. Mexican politicians were all completely corrupt, he said. They were bandits. Only a few years after Mexico's famous oil boom the problems included soaring prices, commodity shortages, the collapse of the peso and even hunger. Only the last was dangerous for politicians. He thought that the most recent elections, which had returned the Revolutionary Institutional Party yet again, were that party's last chance. Next time, surely, one of the opposition parties would triumph at last.

'My friends all say, "José Luis, why don't *you* do something. We will support you." But you can't beat the system. In Mexico the art of politics is the art of eating shit without pulling a face. Look at that tough act we put on when President Carter came down here. What a sham! Look at the reality. The reality is now. Despite all that oil-money, we can't pay our debts. The U.S. has 90 per cent of our trade. So where did all the money go? The politicians had it. Thousands of millions of dollars. Ask anyone.'

This sounded like wild talk but shortly after my conversation with José Luis it was reported that the former director of the Mexican Petroleum Company, who had been replaced at the recent presidential election, was accused of defrauding the state of $34 million. He could not be prosecuted because he still enjoyed the immunity of a state senator.

Before I parted from José Luis and Teresa I arranged to meet him for lunch on the following day. José Luis wanted to show me round Chihuahua. He said he was very proud of it. But he never turned up and the telephone at his dental surgery remained unanswered. The last I saw of them was when they climbed into the comfortable limousines which had come to the station to meet them, Teresa, José Luis, his father and mother, several brothers and sisters, and many others. All disappeared into the darkness of the night and the obscurity of their well-protected relationships. The following week there was another collision on the Chihuahua-Pacifico. It occurred at San Juanito when the passenger train failed to switch into the siding and ran straight into the upcoming goods train. Three people were killed and fifty-six injured. Perhaps Teresa was not on duty that day.

Chihuahua is a town whose name brings a smile to the western lip because of the repulsive little dog that bears its name. Having always tried to know as little as possible about this beast I was surprised on arriving in town to learn that there was another breed of local dog, the *xoloizcuintli* or *tepezcuintle*, a hairless dog descended from a mythological breed known in Ethiopia, Asia and the Andes. The name *xolotl* means monster, so even to the Aztecs these awful dogs were known as 'monster dogs'. They were kept for two purposes, their tender flesh and their body temperature. The Mexican Hairless Dog maintains a constant body temperature of 104°F. and a few of them, placed at strategic parts of the body, are very comforting at night. Nor do they disturb you by panting, for they perspire like humans through their flea-bitten wrinkled flesh. I felt that I should strike up an acquaintance with a Mexican Hairless, but try as I might I could not find one. 'Chihuahua' in Mexico means a university, a state capital, an enormous state. My interest in the dog baffled all with whom I pursued it.

The town can still give an impression of its origins, of one-storey, wood-boarded shacks surrounded by mountains and lesser mountains, crushed by vast skies, lost in what Malcolm Lowry called the 'endless, weary, cactus plains of north Mexico'. The desert winds blow the tumbleweed backwards and forwards, together with the town litter. The litter never seems to get blown more than a couple of miles out before it is all blown back again. In the older part of the town one can sense still that refuge the fugitives sought. From here it is 150 miles to the Rio Grande, which marks the border with Texas, the lost state of Mexico, and 150 miles beyond that to the Pecos river, where the writ of U.S. marshals once ceased to run. And it was in the old quarter of Chihuahua that I eventually discovered something even more interesting then the *xoloizcuintli*; this was *La Quinta Luz*, the house of the widow of Pancho Villa.

Jorge Ibargüengoitia, who was shortly to meet his own death in a plane crash, told me that he had always wondered why all the national heroes of Mexico met violent deaths. This so puzzled him that he once wrote a play about it. Pancho Villa is a Mexican hero and in his case it might even be said that his status is entirely dependent on his violent death.

The first point to note about Pancho Villa is that he was not called that, his name was Doroteo Arango, Dorothy – literally a 'boy named Sue' in the gringo imagination. By his own account, and that is another point to mark, Doroteo was driven into a life of banditry at the age of sixteen when he surprised the local landowner in the act of abducting his sister, and shot him. From then on the words 'and shot him' punctuate all accounts of the life of Pancho Villa. Some doubt has been cast on the romantic story of Doroteo's intervention in his sister's fate, few bandits fail to plead social injustice as the reason for their vocation, but it is at least agreed that as a young man Doroteo was one of a gang of cattle rustlers whose leader was a man called Francisco Villa, known as Pancho. The real Villa was shot by the *rurales*, the mounted police, and Doroteo then adopted his name and his position. He became the leader of the gang.

The new Francisco Villa led his men out of his birthplace in the state of Durango into the less populated northern state of Chihuahua. There was at this stage in his career nothing to distinguish him from the average bandit leader. He was just another cruel, ignorant and heartless man with an unusual strength of personality. He was twenty in 1900 when, it is agreed on all sides, he killed a man for money in Chihuahua. It could be added that he had grown up at a time when Mexican society was in a bad way. Under the dictator Porfirio Diaz little or nothing was done for the poor. The Church in 1906 was described by a just man like Charles Macomb Flandrau as 'corrupt, grasping and resentful'. In the north of the country in particular the land was owned by a few rich families and the condition of the people who had to work for them was pitiful. Peasants were often paid in food which was sufficient for them but not for their families. In order to feed their families they had to borrow from their employers, and they were soon caught in a web of debt from which they could only escape by unpaid labour. In many cases the only inheritance they left their children was the years of unpaid labour they still owed. And so the next generation had to work for the same rich family on endlessly deteriorating terms. The longer they worked the more they owed. The government of the elderly Porfirio Diaz which presided over this situation made itself so hated that the armed uprising of the oppressed which eventually overthrew it is still the cornerstone of the modern Mexican constitution. Before the destruction of that system, one way to escape a lifetime of debt-bondage was to take to the gun.

The long-awaited armed revolt occurred in 1910, and Pancho Villa, motivated perhaps by a mixture of hatred for the *federales* who opposed his banditry, an eye for the main chance, and even, who knows, a concern for social justice, joined the uprising, granting himself the rank of colonel in the revolutionary army. Since he brought with him a useful force of armed and desperate men, he was pardoned for his previous crimes by the revolutionary leader Francisco Madero, and confirmed in his rank; and so began the unexpected rise to respectability of Pancho Villa.

In the legend of Pancho Villa two themes are frequently emphasised by modern Latin American revolutionaries. First there is the time of exile in the Sierra. Fidel Castro came down to Havana after several years in the Cuban Sierra. The guerrillas of El Salvador today descend from the hills to rob poor bus passengers. The passengers must pay 'the People's Tax'. This is the Robin Hood theme and it does not bear too close examination. The second theme is that of the time of reflection: life is reduced to hardship and bare necessity, on a sparse diet the mind clears, the future lies bright ahead, and suddenly the foundations of a political philosophy have been laid. So Villa, disengaging briefly from the *rurales* who wanted him for a long string of murders, robberies and arsons, met the future President Madero who had himself journeyed back from exile in the United States, and found himself an officer in *La Primera Division del Norte del Ejercito Libertador*, the first Northern Division of the Army of Liberation. The scene was set for a historic encounter. Madero, a high-minded man in need of troops, granted Villa an amnesty 'considering that the outrages of the representatives of the dictatorship obliged him in self-defence to commit certain acts'; an explanation that reads very like one written at gunpoint. How did Villa respond to his new leader? He said, 'Madero is a rich man who fights for the good of the poor. He looks small in body to me, but I believe he is great in spirit. If all the rich men in Mexico were like him nobody would have to fight and the sufferings of the poor would not exist, since we would be doing our duty. Because what should be the occupation of the rich if not to work to raise the poor out of their misery?' Ten years of pillage, slaughter and intellectual effort in the Sierra Madre had borne fruit.

But Pancho Villa did not allow his social conscience to make him flabby. According to the Mexican general Luis Garfias M., who has written a rather hostile account of the life of Doroteo Arango, Villa was intelligent, shrewd and masterful. He was also unusually violent, even for a Mexican bandit leader. Throughout his time as a colonel in the Army of Liberation Pancho Villa shot his prisoners. He also shot civilian witnesses of these atrocities. Once, when acting as state governor of Chihuahua, he shot a British rancher; the man had come to him to complain about cattle rustling by Villa's 'troops' and had spoken insolently. Another time Villa ordered a Mexican doctor and two nurses who were tending enemy wounded to be shot. They were saved at the last minute by outside intervention. Regular army officers did not approve of Villa's behaviour and at one point Colonel Villa was himself ordered before a firing squad by a superior officer who had become exasperated by his horse thieving. He was reprieved when the order 'Ready' had been given, but not before he had sunk to his knees in fear. There is one anecdote which throws a dreadfully clear light on what it must have been like to face Pancho Villa from a position of weakness. His men blew up a government train and captured the brakeman's apprentice. 'How old are you, lad?' asked General Villa (he had been promoted).

'Seventeen, General.'

'Oh, how I would like to be young like you, to fight so many more years,' said Villa. He patted the boy affectionately on the back twice, then ordered him to be taken away to be shot with the other prisoners. Writing of this incident, Luis Garfias M. says, 'Anecdotes like this dot the life of Francisco Villa, filling with blood and cruelty the existence of a man who did not know how to be equal to the occasion.' This is a gentle judgment. The truth is that Villa was drunk with death.

Despite the rather unattractive side to his character, the city of Chihuahua holds Villa in high regard today. Towards the end of his life he married a local girl. She was called Luz Corral and her house, La Quinta Luz, has become a museum to the great man's memory although he never lived there. Going around the museum it becomes clear that the revolution did at least allow one of its children to escape 'the sufferings of the poor'. It contains, among many other of Villa's possessions, a white leather saddle with ornamental pommel, a 1919 Dodge automobile with open sides and wooden-spoked wheels, and even an 'AutoStrop safety-razor, made in the U.S.A.'. The attractive garden is not so much walled as fortified; there are rifle slits cut into the ornamental stone mirador.

Mrs Luz Villa survived her husband by some years, long enough to benefit from the full process of rehabilitation. She lived to receive a delegation from the Los Angeles Press Club, who presented her with a brass plaque. This now stands near the framed '$5,000 Reward' poster issued by the Chief of Police of Columbus, New Mexico, on 9 March 1916. There are pictures of Luz Villa with Anthony Quinn and Clark Gable, a framed poem by Eileen Rockefeller, 'To Mrs Villa . . . Where others would have shrunk from publicity, You ask us in . . .', and a framed papal blessing dated 1933. In general the old boy's picture, which is widely displayed, makes him look frightfully respectable. One of his impromptu little speeches is also displayed. 'I am a fighting man, I am not a *politico*. I have not studied Laws. I know nothing of such things.' Very true. The polite young man who guided me round the house was clearly a devotee of the cult. He wore a grave expression and a Mao cap and he refused my tip with dignity. He had been fulfilling a duty. Villa would probably have shot him.

So what happened to Pancho Villa in the end, what prevented him from kissing the hand of Eileen Rockefeller and opening a few bottles with the delegates from the Los Angeles Press Club? Where was he when the papal blessings were posted off in 1933?

As the revolution wore on Villa began to revert to type. His brutality and indiscipline made him an outcast among army officers so he simply resumed his former career. He defied the forces of the Army of Liberation, now called the Constitutional Army, just as he had defied those of the much-hated Porfirio Diaz. After one train attack too many Pancho Villa was declared 'a reactionary rebel', outlaw and fair game. If he had been shot at this point few people today would remember his name. But he was not. Instead he launched the action which led to the $5,000 reward being offered by a gringo police chief.

When his official supply of weapons was cut off Villa started to buy guns from Samuel Rabel, the owner of a hardware store in the small border town of Columbus, in the state of New Mexico. Eventually Rabel, no doubt thinking himself safe in the United States, took some of Villa's money and refused to supply him with any guns on the grounds that he was nothing but a bandit. So one night Villa stole across the border with a large force and attacked the town of Columbus. He burnt several buildings and killed people in their sleep, but he failed to find Mr Rabel who had gone to El Paso to be treated for toothache. It was this outrage which led to the famous expedition by General Pershing. Two brigades of U.S. cavalry, infantry and artillery roamed around the state of Chihuahua for ten months. They did not once succeed in making contact with Pancho Villa but they triumphed in several engagements over the Mexican army.

For four more years Pancho Villa terrorised the north of Mexico, then he decided to take advantage of an amnesty and retire. Surprisingly, even at this stage, Mexico gave him a generous pay-off for his revolutionary services, as well as a bodyguard. He bought a *hacienda* in his home state of Durango, where he had killed his first man, and settled down with Luz. But by this time north Mexico was full of the relatives of men he had murdered, and they did not intend to pardon him. In 1923 a conspiracy of prominent citizens, including the legislative deputy for Durango, ambushed the open-sided Dodge and riddled Pancho Villa with bullets as he drove himself into the nearby town of Hidalgo del Parral. For this act the legislative deputy was sentenced to twenty years in prison. He only served six months. His lawyers appealed successfully on the grounds that the decree that had once declared Villa outlaw justified the killing, amnesty or not.

It was really by two events, his criminal raid on Columbus and the violent manner of his death, that Villa ensured his status as a Mexican hero. Luis Garfias M. has argued that the raid on Columbus was 'disgraceful and is . . . the fundamental reason why . . . he can never be a national hero'. He adds that it was bad enough that Villa should have killed defenceless people as they slept, 'but what is more serious is that this should have provoked the North American invasion and that Mexico should have suffered the ten-month humiliation inflicted by Pershing's soldiers . . . The erroneous custom exists of calling heroes all those who are able to come out victorious in what they do, and also those who through circumstances of fate fall victims to their cause. But a hero is only he who gives up his life for certain absolutes and imposes his qualities on all opponents.' Here the general is speaking for himself, not for Mexico. For it is precisely the category he condemns, 'the victims of fate', who tend to attract Mexican admiration, provided they are flamboyant enough.

There is a wonderful concreteness about this word 'hero' as used by Garfias M. It is clearly an exact status. The Mexican Pantheon is as solid as the French, though it exists only in the imagination of the Mexican people. What is it that Mexico found so heroic in Pancho Villa? His raid on Columbus is still described, even by some of his warmest admirers, as an outrage. It reduced him to the level of a brute and his brutality is recognised and deplored. But, in truth, that it provoked so strong a response from the United States is a secret source of national pride rather than a cause of continued humiliation. To provoke a Mexican humiliation at gringo hands is not necessarily a disqualification for heroism, provided the provocation was outrageous enough. You don't invade a country that doesn't matter. And by himself evading the pursuit, Villa 'got away with it'. Even Luis Garfias M. cannot resist suggesting that Pershing was only sent in because William Randolph Hearst's newspaper chain used the outrage to whip up the anti-Mexican feeling that existed in the United States.

And then there is Villa's violent death. Here is the man who falls victim at last to his fate and so lives out the Mexican pageant of life and death in a satisfyingly violent manner. Sybille Bedford tells in *A Visit to Don Otavio* of how she read in a Mexican book of *Useful Words and Phrases* the following exchange.

'"Are you interested in death, Count?"

"Yes, very much, Your Excellency."'

Very much interested in death, and particularly in the manner of it, and more particularly so when death is clearly linked to the actions taken in life – as it is so vividly when it appears as a punishment meted out by fate, as it appeared so vividly through the open sides of a white Dodge automobile on the road to Hidalgo del Parral.

Apart from his brutality Pancho Villa's lack of imagination is deplored, as are his lack of nobility or generosity, and his dishonesty, and his criminal origins by those who do not accept that he was driven to this by social injustice. What is left to admire? There is mainly his strength; his strength of personality, even his strength of mind – though it was a narrow intelligence. And he had sufficient sense of his Mexican destiny to continue struggling violently when he might have given up, until he won his early grave.

In 1925 this grave in Parral was robbed of Pancho Villa's skull, an act which, it was subsequently discovered, was committed by a platoon of extremely nervous soldiers on the orders of the local military commander. The head was taken in a suitcase to the house of this general and then flown away in a private aeroplane to an unknown destination. But before the truth emerged the strangest rumours circulated around Mexico. It was said that the head had been taken by the people of Columbus, New Mexico, to be exhibited in revenge. Then it was said to be in the American Museum of Natural History in New York. Then it was said to have been seen in the Ringling Brothers Circus. Wherever it was, it was evidence of Pancho Villa's success as a ferocity who lived on in gringo hearts. So, as the cult of a saint grows from the obstinate unofficial devotion of humble people, did Mexico cultivate this appalling hero.

Mexico is an old country. In 1575 its books were printed in Spanish and in twelve Indian languages. Its first printing press was set up a hundred years before the first press appeared in the British colonies to the north. The Mayan culture, the memory of which still dominates the lives of many Mexican Indians, developed a sophisticated astrology a thousand years ago. Under Spanish rule Mexico, for a time, led northern Europe in art and science. The ruins of that glory lie visibly on all sides in Mexico today. In 1857 Benito Juarez, an Indian general, fought so resolutely against a French army that he and his men overthrew the Emperor Maximilian and expelled the French. Mexico seemed set to be a country that mattered for centuries to come.

Yet today a politician, aged twenty-four, sees Mexico's only hope in a governor from the United States and his despair is not entirely histrionic. Juarez represents only one side of the national character. A corrupt church and a cruel dictatorship were finally overthrown by a Marxist revolution in 1917. The party which has governed the country ever since has made corruption and the pursuit of personal wealth its governmental emblem. The people are once more at the mercy of greed and indifference.

When the Mexican painter Frida Kahlo accompanied her husband, Diego Rivera, to New York in 1930 she looked around her and felt an easy superiority. 'I don't particularly like the gringo people,' she wrote. 'They are boring and they all have faces like unbaked rolls.' She christened the land she was in 'Gringolandia', and she longed to return to Mexican civilisation. The frontiers of Gringolandia have been extended since those days. They lie a long way south of the Rio Grande, somewhere between Chihuahua and Mexico City, and the people who live there are sufficiently demoralised to hero-worship a man because he killed children in their beds.

3

Wired for Sound

'When two cars converge on a narrow bridge from opposite directions the driver who first flashes his lights has right of way.'

Mexican Highway Code

I was seated in the roof garden of the Hotel Majestic, overlooking the Zócalo in Mexico City, when I became aware of a person near by. She had placed herself in the shade of a large umbrella and, while attacking a club sandwich, was trying to gain my attention. The sandwich, pinioned helplessly between the painted nails, periodically forced between the painted lips, had submitted to the delicate attention of her sharp little teeth. There was some evidence that it had put up quite a fight; bits of lettuce and mayonnaise were stuck to her upper lip and scattered around the table. But it had by now given up the struggle and accepted its fate. Just the odd squelching noise and squirt of mayonnaise showed that it was still conscious of what was happening.

She was at first glance a type of Mexican woman frequently seen in the more elegant streets of the capital, about fifty, tight slacks, every hair in a place God never thought of putting it, face made up like a China figurine, beneath her dimpled arm a talcum-powdered dog, borne above street level in order to keep it clean enough to carry. I used to look at these fluffy dogs and consider the life they led. Odd to be carried around every day, thrust up beside those huge, yielding, scented breasts: the scented hands with their razor talons twisted in one's fur, the elevated point of view over the rest of the world's dogs, the lack of a need to place one paw in front of another: not all bad the dog's life. One was transported from bowl of food to bowl of water, occasionally one met another dog of one's own class, circumstanced in equal comfort, but in their case proceeding from bowl of water to bowl of food.

'Psst . . . *Ciao, ciao. Va bene?*' I had a closer look at this person under the umbrella. She was younger than I had thought, too young still for the dog; she was dressed like a hostess in an expensive clip-joint and she was apparently under the impression that I was Italian. I corrected her about that. It made no difference. Effortlessly she drew me away from my postcards and my citron pressé. I found myself seated under the umbrella, a club sandwich before me. She was cutting it up for me, she was telling me about herself. She seemed to be saying that she was a psychiatrist.

Her name was Aurora. She said that her uncle had been the governor of Durango state. I asked her if she liked him. She said that he was 'agreeable', but rather too fond of money. Her father on the other hand, though a Colombian by birth, had been a general in the Army of Mexico. I told her that I did not want a club sandwich. I had already eaten. She reassured me, that was quite all right. She took a bite out of mine and sent it back. She told the waiter to bring another one. I liked more mayonnaise on my sandwiches she said. He, who had taken so little notice of my own views on food, hurried to obey her.

I wondered whether she was a Colombian coke dealer or a genuine doctor. It was just possible that an intelligent woman who was a psychiatrist would dress in this way. She wore a frilly nylon blouse that plunged around on her like a puppy on a trampoline. Her dyed hair was arranged in a mass of crazy bubbles. She was obviously desperate to talk to someone, even to a man who had never heard of her uncle or her father. She said that we would talk in Spanish. She spoke no English and little French. She proceeded to talk in Spanish quite fast. She said that I need not say when I failed to understand her, it was always perfectly obvious from my expression, she was a psychiatrist. I regretted that I was too tired to disguise my incomprehension.

The club sandwich returned, Aurora cut it up again and I found myself feeding helplessly off the pieces which she handed to me. She told me about her psychiatric exams in Durango. She was working in one of the state mental hospitals. When she had taken some more exams she intended to leave the hospital and work with handicapped children. If she was a dope dealer she had an unusual line in banter. The conversation turned to marriage. Aurora was the second Latin American who fed me in this way and then started to discuss marriage. The first occasion occurred in a coffee shop in Panama City when a delightful Peruvian person ordered me a steak, sent it back, and then turned the conversation to nuptials.

Aurora told me that she was not married. She told me that she would never marry a Mexican. The men of Mexico were all so macho. I suggested that there must be a selection of Mexican men who did not suffer from machismo. She *snorted* her contempt at this suggestion. I had to agree with her that machismo is everywhere in Mexico. Driving me at 50 m.p.h. in a cab that lurched even on a straight road the owner had taken both hands off the steering wheel to glance at himself in the mirror and run all his fingers through his hair. His hair had been dyed. I asked Aurora about this. Why, in a country obsessed with manliness, do so many men dye their hair? It is a fascination with them. They dye it jet black, Indian black. Then they grow moustaches to prove that they are not Indians. It is widely believed that pure-bred Indians do not grow facial hair. There is even a restaurant in Mexico City called *Les Moustaches*, where the entire staff wear them. Aurora had nothing to say about this and I began to wonder whether her complaints about machismo were heartfelt. If women did not find machismo attractive it would never have caught on. Aurora started to complain about her boy-friend who was absent from her side for a few hours. She seemed designed for infidelity, not perhaps for the act but for the suggestion. I had an idea that when this unsatisfactory male returned he would be sleek and dyed and hairy and very, very macho. He would inspect the remains of my club sandwich. He would bow to me courteously. Then he would sweep Aurora off to their room and rend her limb from limb in a highly satisfactory manner.

As Aurora rattled on I remembered an engraving by the great Mexican artist Pousada. It is entitled, 'A rustic Don Juan pursued by his victims'. A small and very worried-looking Mexican is running in flat-footed panic from an enraged crowd of women whose faces anticipate the pleasure of the violent encounter they seek. Aurora could have taken her place in that crowd of women, for, like them, she had no one to betray. There was, after all, no boy-friend. She was staying in the hotel alone. Time wore on and it became more and more obvious. Did I enjoy the theatre, she cried. Perhaps I preferred French women to the women of Italy and Spain? This was an insult. She had had enough. Eventually we descended together in the lift. When we reached her floor she left me. I could return, rather baffled, to my postcards.

Of all the wonders I saw in Mexico City none matched my first view of the Zócalo from the roof garden of the Majestic Hotel. It is grotesque, an enormous square laid out on the site of the centre of the Aztec city which Cortés captured at such cost. At that altitude, 7,300 feet, sunlight stabs through the thin air and magnifies an already grand scale. The buildings around that Zócalo form a cliff face of black granite; they are crushingly imperial, built to deploy the brutal force of seventeenth-century Spain. Here, at the heart of its American empire, the power of Spain grew into something frightening to see. It was of course psychologically important for the Spanish to dominate this space and to destroy the memory of what had stood there before. When the Aztecs ruled, their sacrificial pyramid stood near the present site of the cathedral. The steps ran with the blood of humans sacrificed alive, including the blood of all those conquistadors taken prisoner before the city fell. The dwindling band of Spaniards paused in their fighting, looked up and watched them die. They needed no greater incentive to victory. Once taken, the Aztec citadel had to be thoroughly remade, and it was horrifyingly done.

But in modern Mexico ancient grandeur is hard to sustain. In the centre of the Zócalo the national flag of Mexico flies. This flag is the area of a tennis court and is suspended from a pole as high as a television mast. At 6.00 p.m., after Aurora had left me, I watched them haul it down. One of the vast doors in the slablike wall of the National Palace opened and a military band of buglers and drummers emerged and goose-stepped across the square towards the flag. The tinny bugle calls briefly rang out, the vast flag was folded and laid reverently in a plastic cradle. The band struck up an anthem and the scattered detachment sang it, their voices soon lost in the enormous space. Then the senior officer led the march back towards the yawning hole in the cliff face. I wondered if this important task had ever fallen to the general, Aurora's father. This particular officer was a small man and he was escorted by two much larger attendants; one had a vivid impression as the three of them strutted along that the small man in the centre was not in charge of the occasion but under arrest. Their footsteps echoed back in syncopated beat from the surrounding stones and one wanted to laugh, so comically pretentious did this ceremony seem under the shadow of these alarming buildings. And then, without warning, there came a sound which did match the imperial scale of the Zócalo. It was the authentic voice of the conquest, surviving here as defiantly as the buildings. From the turrets of the cathedral the bells began to ring out. There was nothing melodious about those bells, they clanged and crashed in an unmusical tumult for ten minutes, and while they did so it was difficult to hear the man beside you speak. It was as though giants were beating empty gasometers with railway tracks.

My first impressions of Mexico City were all favourable. In the streets around the Zócalo there were barrel organists in khaki uniforms and peaked caps. They were licensed by the authorities, dressed in this way to distinguish them from common beggars. The organs were museum pieces, one still going at full volume bore a brass plate marked 'Berlin 1910'. The organ players did not make much money. The Mexicans gave frequently but in very small amounts. I sat down in a café for lunch one day beside an elegant old man who blew cigar smoke all over my soup. The barrel organist's mate came round the tables and this old gent gave him a 5 peso piece (2½ pence) for which he demanded 2 pesos change. When the old gent rose to leave one saw that, in the manner of urban Mexicans, he had added to his conventional costume the unexpected detail. He wore a blue pinstripe suit and a brown trilby. Beneath the trilby, only visible from the rear, he had knotted a pirate headscarf. Outside the café two little boys who were selling flowers approached him. He brushed them off like flies. They threw their arms around each other and broke into a soft shoe shuffle with vocal chant. They did it out of high spirits, perhaps they were inspired by the pirate headscarf. If they had given away their carnations and sold the dance they would have made a lot more money.

The street theatre spilled over into the cathedral. On Palm Sunday there was a splendidly chaotic high mass. The central aisle was packed with Indian worshippers who before mass had been weaving and selling palms on the steps outside. Two *animateurs* waved their arms at different speeds throughout the service with unfortunate results. Eventually the Cardinal Archbishop seated on his throne threw up his hands in despair and started issuing angry instructions to the master of ceremonies. He, in turn, started rushing around the sanctuary like an ineffectual head waiter. A little Indian boy did good business selling palms to the devout Spanish ladies who were without. When the procession of palms started he begged more palms, pathetically, off one of the robed priests and then started selling those too. In front of me a carefully dressed, severe-faced spinster, her lips moving in continuous prayer, tried to make a space for herself among the Indians sprawled all around. She polished everything she touched: her bench, the kneeler, the back of the bench in front. Somewhere in the crowded congregation a transistor radio was playing dance music. The Indians noticed none of this but joined in the nineteenth-century hymns, their clattering voices impervious to the finer distinctions between the notes. The service reached its climax with a vision. The crowds of tourists battling round the side aisles all the way through mass, taking photographs and calling to each other as though they were in a fun-fair, suddenly parted, and about 150 blond, blue-eyed gringos marched past. They were gigantic boys and girls, all dressed in navy blue trousers or skirts and crisp white shirts. Each wore a large stars and stripes sewn on to the shirt. This was not the low profile of North America. Then they marched out, as suddenly as they had marched in. From the expressions on their faces they looked almost as culture-shocked as the Mexicans they left behind.

One evening, while dining at a pavement café, I watched a man setting out to achieve intoxication with *mescal* and whisky chasers. It did not take him long. The more he drank, the less he moved. By the end he summoned the waiter with just one hand, even his eyes were stilled. He seemed to be chiefly supported in an upright position by the muscles of his neck. He wore a red cravat around his neck and his face gradually changed colour to match it. He looked to me like an Englishman, but not a tourist. The waiters were beginning to wonder how they would move him to the street when I glanced towards the pavement and forgot all about him because I saw a face I knew.

She was called Stella and she was with a friend, Edward. Later that week we went out to dinner and they introduced me to *mescal*, the drink that stilled the Englishman's eyes. The barman dropped a piece of cactus worm into our glasses to improve the drink. Then we took a taxi to the Plaza Garibaldi to hear the *mariachi* bands. In the centre of the square there is a shrine, the statue of Saint Cecilia, the patron saint of musicians. The saint is protected by a glass case and the base of this is heaped with notes and coins offered by those who hope that their visit to the plaza will change their luck or the course of their lives. All around, under the trees and far into the night, stand the bandsmen, trumpeters, accordionists, guitarists, singers, playing to each other or to anyone who will pay for a song. The atmosphere in the Plaza Garibaldi, composed of the raucous music, the dashing style and bandit costumes of the bandsmen and the insulting words of their songs, is relentlessly Mexican.

Distracted by the *mescal* I was surprised to find myself sitting in a booth in Tenampa, one of the few bars which admitted women. I was still with Stella and Edward. A man was singing to us. He had grey hair, a face like a rubber monkey and the most mischievous eyes in Mexico.

'Ayeeeeeeeeeeeeeee . . .' he sang. 'Farewellllllll . . . Oh what drinking. What drinking took place . . . during this night of sentiment!! There can be, no other land like mine. Where you find men who are pee-ure Macho. And where you find the real drunks.'

The noise he made was unbelievable. He was not singing alone. He was accompanied by three guitars, two violins, a double bass and two heart-rending, ear-splitting trumpeters. All these men were dressed in skin-tight black trousers and short waistcoats, and they were dripping with silver embroidery. Silver ornaments were sewn into their bulging trouser seams. They pressed around our booth trapping us still deeper in the extraordinary noise of their music. The voice of the elderly rubber monkey soared above the general racket. The words of the song were most affecting. It was as though we were drowning in the sound and the sentiment. We ordered more tequila and gazed deeply into the eyes of the monkey. From somewhere above and behind his open mouth, from somewhere beyond the torrent of song, his arched blue eyes gazed back at us. I thought I would burst into tears, so overwhelmed was I by the proximity of this genius and philosopher.

Before this could happen the situation was saved by the arrival of another man, not a musician, holding a wooden contraption which looked like outdated stock from the police interrogation room. Edward said that this man was called 'Annihilation'. He had a grey streak running through his hair like a lightning flash and he invited me to attach myself to his electric shock machine. 'He says the maximum strength is ninety,' said Edward. Ninety what?

Looking down at my hands I saw that each gripped a small metal barrel which was attached by wire to the machine. 'Ten,' said Annihilation, moving his little dial. 'Twenty.' Edward and Stella watched me with interest. 'Thirty.' I began to feel an agreeable tingling sensation in my arms. It was probably the tequila, or maybe the *mescal*. Edward had said that at the altitude of Mexico City, tequila did not make you drunk. 'Fifty.' Edward said that you must never drink it at sea level. 'Sixty' – Annihilation was also watching me with interest. But it was all right at 7,300 feet. At 'seventy' I let out a scream and dropped the electrodes. Annihilation beamed with pleasure.

For his next trick Annihilation suggested that we should all hold hands. Edward and I could each hold an electrode and Stella could sit in the middle and be electrified. *¿Como non?* What a good idea, and highly scientific. It was a repetition of an early electrical experiment. Before the court of Louis XV, the Abbé Nollet persuaded two dozen friars to lock themselves to an iron chain along which he passed an electrical current. The audience could trace the progress of the electrical charge as the friars hopped up and down. But we were in Mexico in the twentieth century, not France three hundred years ago, and as Edward and Stella and I formed a human power cable and gazed trustingly up at Annihilation I wondered why we placed such confidence in amateur Mexican technology. Already a bottle of white wine had exploded in the hands of a waiter, powdering my food with glass. And while munching a can of peanuts I had cracked a tooth on a peanut-sized chip of glass.

It was when Annihilation said 'Fifty' that we realised something was going wrong with the experiment. Stella and I felt nothing. We were just sitting there holding hands. My electrode was apparently dead. But Edward, whose hair was at the best of times arranged in a rather spiky and electrocuted style, was behaving oddly. He was jerking up and down like a yo-yo, twisting around, going red in the face. 'Stop playing the fool, Edward,' I said, just as his feet jerked off the steel bar on which he had inadvertently placed them. The short-circuit was thereby bridged and the three of us were fused for one unforgettable moment at 'One hundred and twenty'. Annihilation, unaware of the short-circuit, had flicked another switch and ¡*Que barbaridad*! doubled the charge.

We felt that it was time for a tequila, ¿*como non*? By now our *mariachis* were being paid by two very young men wearing very thin moustaches. In Mexican fashion they had joined in the singing. They were forced to support each other as they stood. Moved by an uncharacteristic fellow-feeling towards foreigners they told us that they were porters at the food market and this was their night out. Then they dedicated their song to Stella.

Like many *mariachi* songs it was concerned more with drink and manhood than with love. Between manliness and love, the Mexicans seemed to draw a distinction. 'You do not know,' they sang, 'you can *never* know, how drunk we are. Or how happy we are. *Ohhhh*, how many times have we been thrown out of this bar. And we have walked the streets, singing our songs, a lump in the throat and the *mariachis* at our heels.' The improbability of the swollen *mariachis* obediently following these two pipsqueak porters around the streets did not occur to the porters. As they swayed in harmony, their limpid brown eyes fixed on Stella, they began to resemble a pair of spaniels gently swaying in and out of focus. One of them held a Polaroid photograph of himself looking fierce in an enormous sombrero. The other clutched something far more valuable: a new tube of toothpaste. For the past three weeks there had been no toothpaste in the shops of Mexico. The government had advised everyone to use a mixture of salt and bicarbonate of soda. Warming to his art the porter put down his tube of toothpaste on the table behind him. One of the violinists started to nudge the tube towards his side of the table with his bow.

All around us the *mariachi* bands were battling it out. At one table a middle-aged woman was persuaded to get to her feet and take a solo. She addressed the song to the girl-friend at her side; the singer had once been a professional, she had a very loud voice and her friend was so melted by her performance that she began to weep. The men accompanying them waited respectfully for the sobbing to stop. Eventually both women rose and retired to the lavatory to compose themselves. No sooner had they disappeared behind the door marked *damas* than two ugly thugs strode into the bar. They looked at every face in the room and then they too headed straight for the *damas* and disappeared from view. 'Police,' said Edward. The men sitting at the next table who had watched this procession without moving, and were waiting for their companions to emerge from the *damas*, began to look rather alarmed. By their side an old man in a wheelchair, a portrait sketcher, gave up the struggle and fell asleep. He had a fine, ruined face. He must have been a strong man once before he lost his leg. He pulled his cowboy hat over his eyes and nodded off, oblivious of the racket all around.

A waiter approached us with more tequila, *¿como non?* He bent over Edward and murmured something in his ear. Edward said that the waiter was called '*Gigantamente*'. 'Gigantically what?' '*Gigantamente Sexual*.' The waiter started to make smoochy noises at Edward. He had the usual dyed black hair and looked about seventy. Stella and I found his pleasure in Edward diverting, but he was a cunning old fox and when we eventually left the bar Gigantically Sexual saw us out then altered course, and it was Stella who got kissed at the door.

The most revered Christian shrine in all Latin America is just outside Mexico City, in the suburb of Guadalupe. Ten years after Cortés conquered Mexico, the Virgin of Guadalupe appeared in a vision to an Indian peasant recently converted to Christianity. The vision was a tribute to the work of the Inquisition. All over Mexico the Aztecs and other Indian people had been forced into labour and belief. Here was divine confirmation that the conquest was God's work. Given the frequency of Marian apparitions in the Age of Belief, that this vision would take place was as certain as the sequence of night and day. Many of the classical features of the mediaeval apparition were present. The visionary was a simple, ignorant man. A rose tree blossomed in winter, a message was sent to an initially sceptical bishop, a miraculous sign was left behind – in this case the face of the Virgin on the peasant's cloak. What was unusual about the vision of Guadalupe was the way in which the story caught on. There are hundreds of places of pilgrimage in Latin America, but none of them match Guadalupe. And in the universal Church its fame equals Lourdes although it has never been known for its cures. Even the Polish Pope chose to make the second journey of his pontificate to Guadalupe. After Tenampa I needed a rest so I drove out to see it.

Today the suburb is a village of churches, chapels and shrines. As in old Jerusalem many of them are run by rival religious orders. Where a building has become obsolete or wrecked by earthquake it has not been demolished and rebuilt, it has simply been abandoned and then replaced. An entire hillside littered with ruins, some leaning at a notable angle, some resembling a heap of consecrated rubble. The most recently abandoned basilica, a lowering example of nineteenth-century baroque, was rendered unsafe by an earthquake but is now being restored and turned into a museum. Its entrance hall is lined with very pretty naive pictures depicting some of the cures and favours that have been associated with the shrine. All these pictures are remarkably alike, in style and size, as though they had been painted by one man. They show sick people cured by a vision at the bedroom window, road and rail accidents, or primitive surgical operations that were judged miraculous by reason of the patient's survival. The pictures were not painted by one man but by anonymous peasant artists who once sat outside the basilica and recorded the stories of the pilgrims who came to give thanks. By purchasing the *ex votos* and offering them for display the pilgrims could express their gratitude and increase the fame of the Virgin. It never occurred to the artists to sign their names or even to indicate their identity by adopting an individual style: just as it does not seem to have occurred to those who had been healed or protected to keep this unique record of the most important event in their lives for themselves. The pictures were both commissioned and executed in honour of the Virgin.

I wanted to see the old basilica but once inside found that entry was restricted to those parts of the building that had been converted into a museum. However, *no hay reglas fixtas*. The same drunken official who announced this restriction promptly led me away from the other visitors through a locked door and into the unlit cavern which had formerly been the cathedral church of Guadalupe. Once inside the extent of the earthquake damage was even more apparent. My guide danced about in the echoing gloom, skipping over the fallen statues and crucifixes that blocked the aisles. Even where there were no obstructions the angles of the paving stones, heaved all over the floor by the earthquake, made progress difficult. My companion was positively excited by the ruination of this once holy place. He returned several times to point out exactly where the sacred relic bearing Our Lady's portrait had formerly hung. The basilica was now a temple of disbelief, the idols fallen, all that was once precious shattered in pieces, its only guardian a jubilant drunk. On the way out he slipped behind a wooden screen and reappeared with a triumphant leer on his face carrying a bottle of Mexican whisky from which we both drank. Then he staggered back to his position outside the locked doors where he once more denied other visitors admission with loud regularity.

The modern basilica of Guadalupe, which stands near by, has evidently been built with earthquakes in mind. It is an enormous concrete dome, like a flattened toadstool, which shelters one of the strangest Catholic churches in the world. Beneath the toadstool dome the people sit on rows of benches arranged in a semi-circle around the point where one would expect to see an altar. Here instead there is a raised and very long stage made of concrete and wood. To the left hang the thirty-two flags of the United States of Mexico, to the right stands fifteen yards of aluminium organ piping. On the back wall hangs the miraculous cloak, separated from its public by a depth of twenty-five yards of red leatherene choir-stalls which are banked in the manner of a Mormon Temple. The most prominent visual feature of this church is no longer the tabernacle but the microphones and electric candelabra that sprout all over the raised stage. The characteristic accompaniment is not the organ but a metallic rattling which is ceaseless. For some time I was puzzled by this noise. Then I identified it as coins falling into metal collection boxes. It had been amplified to encourage the generosity of the faithful; were the collection boxes wired for sound?

It must be a sobering moment for anyone who enters this hideous building with the conviction that Christian art has enhanced and encouraged Christian belief to see that, despite the chilling ugliness of their basilica, the devotion of the pilgrims to Our Lady of Guadalupe continues unabated. Giotto and Bellini may as well have doodled strip cartoons if they thought that their life's work was essential to the preservation of the Faith. At Guadalupe an old woman with tears streaming down her cheeks moved towards the altar rail on her knees, as smoothly as though on rollers, apparently unaware that she was performing this penance in surroundings that resembled the warehouse of a trading stamp conglomerate. Between her and her destination a guard, dressed like a commissionaire in a comic opera, fluffed out his gold braid and noisily ordered a party of peasants not to light their candles at the point where they happened to be standing when the inspiration seized them. But the old woman did not even see the commissionaire. All she could see was the face of the Virgin, stamped in some way on to the Indian's cloak. It was the same with the rows of completely silent pilgrims sitting on the benches, and with those peasants who had, after some hesitation, joined the line kneeling at the altar rail. From there they could gaze intently at the distant image in its heavy silver and gold frame. Like the old woman on her knees they were aware only that they were as close as they would ever be to the Mother of God. Many of them were under the impression that the figure in the picture was alive. Indeed for them, to all intents and purposes, she was. She lived with the life their love bestowed on her. This popular belief is not acknowledged by the Church in its publications but it is apparent in many of the legends and 'mysteries' that have grown up around the image of the Guadalupe, that her eyes follow you, that her expression changes, that she acknowledges those she loves. For the peasants this was not a picture. It was a face looking down at them from a window that had opened in heaven.

The strangest part of this church, however, is its crypt. For as the Indians at the altar rail pluck up their courage and explore further they find a ramp leading down beneath the stage. On their way to this they pass a display case containing a damaged crucifix. In 1921, when the revolutionary government closed the churches in Mexico and the religious persecution was at its height, a socialist fanatic entered the old cathedral and placed a bomb disguised as a vase of flowers on the altar. In due course the bomb exploded damaging this crucifix, but quite failing to harm its target, the miraculous image. Another miracle! Now as one enters the crypt one sees how the Virgin today is rendered safe from vases of flowers. The roof of the crypt has been opened directly beneath the back wall of the main church on which the image hangs. Those standing in the crypt can therefore gaze up about fifteen feet into the air and see it directly above them. But in order to avoid congestion they can only reach the closest point to the image by means of a moving pavement. When they reach the end of it they can transfer to another pavement, parallel to the first, which will carry them back to their starting point. Then a third moving belt will repeat the process, and a fourth complete it. And so the pilgrims stand on these flat escalators, being carried sideways in alternating directions, looking not where they are going but always upwards at the image, their lips moving in muttered prayers. Directly against the base of the wall, beside the first escalator, a steel trench receives any coins they wish to toss down. And by a trick of acoustics the noise of these falling coins is carried all round the church.

Above the crypt the commissionaires wander around the sanctuary, carrying silver ice buckets, and dressing the altar with enormous sprays of gladioli. A sign near the entrance to the church forbids anyone to take drinks inside; so of course many people do so. But a supreme effort has been made. There was only one sign of commercial activity on the premises. Just inside the shade of the dome a solitary Mexican nun in a powder-blue habit sat at a table. She had a tray of money before her, a basket of cakes and a pile of holy pictures. 'How much?' 'Limosna', for alms. I gave her 15 pesos. She watched carefully, then rewarded me with a card and a cake. On the outside wall behind her the authorities had been obliged to erect another sign. 'Do not use this place as a lavatory.'

4

Holy Week

'Every blasphemy is, ultimately, a participation in holiness.'

Camus, *The Rebel*

In Mexico City, Trotsky was murdered. The details are notorious. The disciple who was really a Stalinist agent; the blast-proof steel doors, which opened to welcome the assassin; the ice-pick, suddenly produced from beneath a raincoat; the weight *post mortem* of the great man's brain. I heard the story first from a follower.

'Did you know that after his death they weighed his brain? It was vast. It weighed three pounds.'

I remember the awe in the voice of this normally cynical man. Now that research has shown that brain size is unrelated to intelligence, the myth of Trotsky's brain may have begun to die. But it takes more than facts to destroy a myth. Something of my friend's awe remains with me still. It became my obsession to visit the house of Trotsky, where this vast brain fed and grumbled and snored.

Mexico City is extremely large. Exhausted by the altitude and suffocated by the pollution, I found my resolve to visit it weakening day by day. Anyway it was Holy Week. The newspapers were full of the impending holiday carnage. 'Already – 1,350 accidents, 152 dead!' In a country where children are given little chocolate skeletons as *memento mori*, the public holidays have a special entertainment value. Roused eventually by the carnival atmosphere, I decided to seek *la casa Trotsky*. I asked a travel agent how to get there but it was not on his itinerary. He thought that it was in the suburb of Coyocán,

'Coyote'. He assured me that any taxi-driver would know it. This was not true of mine. For over an hour we enquired our way around that suburb. It was frequently stated that the Trotskys still lived there and I began to believe this. Eventually we found it.

The house is just as it should be. It has a watch tower and steel doors, and there are gun slits in the watch tower and bullet scars on the doors. When He lived there, the house stood alone. Now it is surrounded by pleasant villas with gardens and garages and in the streets clean cars are being washed yet again. Coyacán is a fashionable address. The district around the house has been gentrified, like the ideas of its former occupant.

I knocked on the gate. No answer. My taxi-driver, by now completely committed to my quest, knocked much louder. A steel peep-hole slid open in the steel door and an eye looked out. It filled the vacant space. It was a brown eye. I thought what a wonderful target it would make. It looked so vulnerable, one soft brown eye piercing this expanse of grey steel. A voice rendered sinister by the unblinking eye said '*Cerrado*'; closed, now *and for Holy Week*. The peep-hole snapped shut. We drove back to the city, through the stinging yellow murk. I paid the driver a very large sum. The quest for Trotsky was not cheap.

On the advice of Sonia de la Rozière, the author of *Mexico and the Agony of Christ*, I avoided the more notorious Passion centres during Holy Week. Instead I went to the little town of Amecameca where the most fervent religious devotion could be observed unaccompanied by tourists. I hired a car and drove there on Good Friday.

The road to Amecameca was extremely slow. It was formerly the main road to Veracruz and once the route chosen by Cortés for his invasion. Now it has been superseded by a motorway. There should have been very little traffic on this road. When the turning to Amecameca appeared, the whole traffic jam took it – one slow-moving line of cars, all Mexican, all packed with families and all heading for this little town. I was impressed with Mexican devotion. For so many cars to leave the city and come here on pilgrimage on a day which the rest of the Christian world treated as a mere holiday seemed rather remarkable. At the entrance to the town the traffic jammed solid. There was a dirt track leading off to the right, and by following it I was able to work past the deserted shanties on the outskirts and so round to the central square. Here I discovered that the queue of family cars was passing out of town again on the other side. Mexico City was not going on pilgrimage to Amecameca after all; it was merely passing through Amecameca and on to the recreational area beyond it. The entire delay was caused by the distracted efforts of a single policeman to allow pedestrians to cross the road; something they were quite capable of doing without his assistance.

Good Friday was market day in Amecameca; the stalls, huddled together in the plaza in front of the church, were selling everything from cooked food to full suits of conquistadors' armour scaled down for children. In the church a service was in progress. So many people were trying to get into it that they were queuing right out into the market. The crowd, to the last worshipper, consisted not of car-drivers from the city but of Indians, the people of the countryside who had come to town to trade and pray.

It was midday. To the side of the church, around the walls of a small cloister with Romanesque arches and octagonal pillars, the Indians rested in the shade. They lay on the stone flags and slept, their heads pillowed on the sandals they had removed from their feet. Inside the church a terrible black figure had been raised on a high cross. He was supported by the two thieves. Unlike the Christ, the two thieves appeared to be gringos. I wondered if the Indian carver had derived some secular pleasure from crucifying these two white men. The Indians have a knack of turning a wonderful tale from a distant country to bear an unintended and very local meaning. On the high altar the voice of the priest giving out the stations of the cross boomed on. He was a gringo too.

The Indians of Amecameca bury their dead on a hill outside the town called Sacromonte. The dead Christ is called 'the Lord of Sacromonte'. On Good Friday, before the evening procession, the pilgrims carry their picnics up to the top of the hill and spread the food out on the gravestone of a relative and tuck in. Some of the graves are shaded by the branches of trees, or by large awnings, that catch the wind blowing across the lip of the ridge. All the way up the hill the stations of the cross are picked out in coloured tiles. It is a very dusty track in the dry season and on Good Friday it was very hot.

The children wandering up with their parents were garlanded with white flowers, spiky white daisies. Bound loosely round the head they looked more like stars than thorns. Some of the men also wore these garlands; they resembled ancient pagans on their way to Bacchic celebration. Good Friday is a black day in the Christian calendar. It is the one day of the year when mass cannot be said; altars and images everywhere are decked in purple. But not so in Amecameca. The Indians of Mexico are well aware of the horror of death, but it is precisely that horror which they wish to celebrate: it lifts their spirits. On the track up the hill the children with their flowery 'crowns of thorns' bought paper windmills or candy floss or holy pictures. These holy pictures were not the usual reproductions of sacred art. Here the pictures were printed in such a way that the eyes moved. You could get the Pope or the Virgin with eyes that followed you as you passed, and there were close-ups of the crucified Christ, eyes closed in death, then eyes and mouth open in agonised greeting. If the children got tired of that, they could try on pink plastic fangs which fitted over their own teeth to sinister effect.

On the hilltop I found an empty tomb and lunched on it. It contained Francisco Ortega who died in 1841. For some reason his descendants had not turned up that year.

The afternoon wore on and still the penitential procession did not form. The Mexico church authorities have had some success recently in controlling the enthusiasm associated with Holy Week. Live crucifixions have been restricted to once every seven years, but flagellants are still quite frequent. One Mexican newspaper carried a report from the Philippines stating that in a suburb of Manila nine devotees had been nailed to crosses by four-inch stainless steel nails soaked in alcohol. It was a detailed report. One of those nailed up was a woman. Another was the illegitimate son of a wartime G.I. who was trying to attract his father's attention. Needless to say, the G.I.'s boy was a carpenter. Now aged thirty-six, he had hung there for less than a minute and had screamed when the nail was pulled out of his left palm. Blood had flowed from his left palm but not from his right. There seemed to be something wistful in the minute observation of the Mexican news-report: those were the days.

After a while I grew tired of the confusion and disturbance of the town. There were several bars open; one offered a *cocktail femenino* which I was curious to know more about. Instead, I decided to remain sober and drove out of town and up to the *Paso de Cortés*, the high pass by which the conquistadors had broken through the Aztec defences. These are the foothills of the Sierra Madre Oriental and on a clear day the view from Amecameca is dominated by the two volcanoes, Popocatépetl and Ixtaccíhuatl. This was not a clear day. The heat haze pressed down beneath a layer of high cloud which hid the mountain peaks. The road started to climb through thick woodland. Indian women stood in some of the clearings, tending fires. They held out the tortillas they had been cooking, hoping for a sale. Their horses were tethered near by; presumably they were on the last stage of their journey to the fair. They would be in town by nightfall, in time for the procession.

As I emerged from the woods, the clouds, which had hidden Popocatépetl for several weeks, suddenly lifted and the volcano stood distinct in the cold blue air. The cone was covered in snow and from the tip of this rose a thin plume of smoke. Below the ring of snow the volcanic slopes were rumpled into pleats of soft brown and grey. Not a tree or a blade of grass could be seen on those slopes.

The Aztecs believed that Popocatépetl was a former king and that Ixtaccíhuatl, the 'Sleeping Woman', was his faithful wife who accompanied him in death. I wondered what Cortés would have thought of all this beauty as he was guided between the volcanoes and knew that the guardian saints of the Aztecs were nothing more than volcanoes. It was as deserted now on the brown windy plateau as it was on the day he passed. Cortés is not honoured in Mexico – there are only two statues to him in the entire country – but on the *Paso de Cortés* a small bas-relief has been set into a stone. This shows a knight advancing, mounted on an armoured horse, a crowd of men around him and the Indian interpreter, Princess Marina, who bore his son, showing him the way. Without Marina, the Spanish could never have left the coast. They numbered only five hundred, but their arrival had been prophesied in the Aztec religion, and with

Marina's help they were able to take advantage of this and save themselves from Montezuma's sacrificial altars.

In truth Cortés needs no monuments in Mexico; the whole country is the result of his restlessness. Every church in Mexico is his monument, just as much as the mediaeval suits of armour which were being sold to the children in the town below the pass. A chill wind from the volcano started to blow and I returned to the warmth of the forest and the mist. Outside the church as dusk fell, festivities took on a new life. The fair was now lit by neon signs and flares. Where there would once have been a band of trumpeters there was a loudspeaker blaring out pop music. A snake pit had been set up on the churchyard steps. One could not see into their open-topped trough until one had paid for a ticket and then climbed a wobbly ladder on to an equally wobbly platform. Most of the snakes were fast asleep; the Indian children, on seeing them, jumped up and down in excitement. This was not a country with very high standards of public safety. It was easy to foresee the chaos in the crowd when the platform collapsed, the trough tipped over and the sleeping snakes woke and made their bid for freedom.

The last light of Good Friday picked out the chequerboard façade of the church, white and ochre. One could still see the places where the ochre had run and stained strips of the white. On the churchyard wall a notice banned all commerce in the churchyard, by order of the Federal District. By now the fair had spread inside the walls and right up to the church. So often in Mexico the simplest way to discover where a particular event will take place is to find the notice forbidding it.

In the darkness, people started to leave the fair and crowd back into the church. The cloister was packed. For the poorest pilgrims it would provide a roof for the night. Some of them had spread matting on the flagstone floor; others, still poorer, had spread cardboard. On this they lay, wrapped in their blankets, whole families together, mothers feeding babies, slightly older children nursing younger ones. The evening service was amplified so that it could be heard in the cloister and many of the Indians were sitting up on their improvised beds saying the responses to the litany. They made a considerable noise but the sleepers, like the snakes in the trough, dozed on.

Inside the church the altar was hidden by a roll of Lenten

purple suspended from the ceiling, giving the raised sanctuary the appearance of a stage. The performance now proceeded as, once more, the Black Christ was taken down from the cross and carried around like an outsize doll. The lights flickering in the cloister, the lulling responses of the rosary, the quiet laughter among the sleepers, the occasional shouts from children playing in the darkness outside, the women oblivious to all this, holding their babies and murmuring their prayers – somehow it drew to mind the fantastic comparison with a house in Somerset thirty years earlier. The cloister, the rosary, the shouts of ten-year-old children, the devotion and inattention mixed, the carved stone pillars and the flagstone floor: I sat by the base of a pillar and tried to remember exactly what it was about Lent in an English boarding school that should have sprung to life again.

An Indian girl, aged about seven, in a red gingham dress and a red shawl with a pigtail hanging down her straight back sat down beside me, cradling a sleeping baby half her size. The baby was invisible within the shawl except for one white shoe and sock sticking out. The girl, her back still straight, still holding her burden, fell asleep, head slightly to one side to ease the weight she supported.

Opposite us a young couple spread out their mats. They had two children of their own and were accompanied by the mother of the sleeping girl and baby. On top of their mat they spread a quilt to add to their comfort. Sometimes the woman sat at her husband's side, leaning her back against his knees and holding his hand. Sometimes she lay down beside her children and tried to sleep. Sometimes, catching the words of a litany, she joined in. Noticing that her niece, the seven-year-old beside me, was falling asleep, she called her across and put the baby down on the already crowded quilt. There was no room for the girl, who spread some sacking of her own. It was far too small for her to stretch out on, so she curled up and was immediately asleep again. A moment later her mother returned from the church and woke her. The girl sat up and smiled again, but looked tired enough to cry.

'*Perdona tu pueblo, Señor*,' said the distant voice of the priest.

'Pardon us, Lord,' the Lord's people replied.

And in the sermon the priest introduced the familiar reflection about Mary's reaction to the death of her son. 'What can she have thought? How can we imagine her suffering?'

In the cloister another woman wrapped herself in a striped blanket. Her husband crossed himself, then lay down on his back in the space beside her. He closed his eyes. She, supported on one elbow, glanced down at him and stroked his face. They noticed no one around them. It was as though they were at home in bed. It was how they slept every night. In the centre of the cloister there was a flower garden; above it, the stars stood bright in a moonless sky.

It was by now quite dark and the high point of the devotions had been reached. Slowly a procession began to form up behind the Cristo, once more recumbent in its crystal bier. The litany had stopped and the priest was nowhere to be seen.

They carried the life-size wooden figure lying in the glass case out of the main doors of the church and into the churchyard. Everyone in the congregation joined the procession. Sixteen men staggered beneath the weight of the bier. One of them was the young husband who had been sitting opposite me in the cloister. He had fought his way at the last moment to the altar rails to secure this honour. Immediately behind the Cristo other men, who had been pushed aside in the struggle, pressed forward, eager for signs of failing strength among those who had succeeded. Behind them, sixteen women staggered in the same way under another litter supporting the rocking but upright statue of Christ's mother. Behind them trailed the rest of the penitents. The procession was lit by a few candles. Beyond the churchyard wall was the noise and brilliance of the fair. Against this explosive background the dark figures of the worshippers seemed all the more intent on their unlit purpose. What they were doing had to be done in the dark space between fun-fair and church. There was a terrible determination in the scattered chorus of voices that sustained a mournful hymn against the thunder of commerce. Real grief was evident. It was as though a real mother was following the dead body of her real son. If the sixteen men had been carrying one of their own family, they could not have mourned him with more passion. This was what the Indians understood by belief. They did not merely believe in Christ. They went further. They *invented* Him. From the shadows at their feet occasional voices still called out, traders rattling rattles, offering food, crying their wares to those who processed by. And yet there was no feeling of irreverence. The Indian imagination could as easily manage the discord of commerce and religion as it could bridge the space between grief for the dead of today and grief for the dead God.

An onlooker could be moved by the feelings of this wild congregation, but he could not share them. Mysteriously these Indians, while observing a Christian rite, managed to exclude the Christians who were foreign to their world. They had taken the characters of Christ and Mary out of the Gospel story and recast them in an entirely Indian tragedy. To an outsider the words of the drama seemed familiar, the figures in the cast were authentic. Nothing had been omitted, but inaccessible meaning had been added. The grief of this *pueblo del Señor* was far too genuine and far too private. Cristo had been kidnapped, overwhelmed, diminished.

The procession ended, the penitents disappeared silently into the night. The bier was laid down again beside the high altar. Those still awake queued up to touch it. They held their children up, as they had done by the snake pit, to gaze down at the sight within. Then they crossed the children with their hands. Their lips, in supplication, moved constantly. Like a corpse at a funeral, the Lord of Sacromonte was surrounded by flowers; lilies, roses and thistles. What the children saw as they looked down was a twisted body; black, matted hair thinly spread; the face blackened and dead, blank, rejecting, caved in. It was more the corpse of a man dug up than one due to rise on the Third Day. There was nothing supernatural about the figure who had died again in this town. He seemed as powerless as Popocatépetl and the Sleeping Woman who had been powerless to stop Cortés.

After Holy Week I returned to the house of Trotsky and knocked again. This time when the peep-hole opened it was for a blue eye. I asked if I could come in. The blue eye remained silent but the steel gate creaked open to reveal a slight figure wearing a powder-blue jump suit. She had curly brown hair and rosy cheeks.

'Do you speak English?'

She replied in a clear Scottish accent that she ought to. She had only been living in Casa Trotsky for a few months. Behind her I could see a lawn on which two small blonde children were busy at play. The house of Trotsky seemed to be occupied by an au pair girl from Ayrshire. On the wall of this once pleasant villa a great cluster of climbing roses hides a small steel door. You enter the house by this door, and by stepping over a steel plate which has been cemented into the wall. It is like entering a submarine. You can only move through the house by passing through a succession of steel doors, steel steps and steel shutters. Most of this was installed by the Mexican government in May 1940, after the failure of an attempt on Trotsky's life mounted by the Mexican surrealist painter David Alfaro Siqueiros. Siqueiros and his men had attacked with heavy machine-guns but only managed to kill a gringo 'Trotskyist' – who was a secret member of their plot. The bedroom wall is heavily scarred by their machine-gun shells. In the whole house the only unprotected entry I could find was the bathroom window. I wondered if, as he lay there in his suds, Trotsky fantasised about the sudden arrival through the window of some Stalinist Charlotte Corday. All these precautions availed for only three months. Ramón Mercader, the trusted disciple, carried his ice-pick through those steel gates in August of the same year.

The interior of the house is covered in dust and plastic sheeting, preserved as exactly as possible in the state it was on that day. The deed was done not in Trotsky's bath but in his study as he bent over his desk. On that desk today are *The Statesman's Year Book for 1939* and several books published by Gollancz in the 1930s. One is called *If Germany Attacks* by Capt. Wynn. Beside it is *Trade Unionism Today* by G. D. H. Cole. This is melancholy. Could it be that just before the Brain died it was pondering some footnote in G. D. H. Cole, the Englishman, the old Pauline, the detective-story writer, the Fabian?

It is appropriate that the house is so carefully preserved, for this too is a major shrine. Time has nothing to add to the truth as it was discerned within these walls. The steel doors, like the doors of a tabernacle, protect the mystical body of correct conclusions. Throughout my tour I had the feeling of being watched very closely by my guide, the au pair girl. It was almost as though she were trying to read my thoughts. You could not help remembering that a man was once admitted to this room who had been trusted with a hideously misplaced trust; and under the eyes of this guide, you could not help feeling slightly in the same position yourself. The house was as much a period piece as any Spanish colonial church, and its guardians were as devout as any Indian congregation. The red and yellow roses pouring over the steel door symbolised what happens to an idea whose time has passed, though once it was bullet-proof, strong enough to move the world.

On my way out the Scottish girl showed me the stone column in the garden which stands beneath a tall tree and marks the place where His ashes are interred – last resting place of the Brain. The column is engraved with the hammer and sickle, the emblem of the state whose agent murdered him.

Before I left Mexico City I returned to the house once again; I could hardly keep away from the place. This time the gates were opened by the presumed owner of the original brown eye, the curator in person. He was a youngish Frenchman wearing a white beret and a lugubrious expression that was somehow professional. He would explain some detail of the furnishings and then look at me in unspecified sorrow, like an ideological mute. Once again I had a sense of a shrine in a parallel church. Unconsciously I searched for an alms box at the exit. In the course of time an Indian Trotskyist may succeed the Frenchman, the missionary will be replaced by a native priest. One can see how the legend of the Great Brain might appeal to the Indian mind; and how Trotsky may be absorbed into an Indian version of the past, to sit with Cristo and Popocatépetl, one day.

5

Controlling the Universe

'The people had desired money before his day, but he taught them to fall down and worship it.'

Mark Twain, on Jay Gould, the North American railway baron

One evening I arranged to meet Stella in the lounge of the Del Prado Hotel in Alameda. I expected her to be late, she was always late, but it wouldn't matter in the lounge of the Del Prado because there was a painting there which people spent years of their lives looking at.

'The Dream of a Sunday Afternoon in the Alameda' is by Diego Rivera. It was painted in 1947, when the muralist was at the height of his fame. It is forty-eight feet long and fifteen feet high, and its subject is the park outside the hotel which is a popular Sunday resort. But in Diego's work the usual crowd has been transformed. The park is peopled by figures from the history of Mexico and from the mythology of revolution. To the left, the Inquisition is once more at work. The friars are burning their victims, whose backs have been stripped of flesh by scourging, and who are wearing long, pointed witches' hats – but hats painted a rather jolly shade of green. Near by Sor Juana Inés composes her poetry 'about the evil of men'. A conquistador with his hands covered in blood, apparently Cortés, is dominated by the swollen figure of Benito Juarez, Mexico's only Indian president, holding the country's first democratic constitution. The poor slump, exhausted, on a park bench, beside the dozing figure of the elderly dictator Porfirio Diaz. In front of the slumbering president's face an urchin picks the pocket of an elegant gent. All this occupies a mere ten feet of the fresco.

All the life and wit which Diego brought to his work is in this fresco, it instructs and amuses and delights in the simplest terms. But the hotel was not always so proud of its treasure. For years it was concealed as a scandal. It is not clear today what exactly about this picture was so scandalous. Possibly the disrespectful attitude to authority, possibly the image of a woman dressed in fashionable clothes lying back in abandon, her legs separated by a tree. It is said that somewhere in the picture there was once a placard which contained a blasphemous headline, but if so it would have been lost among the 130 life size figures crowded into the fresco. And Mexico is in any case a country whose government has denied the existence of God for the last sixty-three years.

Today, once more exposed, 'The Dream' stands oddly in the world of those who come to honour it. Up and down the cocktail salon of the Del Prado move the cocktail waitresses, overlooked by the grotesque inhabitants of Diego's world, and serving two distinct groups of customers. As I waited for Stella the predictable parties of package tourists were suddenly reinforced by the mass apparition of Palm Sunday, the lightly tanned blonds who had carried the flag with such distinction round the cathedral. Now, departing for a mass steak-in, the girls wore trim grey suits, pleated skirts and white socks, the boys by way of contrast were in navy blue suits. But all remained six feet tall, eighteen years old, in crocodile file, and highly-disciplined. Again struck dumb I watched the crocodile disappear into the heat of the night, then I asked a cocktail waitress who they were. 'Un grupo de scolares de los Estados Unidos,' she replied, as though that said it all.

The second group of customers were the solitary Mexican men who sipped whisky and gazed at the fresco. By choosing a table in a different part of the room they could study at leisure an entirely different part of the fresco on each of their visits. If they tired of their study they could turn instead to the cocktail waitress who served them. She had ash blonde hair and black eyebrows, and wore an ankle-length red velvet skirt split to the hip bone. Her name, pinned to her left tit, was 'Guadalupe'. The cocktail lounge had a trio. The members of it wore dinner jackets at tea-time and two played zithers. They were placed on the opposite side of the room to the art. The zither players, with a keen sense of publicity, searched round the room constantly for a friendly face at which to smile; they were chubby, happy, personable people. The bass player, a man in his seventies, hair dyed a very black black, his thick horn-rim spectacles concealing the squint, drooped over his instrument with an air of terminal gloom. This was not so burdensome as to prevent him when the time came from mouthing out the enigmatic message

Guapa Pa Pa
Guapa Pa Pala
Grazie! Grazie!

But on the evening when I sat in the Del Prado, waiting for Stella, nothing, not the picture, not the band, not even Guadalupe could match the most astonishing sight in the room. Two English girls with cropped hair sat sipping their drinks. The first, a slight, self-contained figure, wore a mud-coloured T-shirt and trousers and drank lemon tea. The second, a mountainous person, chose chilled beer. She wore a scanty, white, sleeveless blouse, blue mini-shorts and muddy flip flops on muddy feet. Her biceps were like bowls, her blouse gaped to reveal the roll of muscle beneath her bra, her thighs were the size of middle-aged oaks but dimpled and smooth. One by one the Rivera worshippers lost their concentration and gazed instead at this remarkable young person, a sight they had never expected to see, a sight more arresting than the crocodile of blonds, or Guadalupe. They were looking at the Englishwoman, abroad and at ease. Inexplicably, the band, the waitresses, the blonds, even the customers had all taken on a fantastic air, almost as though we were become characters in Diego's *Dream*.

I wanted to see more of Diego. Almost all of his work is in murals so it is necessary to go to Mexico to see it. And the pictures at first sight are overwhelming by reason of their size, their success and their unabashed politics.

After the Del Prado I went to the *Museo de Bellas Artes*, a little further down the same street. The *Museo* is a pillared, domed and marbled hall which was originally built as a pleasure palace for a dozen of Mexico's richest families. It dominates its surroundings even today though they now include the tallest skyscraper in the city. In its original setting it must have been one of the most tactless statements of private wealth ever erected. Its owners intended it as the setting for their receptions and courts and balls. But hardly was it complete when the Revolution took place and ownership was transferred to the people, who turned it into a place of culture, culture being the only activity appropriate to the building which the directors of a Marxist revolution found morally acceptable.

Unfortunately the *Museo* is so heavy that it is sinking into the lagoon on which Mexico City stands. The passer-by looks down on what was originally intended to be seen from below, the ground floor has become the basement. In style it is neo-Egyptian, it could have been the largest neo-Egyptian Odeon in the world. Those wishing to see the Diego have to climb up several flights of marble stairs until they are confronted with another unforgettable experience, '*El Hombre Contralor del Universo*', painted by Diego in 1934 when he was aged sixty-eight.

The picture spreads out from a central figure, a fair-haired, grey-eyed, supersized superman, dressed like a steel-worker, who is driving a machine which projects suns, sea anemones, light bulbs and corn on the cob. Around him are the lesser mortals; they are playing cards, dancing, flirting, wearing monocles. They are no match for the Controller.

Once again the picture covers a large wall, and is divided into several stories. Diego Rivera went in not so much for narrative art as for epic narratives. To the right of the Controller massed ranks of Red Soviets advance; they have no weapons, they are armed only with red flags and with the passionate belief that shines from their eyes. They are advancing, apparently suicidally against the forces of evil, men wearing gas masks and carrying fixed bayonets. In other parts of the picture one can see Lenin, surrounded by clenched fists, nations of the world and athletic youth. In another Trotsky, Marx and Engels, holding on to the banner of the Fourth International, are surrounded by workers. All are gazing at the Controller, at Man armed with knowledge, controlling the machinery of the universe, everything from the cultivation of fruit to the movements of the planets.

The painting is naive, passionately trusting and very powerful. It is an artist's view of politics, ridiculous in its sincerity but a wonderful illustration of the appeal of communism in the 1930s. This picture is saying – the world is terribly complicated, the enemy is terribly powerful, but because they have to be controlled they *will* be. How? Well . . . well through science and communism of course. If you painted flags defeating gas and bayonets, and believed it strongly enough, then it would happen. It had to happen. And the element of belief is confirmed by the positioning of the Controller, for he is exactly where a sixteenth-century muralist would have placed God the Father, riding on a cloud and controlling destiny in just the same way. And one sees what has happened to the twentieth century; God the Father has become a youthful Aryan steel worker.

The interest of this picture is increased if one knows two stories behind it. The first is that the fresco in the *Museo* is actually the second version. The original was commissioned by the young Nelson Rockefeller to stand in Rockefeller Center in New York. Diego had been working on it for some time, and his patron knew all about his politics, when word got around that the picture showed the figure of Lenin in a sympathetic light. That was enough to stop it. Overnight, uniformed men arrived, forbade Diego to return to Rockefeller Center and covered the picture up. It was later destroyed. The story is all the more curious when one considers that another section of the picture, which drew no objection, shows New York mounted police clubbing hunger marchers on Wall Street. Oddly, among the hunger marchers Charles Darwin can be seen with his parrots and a monkey. Near him a naked white child stands in front of an X-ray picture of the human skull. It is extraordinary the ingenuity shown by a Mexican artist who wishes to introduce a skeleton into his work.

Diego's anger with the Rockefellers for needlessly wrecking his work was triumphantly dispelled by recreating in the *Museo* all that had been lost in New York. Needless to say, in true Mexican fashion, it has since been rumoured, and possibly with some truth, that the Rockefellers never did destroy the original mural. They stored it away for the future. The Rockefellers, it is pointed out, did not get where they are today by chopping up artistic masterpieces.

The other story behind the picture is that Diego fell out with both the heroes he included in '*El Hombre Contralor del Universo*'. He was a close friend of Trotsky and even arranged for him to take sanctuary in Mexico when he was driven out of Europe by fear of assassination. Then his wife, Frida Kahlo, had an affair with Trotsky. Finally Diego quarrelled with him so fiercely (but on political grounds) that when Trotsky was murdered Diego was one of the prime suspects and had to go into hiding to escape interrogation. Previously Diego had been thrown out of the Communist party of Mexico by the Stalinists. He was at the time secretary of the party so it is not quite accurate to say that he was thrown out since he himself had to sign the order by which he was expelled. When he did so he made a little speech which ended, '. . . therefore the painter Diego Rivera should be expelled from the Communist party by the general secretary of the Communist party, Diego Rivera'. He threw himself out.

I was so impressed by '*El Hombre Contralor del Universo*' and 'The Dream of a Sunday Afternoon in the Alameda' that I decided to visit the Ministry of Education. Here, in the arcades and courtyards of the colonial palace that now houses the Ministry, Diego was able to work out his obsession with science and the hope it provided for mankind. It would be impossible today, knowing what we now know, for any great artist to paint this subject with Diego's simplistic conviction. He had the childish faith of a Stanley Spencer but he applied it to rather larger and more topical themes. In one of his dozens of small murals in the Ministry, men, almost featureless, with rounded faces, are bending over a microscope. It is executed in grey on grey. The title is '*Los Investigadores*'. There is no more to it than that, but such is Diego's power that one is moved to pity by the blind hope displayed in this picture. These men, featureless because they are not individuals but the tireless servants of the Method, are investigating something vital to the future of mankind. Even the microscope does not seem to be a neutral technical device; it is beneficent. It guarantees the value of the investigation, it has a religious importance. In Diego's art one finds all the certainty and rude confidence once reserved for sacred art. His murals make a startling contrast with the tacky showiness of Guadalupe.

His inexplicable power to make inanimate objects or apolitical activities line up on his side is constantly demonstrated. In another grey on grey panel, '*La Geologia*', the investigation of Mayan remains by archaeologists becomes, beyond a doubt, a socialist enterprise, a triumph of progressive forces. All knowledge, in Diego's art, is progressive knowledge, it is a socialist monopoly. He is the teacher, and there is no room for unorthodoxy here. It happens in the Ministry murals again and again. In *La Operación* even the surgeons have become the servants of a political cause. They wear masks, that is normal, but they also appear to wear not spectacles but goggles; they are inhuman, they have the faces of insects. But they are not so much inhuman as superhuman. Facelessness is notoriously a penalty of socialism; Diego turns it into a prize.

All these panels, in grey on grey, achieve a more romantic effect by their positioning. For they run beneath much larger murals which are brightly coloured. This gives the small panels the power of a commentary, *sotto voce* and intense.

The story told by the larger pictures is a more familiar one. It starts as one ascends the staircase to the first gallery. Indian women bathe in a river, some naked, some clothed. One sees a similar sight all over Central America, but these women clearly belong to an earlier time. They are human but innocent. In another panel they sit before a witch-doctor or *shaman* in a forest glade. They are overlooked by a forest bird. Here is the romantic view of the Indian life before the coming of evil, the coming of Spain; and it is a reminder of one of the unresolved national paradoxes, for Spain was the mother of Mexico, and the mother of science in America. We reach the gallery, where the sombre grey text runs beneath the vivid colours of ordinary Mexican life. In one scene a revolutionary woman, modelled by the painter's wife, Frida Kahlo, hands back to men the guns they have just made. The picture is blocked out in bold paintbox and crayon colours. There is a wonderful symmetry in the lines of armed figures, individuals bending together, like corn stalks in the wind of change. This is the Ministry of Education, not Rockefeller Center, and Rivera allows free rein to his portrait of capitalism and greed. A bourgeois gringo woman in evening dress is handed a broom by a stern-faced female Indian warrior. The title is, 'Who Wants to Eat, must Work.' Next door, even more cheerfully, a bloated capitalist sits on a large safe. His throat has been cut.

In *'La Cena del Capitalista'*, one of Diego's most famous pictures, a certain amount is said on the subject of bloatedness.

There is a dinner party in progress. Around the table sit a woman, several wealthy men, and a child crying. Everything seems normal, until one sees the explanation for the brat's tears. The plates in front of the guests are piled not with food but with gold coins. Outside the window the workers pass unheedingly by, burdened with fruit. It is a cliché, but it works. Further down the gallery one finds '*La Orgia*' and again one is caught by Diego's simple, romantic vision of capitalist evil. The peasant cadres burst through the door of the mansion and interrupt an orgy of drink and drugs. Young men, who should be strong and lustful, are collapsed and drunk. Old men, who should be detached and dignified, are lechering absurdly. The girls who are submitting to their attentions are beautifully dressed, but their dresses are dishevelled and pulled tight over their Stanley Spenceresque thighs. Ah yes, the familiar bourgeois family evening, one remembers it well. There is something almost wistful about the way in which the painter has chosen these frivolities – to which he was himself no stranger – as the symbol of selfish corruption. And again one has to admire the mysterious skill by which he manages to transform a tailcoat or a bottle of whisky, even a cigarette, into the epitome of wickedness.

I turned from these vivid scenes of corruption and violence, from this extraordinary impression of human comedy, to the tranquil courtyards of the Ministry of Education. It was a holiday, and the country had begun to close down. A bored soldier at the entrance to the first courtyard had waved me through, but inside the palace the bureaux were deserted by their bureaucrats. I could admire the flowering trees undisturbed. A few birds fluttered round the arcades as though trapped in some vast stone bird cage. They hopped up and down the stone staircase between the scenes of primitive innocence and the painted birds on the wall. Somewhere, in more distant passages, late-departing administrators hurried with their files to discreet assignations. It was two hours before closing time on the last afternoon before the holiday, and the pundits of the ministry had already departed. Perhaps they were seeking a little more leisure, hoping to gain a little more strength, in order to spread a little more education, that little extra knowledge which would bring to life the political dreams of Diego

Rivera. I looked back at the pure enthusiasm of those inspiring pictures and then again at the delightfully uninspired Ministry and thought that perhaps the men in Washington, who are so obsessed with the revolutionary fervour of the Sandinista régime in Nicaragua, should remember what Mexico did to socialism. On my way out of the Ministry I thanked the sentry and said that the paintings were very beautiful. 'Thank you,' he replied as though they were his own.

I wanted to see Cuernavaca. It is the town where Malcolm Lowry set *Under the Volcano*. It is the town where Cortés chose to live. And it is the town where Diego Rivera made a fresco on the subject of that conquest. In this painting he expressed his political views on the Indians. Cortés chose to live there for the same reason that the Aztec nobles preferred to live there. It is 2,500 feet lower than Mexico City. Even today, though it contains night clubs, health clubs and a golf course, and has become a gringo dormitory town, Cuernavaca is a beautiful place. In the more elegant 1930s the gringos did not throw so much litter about. Cuernavaca then was a haven for artists, drunks and other exiles and misfits, Lowry among them. *Under the Volcano* is far more a book about drunkenness and a broken heart than it is about Mexico, but its Mexican setting is none the less unforgettable. At the time Lowry lived in Cuernavaca there was a struggle going on for the soul of the country. The Marxist government which persecuted the Church faced an armed uprising from '*Cristero*' guerrillas who fought to return Mexico to Catholic rule. There is no direct reference to these events in Lowry's book, but there is an oblique one. The *Cristeros*, or Soldiers of Christ, were active in the countryside outside Cuernavaca. Occasionally the Consul, the drunken hero of the book, is made aware of this.

'"*¿Quiere usted la salvación de México?*" suddenly asked a radio from somewhere behind the bar. "*¿Quiere usted que Cristo sea nuestro Rey?*" . . .

"No."'

It comes again on the radio, and the Consul remains adamant.

'Do you desire the salvation of Mexico?' 'No.' 'Do you want Christ to be our King?' 'No.'

The *Cristero* revolt was in due course crushed and on the day I reached Cuernavaca the end of a rather different religious intervention was being marked. The famous red Bishop of Cuernavaca, Sergio Mendez Arceo, had retired, and his successor was being installed. Bishop Mendez Arceo regarded himself, correctly, as a progressive. It was another view of him that he was a 'useful idiot manipulated by Marxists'. Outside his diocese he was known as the bishop who had brought the *mariachi* bands on to the altar. Inside it he was remembered for having removed the statue of Our Lady of Guadalupe from the cathedral. I was told that the statue had been replaced by the congregation as soon as he had departed. Mendez Arceo was truly loathed by conservative Catholics in Mexico; 'a monster,' one of them called him.

For the induction of his successor a large congregation queued to shake the hand of the man in the gold mitre who sat unattended on the high altar. In the body of the church a priest, identifiable only by the cross he wore in his lapel, had been trapped by a gossipy woman into hearing her confession. For anyone who has ever wondered about the expression on the face of the priest as he sat behind his grille, this man looked bored and embarrassed. He gazed into the middle distance while the confiding chatterbox sitting beside him on the bench poured it all into his ear. In most parts of the world the priest's civilian clothes would have identified him as a progressive, but in Mexico it is actually forbidden for the clergy to wear clerical dress in the streets. It makes it all the stranger that the modern church should have adopted as its preferred dress the anonymity traditionally imposed on it as a form of persecution. Today no Mexican politician in search of office can be photographed on his way to church – the exact opposite of the position in Europe and the United States where the most surprising politicians flock at election time to be photographed at some place of worship. In Mexico, so many years after the revolution that overthrew the temporal power of the church, priests and nuns are denied many of the normal rights of citizens; they are not for instance allowed to travel abroad without special permission. And yet the wife of the President of the Republic is known to be a devout Catholic, and he himself is generally thought to be one. And the vast majority of Mexicans remain Catholic in more than name.

I left the cathedral and went to the gardens of Maximilian, near the palace which the Emperor's valet called '*Das Lust Schloss*', because his master preferred to spend the days here with his wife Carlotta than fending off the murderous savagery of Juarez. In Cuernavaca, Lowry had written 'What is there in life besides the person whom one adores and the life one can build with that person?' For Maximilian, who believed that even an Indian revolutionary would be a chivalrous victor, there was the firing squad.

And here Lowry had written, 'His passion for Yvonne . . . had brought back to his heart, in a way he could not have explained, the first time that alone, walking over the meadows from Saint Près, the sleepy French village of backwaters and locks and grey, disused watermills where he was lodging, he had seen, rising slowly and wonderfully and with boundless beauty above the stubble fields blowing with wildflowers, slowly rising into the sunlight, as centuries before the pilgrims straying over those same fields had watched them rise, the twin spires of Chartres Cathedral.' There were no *mariachis* in Chartres Cathedral. It was to an older idea of the Christian God that the Consul prayed. He was absorbed in a personal passion, and he argued that it was in such private adventures the human spirit would, if anywhere, survive. It was the Consul who said, 'What in God's name has all the heroic resistance put up by poor, little defenceless peoples . . . to do with the survival of the human spirit? Nothing whatsoever. Less than nothing. Countries, civilisations, empires, great hordes perish for no reason at all, and their soul and meaning with them . . .' Three such empires, the Aztec, the Spanish and French, have perished in Cuernavaca in the last 400 years. But still the gardeners are cutting the grass and weeding the flowerbeds, and the ponds are full of contented ducks. I left Maximilian's gardens and went to the house of Cortés.

Cortés never received the reward he thought his due for the conquest of Mexico. But he was at least able to build himself a fine palace in Cuernavaca where he installed his wife. (He did not get on with her very well, and after she died, rather suddenly, he married again and installed a second wife there.) The house, a solid, Spanish colonial structure with few extravagant features, is now a museum dedicated to the memory of the

Indians and to 'the struggle of man against the exploitation of man'. The Diego Rivera fresco stands in a gallery at the back, a long, three-sided space with a balustrade on the fourth side open to the air. Diego's heroic account of the history of the Indians starts on the short right-hand wall and runs the length of the gallery, ending opposite where it started. It opens with the attack on the Aztec empire, the city protected by lagoons and ringed by volcanoes. As the few Spaniards, with their fearsome technology of armour, horse and cannon, advance we see in the background at the top of the pyramid steps a Spanish sacrificial victim, his beating heart being held up by the Aztec priests who offer it to the Gods who have sent these conquerors.

In the second section Aztec temples are wrecked, mines are opened, sugar cane is planted and cut by Indians, now become *peones*. As the cane cutters sweat, a Spanish planter lies in a hammock, watching them. There is no element of satire here. But in the last panel, which concerns the rule of the church, friars set about their task of converting the Indians, then become distracted by a gift of lapis lazuli which is offered to them. In the close attention with which they examine the stone one can see that the painter's wit has escaped again. Then scenes of the Inquisition and of torture are followed by the final panel. An Indian peasant, a bloodstained billhook in hand, is holding the head of a riderless horse. Beneath the horse's hooves lies its dead Spanish rider. So the animal which helped to enslave the Indians has now become their trophy. The story of the Indians, or 'the people' of Mexico, ends therefore on a triumphant note.

The political interest of this picture is in the light it throws on Mexico's official attitude to the Indians, and the extraordinary, uneasy complexity of the country's view of its own identity. In one sense Mexico has no reason for guilt towards the Indians. Post-colonial Mexico never tried to exterminate them, as they were exterminated in Uruguay and Argentina. There are many Indians in Mexico; it must be one of the biggest Indian countries in or out of America. AmerIndians are to be found from the Arctic to the South Seas, and in Mexico they are better placed than almost anywhere else. Juarez was pure Zapotec Indian, and he became president of Mexico.

Zapata was also a Zapotec Indian and he is a more famous guerrilla leader than Pancho Villa. None the less the Mexican view of its relationship with Mexican Indians is flawed and false.

Throughout Diego's Cuernavaca fresco a racial symbolism is used. The oppressors (with the exception of one good friar) are always white. The Indians (with the exception of Cortés's interpreter, Dona Marina) are always victims. This is a misleading statement of Mexican history. Mexico is proud of its Indians and extols their virtues but they remain an impoverished racial minority. The failure of the Mexican racial fusion is illustrated by the population statistics. In 1953, there were 3 million Mexican Indians, 25 per cent of the population, 17 million *mestizos*, people of mixed Indian and European descent, and a negligible number of whites, 40,000. Today there are 17 million Indians, still 25 per cent of the population, and there are 40·8 million *mestizos* but they now form only 60 per cent of the population. The white group on the other hand has grown from a fraction to 5 per cent of the population, or 3·4 million people. What has happened? Has there been a vast white immigration into Mexico? No. Have 40,000 Mexican whites bred 3·4 million descendants in thirty years? Probably not. Instead over 3 million people who were happy to classify themselves as *mestizos* in 1953 have caught up with the rest of the world and decided to fit into it if they could; they are now calling themselves white.

Although so many Mexicans are proud to be white they live in a state which does all it can in public to slight its white ancestry. Most of the people of Mexico are the children of Cortés. The Conquest took place 400 years ago, and yet Mexico continues to abuse one partner in that union and extol the other, almost as though people who would not exist if it had not been for the conquest, lament the fact that the conquest ever took place. By lamenting this they are lamenting their own existence. Furthermore the partner they choose to praise is not the partner whose way of life they strive to emulate. There is an ambivalence here which goes deeper than *no hay reglas fixtas*. The Spanish colonial rule of Mexico ended in 1821. Post-colonial societies usually express ambivalent feelings towards their former colonisers but it seems that a Spanish colonial experience leaves such a bitter memory that it has to be vilified even 160 years later. It is in tune with the Spanish character to express a truth violently and without compromise or regard for any qualifying truth.

The exhibition which occupies the rest of the museum further illustrates Mexico's tortuous official attitude to its Indians. Near a display of Indian huts there is a notice: 'By ignoring the condition of the indigenous poor the colonialists ensured the survival of their culture, so that we today can see what their life was really like.' This explains why the huts in question have been carried from the fields of Mexico and plonked down on the floor of the exhibition. For Indians in Mexico still live in such shanties. From the exhibitors' point of view, the question then becomes, What have we here? Is this a good thing or a bad thing? Ignoring the poor is bad. But colonial attentions are also bad. Indigenous culture is good. But modernisation, which means the destruction of indigenous life, is also good. Perhaps a fuller statement of the official position would be: 'Typically the colonialists ignored the poor, but for once this was fortunate because in the survival of primitive life we are able to learn about the culture of the indigenous people, before we destroy it with our superior, post-colonial attentions.' But that would be rather a lot to say on a notice in the museum.

One of the earliest dances the Indians performed, in the New Spain that they unexpectedly found themselves a part of, is known as *Moros y Cristianos*. Another exhibit shows the satirical masks and costumes of this dance, which were worn not to depict any Indian subject but to tell a story that the Indians had heard from their Spanish conquerors, the story of the glorious Christian victory over the Moorish kingdom of Granada. It was this victory which enabled the King of Spain to pay for the discovery and settlement of 'the Indies'. The fall of Granada led to the downfall of the Aztec empire. And yet all over Mexico this dance is still danced on feast days by non-committal Indian performers. The internal complications of this relationship seem to have been there from its earliest days.

Few of these ambiguities bother the Mexicans who examine them today. Perhaps Mexicans do not notice ambiguity and paradox because they are so comfortable with them. Below Rivera's terrific statement of the way it was, and his implied hopes for the Way It Will Be, passes the way it is. A girl, aged about twelve, hurries down the length of the mural, hardly glances at it, asks her mother if it is about Pancho Villa, and on learning that it is not hurries out again. In the street below the gallery the buses roar around the corner and away up the hill, their smoke and noise all unheeding of Diego. Only Lowry's 'vandals in sandals' peer into their guidebooks and ponder the artist's message. Then, reassured that it is a message which has no more application to their lives than it has to the life of contemporary Mexico, they return to their air-conditioned buses and are carried away from the house of Cortés to the nearest fast food counter.

The remains of Hernando Cortés, the founder of the country, and of this house, were secretly buried, and have since been lost, unlike those of Francisco Pizarro, the conqueror of Peru, which are displayed in a glass coffin in the cathedral in Lima. And the only public statue to Cortés stands in Cuernavaca, behind the wall of the very expensive and heavily-guarded Hotel Casino de la Selva. The figure, mounted on a horse, cast in copper, sits on top of a stone pillar which is covered in ivy. It is not even in a much-used part of the hotel grounds. Cortés is riding up the disused drive of the hotel, with his back towards the town where he chose to build his house, and looking, if anything, rather lost.

Poor Cortés. One of the boldest, most successful and least rewarded of Spanish generals. Because of the success which his tiny expedition enjoyed over the Aztec civilisation he has come to symbolise all that is supposedly despised in Mexico's past. One suspects that this disdain is commoner among educated people than among the peasants. The Indians originally venerated Cortés as a god. They respected strength, they were ruled by very powerful gods, and a man who could overthrow those would be acknowledged. Perhaps the Aztec Indians could see a simple truth in a way denied to official Mexico.

For there are some who say that there is another image of Cortés in Cuernavaca. Carved on the portico of the Tercen Orden church, beside the cathedral, there is an endearing little fellow who may or may not be the great general. He is the keystone of the massive doorway, placed there by the Indian carvers and bearing the terrible weight of the much larger figures of the bishops and angels on his shoulders. He shows no sign of strain. But, as you drive out of Cuernavaca, there is a statue of a man on a horse which can be seen by everyone. It is enormous, the superhumanly large figure of yet another *bandido* at full charge, *sombrero* bent by the wind, *machete* drawn. Is it Zapata, is it Villa? Either would fit the bill in the town where Cortés, as a matter of policy, is forgotten.

It was time to leave Mexico City. Easter came and went. The people returned and with them a terrible smog. Mexico City either has fifteen million people and two million motor cars or eighteen million people and four million motor cars: all figures are official. One morning, driving in from a visit to the suburbs I saw ahead of me in just one area of the city what appeared to be a desert sandstorm. It had distinct boundaries. Soon we were in the middle of it. This was not sand, it was the famous smog that makes the capital the most polluted city in the world. Shortly after entering it I could feel the grit clinging to my arms and my face. The inside of my mouth was coated with it. I began to cough. Then my eyes started to sting. Visibility in the traffic ahead fell to 300 yards, then to fifty yards. Tall palm trees vanished up into the darkness of the day. My eyes dried out, then began to stream again. There was a rich cocktail of chemicals descending or rising, perhaps both, to form this greasy yellow air. My hair filled with grit. I got back to my hotel and started to swill it out of my mouth and scrape it off my skin, but I did not feel entirely clean again until the following morning. An hour after the smog first formed, it was gone. An hour later it was back again.

I went to the Guatemalan consulate to get a visa. It was high up in a tower block: there was a crowded lift and a patient group waiting to use it. I had to visit the consulate several times, and no matter how many people were in the lift I was always the only person who went to the Guatemalan consulate. Inside the consul's door sat a seedy and bespectacled figure in a memorably dirty suit. It might once have been a white suit. He issued visas. He had the vital rubber stamp before him. The fee was two American dollars. He wanted ten. I had been warned about this. You just waited and eventually he came down to the proper price. I argued with him. I said I wished to see the vice-consul in charge of visas. 'I am the vice-consul,' he said. He added that he was not interested in travellers' cheques. He wanted ten dollars in notes. On my third visit I conceded. He smiled a rather pleasant smile. We both considered how much time I could have saved if I had believed him the first time I came. I remembered, but did not mention, the old axiom that in Latin America officials expect to be bribed to do their jobs. They do not expect to be bribed to break the law and if this is suggested to them they become upset.

I never took the lift when I left the Guatemalan consulate, I used the stairs. There was a glass-fronted mail shaft let into the side of the stairwell. The idea was that if you worked on the fourteenth floor you posted your mail in this and it plummeted all the way down to the sack waiting on the ground floor. It is a perfectly simple system, standard all over the U.S.A. and in use since the 1920s. In this building, somewhere between the fifth and fourth floors the mail shaft was blocked. Someone had forced in a large package and it had become wedged at this point. Above the blockage, through the glass front of the shaft one could see piled up all the packages subsequently posted from the floors above. I walked down that staircase three times and each time the pile had risen higher. I wondered how long it had been there. Each of those letters had been written more or less carefully and then addressed. I came to dread passing that point. If you are travelling, you need to believe in the postal system.

Before I left I called on the military attaché of a European embassy. It seemed sensible, before going to El Salvador, to hear the latest analysis of battle positions. As our discussion got under way it became clear that this naval person had it firmly in his mind that I worked for the London *Daily Telegraph*. This was, in his view, the right start. He got out his maps and warmed to his theme. He became quite heated after a while. He sucked on his pipe rather noisily and abandoned the military exposition. He referred to the political situation and started shouting the odds about communism. There was another person present during this performance, his successor, a quieter man. The attaché began to beat on his desk to emphasise a point. A heap of papers balanced on the edge, fell off. 'Damn.' He paused for a moment to recover the papers, then moved over to a map of El Salvador on the wall. He became heated again and began to jab the map with his finger. I could see what was about to happen. While jabbing he looked over his shoulder towards us. He misjudged the jab and his finger bent upwards against the wall. 'Damn.' He was shaking his hand in pain. His colleague and I watched him for about twenty minutes in silence. Then the attaché reached the climax of his argument. 'You know,' he shouted, 'YOU could do a great service for world democracy – if you wanted to.' *World* democracy? He meant that I should write in support of the Government of El Salvador. As I left, his quieter successor murmured, 'I think that proved as useful for me as it was for you.'

My last appointment was with another diplomat, a man who had lived and worked in Mexico City for too long. He was no longer amused. He said, 'It's all right for you. But I have to *live* here.' He spoke contemptuously of Mexico. They called this the third largest city in the world, he said. Had I seen the slum of two million people who'd just arrived because they were starving in their villages? They were included in the total. The country had a capital debt of $80 billion. They had a new loan on which they could only repay the interest, and this was one of the richest oil countries in the world. They were supposed to be a socialist state. They had one trade union, it was run by the government party and it had been led by the same man since the 1930s. He was now eighty-five. Opposition figures were starting to disappear, nobody ever wrote about it but their mothers had formed a human rights committee just as in Argentina. The country was split in two. In the south the poor drifted to the City, in the north they drifted to the U.S. border. The rich had gone on a six-year binge under Lopez Portillo, the previous president, and got their money out when the going was good. Portillo had built himself a palace with stolen money. The poor had christened his private estate 'Dog Hill'. They remembered his famous remark, 'I will defend the peso like a dog,' made shortly before he devalued it. Portillo's chief of police, General Arturo Durazo, had built himself a private tourist resort in Zihuatenejo, not far from Acapulco. *His* private villa was modelled on the Parthenon. The only trouble was that under his direction the police force had robbed so many tourists that he couldn't fill his resort. Had I heard the Mexican joke: 'There's good news and bad news. The bad news is I've just been robbed and beaten up in the street. The good news is that I got away before the police arrived'? It was true. Had I heard all the talk about prosecuting Jorge Diaz Serrano, the former head of Mexican oil? It was just hot air, the man was a state senator, he had immunity. He also had at least $34 million of the country's money. He'd done it by taking 5 per cent. He'd taken 5 per cent of the price of a petrochemical plant made in Houston which had been shipped down to the oilfields in the south and was lying there today, rusting. It had never been screwed together: *an entire plant*. In the Chiapas oilfields the main pipeline was rusting away. Señor Serrano was untouchable. If a Mexican newspaper published any of this it was banned. This diplomat said the country was rotten and the city stank. He said he had tried to get a transfer on grounds of mental strain but nobody paid any attention. It was all right for me, he repeated. I could leave. But he had been there for seven years. By the end of our interview he seemed as wound up as the military attaché but less exercised about my role in advancing world democracy. The two men worked in the same corridor. I began to wonder if I had missed an essential part of the Mexican experience.

I left the embassy and strolled in the Alameda, the long, leafy park which has replaced the execution pyres of the Inquisition. There was a crowd round the bandstand in the middle; a bunch of desperadoes had captured it and were singing of love, death and the inevitable connection between the two. On the edge of the park a political demonstration started. It involved about 100 students and caused a serious traffic jam but the police tolerated it because it was directed against the United States rather than a Mexican target. The students were dressed in gringo fashion, like students all over the world; they wore jeans and college sweaters and walked around in circles so as not to cause an obstruction, just as students do north of the border. The issue was the death of 'Comrade Ana Maria', a Salvadoran guerrilla leader found murdered in Nicaragua, her place of exile. The students were confident that her death had been arranged by the C.I.A. Their banner read, 'the people of Sandino are not alone, the people of Zapata are behind them'. After a while, tired of obeying the law, the students stopped walking around in circles and just sat down in the road. The traffic jam was now over the horizon but still the police did nothing. A little cripple with the whitened face of a circus clown struck up an anti-gringo patter. Police and students looked on, equally amused. From the spacious limousines that crawled past, rich men peered warily out. One could see them any day of the week whistling home down the boulevards, usually sitting beside the chauffeur bent over their reading lamps, while a burly decoy, not a member of the company board, sat alone in the place of honour behind the glass partition. The burly man was the *gardero*; the business community of Mexico are terrified of left-wing kidnappers. Bored, at last, of the uneventful demonstration I got up and found that I had been sitting on the upraised, naked bottom of a kneeling, female figure labelled 'Despair'.

The contrast between rich and poor in Mexico City is not hard to find. The city is said to be a dangerous place, but I was bothered only once, by an old man sitting in a historic square. He shouted at me from the shadows where he crouched that had he worked every day of his life he would never have earned enough money to have bought clothes like mine. Why had I come from so far wearing clothes like that to look at people like him? I had not been looking at him and I was wearing cheap clothes, but I could see his point. More often the poor provide a gentle backdrop to life in the centre of the city. They come in for a day's work from the enormous shanty town of Netzahualcóyotl. Nobody knows how many people live there. At 1 a.m. the paper-stall in Avenida Madero was usually still open, though the vendor in charge of it had fallen into a sober sleep on the pavement. Beside him a street sweeper stood staring, rapt, through a restaurant window at the scarlet figure of the singer with the band, a woman in a long dress dancing frantically but silently and by herself – as far as the shortsighted sweeper could make it out. On the opposite side of the street another old gent was turning in for the night. He unrolled his strip of cardboard in front of the glass-fronted arcade on this fashionable street, then slipped out between the parked limousines for an unfurtive last leak. He was gone very early every morning. There is a North American phrase, 'What's the problem?' It's a comforting phrase; every 'problem' has a solution. The Mexicans comfort themselves with a different phrase – '*No hay remedio*', 'There's nothing to be done'.

There was something familiar about the shop window dummies the tramp chose to sleep with. They were reminiscent of the devotional carvings found in every Mexican church. Perhaps they came from the same factory. Searching for the familiar wooden tears on the painted cheeks, or the wounds in the hands, one found only nail varnish and price tags, the blood and tears of the rag trade. And after a few tequilas the nylon hair glued to their skulls recalled the ringlets and locks gathering dust on countless unlit altars in Estremadura and Castile, offered for the safe return of a Spanish colonial soldier.

My plan had been to go to Guatemala on the train. There was a service via Veracruz, the town from where Cortés had marched. It is a fishing town, famous for its fish restaurants, and before Texas was civilised it was the traditional European gateway to Mexico. Maximilian's French soldiers had retreated through the port at Veracruz, leaving their young Emperor to Juarez. Maximilian had originally been imposed by the European bankers because Mexico had defaulted on its international debts. Bankers were more powerful in the nineteenth century. There seemed a symmetry now, in a visit to Veracruz, after my conversation with the disturbed diplomat.

At the rail station there were long queues at every window, and every window was shut. They told me once again that tickets would not be sold until shortly before the train departed, which was seven hours away. I thought there must be a way around this and approached the only smartly dressed man I could find in the booking hall. He would know how to make the journey comfortable. This man turned out to be not a passenger but a senior official of the national railway company. He said that what I was suggesting was madness. It was true that trains did still run to the Guatemalan frontier. There was an overnight train to Veracruz, but it was not very comfortable, not recommended, even in a first class sleeper. There was also a connecting train from Veracruz to Guatemala. It was scheduled to take twenty-four hours but it rarely took less than forty-eight. There *was* an air service, he said rather sarcastically. No one like me thought of taking a train to Guatemala, he said. The train was not intended for people like me.

So this rail official succeeded in discouraging me from taking the train. I decided that I would fly, but not to Guatemala, to Oaxaca, the Indian town on the road to Chiapas. From there I could go by bus to Guatemala. And so I left Gringolandia, where the United States gives the word for everything, for industry, trade and politics, and crossed the real frontier, to the next place.

PART TWO

Indian Country

6

Going to Seed

> 'The Indian way of consciousness is different from and fatal to our way of consciousness. Our way of consciousness is different from and fatal to the Indian.'
>
> D. H. Lawrence, *Mornings in Mexico*

In *Under the Volcano* Malcolm Lowry describes Oaxaca as 'the saddest sound in the world'. What he omits to describe is the pronunciation of this sound. I tried it out while reading Lowry's book. 'O-ax-aka, Oh axe acka,' it did not sound so sad. Then I discovered that it was pronounced 'Wa-hah-ka'. That did sound sad, and the town was better still. Here after the forthright, brassy Mexicans of the capital and the north, one is suddenly among Indians. But not the familiar village Indians of 'underdevelopment'. These people are Indians of an Indian city. Oaxaca has a population of 180,000, which must make it one of the largest settlements of AmerIndians in the world. It is certainly an improvement on the pathetic reservation settlements of the Indians of Canada and the United States. In Oaxaca, Mexico is right to be proud of its Indian heritage. At its centre is the most beautiful plaza or zócalo, cool and roomy, a handsome bandstand shaded by tall trees and, in the evenings, a military band playing Strauss and Mozart. They made a restful contrast with the muscle-bound *mariachis* of the City. I booked into the hotel overlooking the bandstand and walked over to the usual handsome colonial cathedral. As soon as I passed into its cool air I felt at home.

There was an old Indian couple in the cathedral, just ahead of me as I walked in. They were making towards the High Altar up one of the aisles when the woman took her husband by the hand and led him aside to greet John the Baptist who looked down at them from a niche high up the wall of a chapel. The old man approached the saint, peering up shortsightedly as though uncertain which old friend he was about to meet. She continued to urge him forward until he recognised the statue. Then he removed his hat from his head and both crossed themselves.

I left the cathedral and began to enjoy Oaxaca. At 4,600 feet it is warmer than Mexico City by day and cooler at night. The place is a continual surprise. One can see from the air that it is surrounded for ever by the brown, bare plains of the uplands of Oaxaca state; nothing more than a village for miles and miles, hardly a green field. Then one finds that the main road into town is twisting and slow and full of holes. One is hardly expecting a proper town at all, instead one finds a town still encrusted with the wealth of an empire.

To one side of the *zócalo* there was a colonial palace, still in use as the administrative centre of the state. On the other three sides were arcades and cafés, the onyx tables set out between the pillars so that shoppers had to brush past those being refreshed. But this proximity did not give one a sense of being crowded. Indians seem to need less space than other people, and the streets and trees of Oaxaca are as clean as the air. Even its vestigial shanty town on the bare hillsides beyond the city limits is neat and airy, and many of its inhabitants successfully cultivate little flower gardens in front of their shacks, something I had not seen in shanty towns.

Oaxaca offers onyx everywhere. The Indian children hawk tiny carvings of animals made from green onyx chips and the floors and staircase of the airport are made of it. The other chief beauty of the town is the church of San Domingo, which must be one of the most beautiful churches in Mexico. I walked down the Street of the Holy Blood, past a shop where they sold toys for children, toy skeletons arranged as a miniature band. The Mexican enthusiasm for the macabre knows few limits. Frida Kahlo, who was unable to bear children, was comforted by the gift of a human foetus in a bottle. She called it 'my baby boy'.

There were also several shops that sold only a particular brand of *mescal*. The entire stock was lined up on the shelves, each bottle bearing an identical label and arranged one deep on each wall and from floor to ceiling. The Indians staggered in to be served by the intoxicator but they never bought a bottle; instead their jug was filled from a tap beneath the counter. The *mescal* was for strangers. The Indians drank the coarser *pulque*. The liquorist and his customers were both invariably drunk. They grunted at each other while the transaction was taking place, each face wearing a smile of intimidating determination.

People in Oaxaca rose late, another reason why I felt at home there. Life in the *zócalo* did not start until about 9.30 a.m., when the first shoppers would take the shutters down and the ice cart would come round. I watched an Indian trying to manoeuvre a large block of ice on to a porter's trolley with a pair of outsize ice tongs. Eventually he got bored and hoisted two large blocks up on his shoulders without even bothering to use gloves. A little boy was attempting to run down pigeons in the deserted square. Try as he might, he could not run fast enough to force the pigeons into a trot. They strolled away from him. His brother had lost a balloon in the lower branches of one of the tallest trees. He threw sticks to get it down and went on for twenty minutes before he succeeded. No one applauded but he looked pleased enough.

Stella and Edward were in Oaxaca and one night there was an incident in their hotel. A drunk followed one of the American guests home and attacked him with a brick in the lobby. The landlady and several guests drove the attacker into the street. Then every time he saw the American he became enraged and attacked again. The landlady kept on pushing the American back into his room; he kept coming out again. Eventually they succeeded in locking the American into his room and the drunk out on the street. Then the drunk started to break down the door. The landlady did not seem too shocked by this incident. Next morning she displayed the cuts on her arm and said rather proudly to anyone who did not know, 'I got it defending my guest.' It had never even occurred to her to call the police until the drunk attacked the door. Fortunately he went away before the police answered the telephone.

Stella and Edward took a bus down to the coast after a few days in Oaxaca, they were not tempted by Guatemala, and I drove to Monte Alban, a hill outside the town on which there is a very large and mysterious pyramid site. It is known that this site was once the capital of a Zapotec Indian civilisation and that it was a sacred place. It was an incredibly hot day, the only shade available was offered by the tiny little rooms which had been left in the centre of the stone pyramids. The ruins were on a vast scale, one climbed to the top of a hillside at one end of a beaten plain and the enormous pyramids at the far end became indistinct in the shimmering haze. I could make little sense of what I could see but neither could anyone else. Almost nothing is known for certain about the life of the people who created the ancient Indian civilisations. They were masters of mathematics and astronomy; they were gold and silversmiths; they practised a religion based on worship of the sun and human sacrifice. On the merest hint, imaginative theories have been advanced about the trivial details of their lives, but the scholarly answer to most questions is still 'We do not know.' It is somehow comforting that a people could make so enduring an impression on the face of the earth and leave so few clues behind them. One finds oneself hoping, as one gazes at the silent, vast and apparently pointless constructions, that they will keep the secrets of those who built them, and that the truth of AmerIndian civilisation will remain as obscure as do the thoughts of Indians today.

I walked the length of the site and started to climb the steps at the end. Each was about one foot high; there were forty-two of them. The flight was steeply pitched and some of the steps were crumbling away. Slightly dazed by the heat I wondered what it would be like to fall. One would fall all the way. The steps were too narrow to act as a ledge. When Cortés and Bernal Diaz mounted the great pyramid in Mexico City they counted 114 steps. They were made dizzy and exhausted by the climb, and they were sickened by the sight they found at the summit. There were no altars at the top of these steps but there were a number of caves. From one of them a rascally-looking 'guide' emerged. When I refused his suggestion of a tour he offered to sell me his genuine pots and carvings found in the ruined pyramids. The little chips of pottery did not look very genuine but the rascal was not starving. There were enough tourists on most days to feed him. From the highest points of Monte Alban there were magnificent views of the desolation all around. The people of this part of Mexico have to live from the soil but little grows in it before the rains. Looking out over the valleys the first impression, of a city surrounded by a wilderness, returned. There were very few animals to be seen. A couple of donkeys, a few goats, no cattle. I left the drunken genie of the pyramids, last inhabitant of the sacred city, and swam back through the heat to Oaxaca.

There was another place near Oaxaca which seemed worth a visit. At Mitla, in the ruins of an Indian palace, there stands the Column of Death. The Indians gathered there on New Year's Day to put their arms around the statue. The space they could not enclose represented the number of years they had left to live. I thought I might go out there and put my arms around the column. Then it occurred to me that the arms of the average Indian were considerably shorter than my own, so I decided instead to take a plane to Tuxtla Gutiérrez. From there on, I would be taking the road.

Waiting at the bus terminal in Tuxtla, sipping from a bottle of warm soda, I felt something behind me and turned to find a boy aged about five, an Indian, with two fingers in my hip pocket. He froze as I turned, his fingers still there. I looked down at this incompetent apprentice and he looked back. He was mildly embarrassed. I had not caught a thief red-handed since I was aged five myself. For some time we looked at each other. He could not have been described as the panicky sort. Somewhere among the other passengers his tutor – his father or an elder brother – must be looking on, awaiting developments. Nobody else seemed to have noticed his activities. I pulled open my hip pocket to show him it was empty, then I turned away. He remained frozen to his seat. Eventually I gave him the remains of my sandwich. He ate it thoughtfully, then rose and left the hall. We queued for the bus beside a prominent shrine to the Virgin. There was another, with a light burning in front of it, at San Cristóbal de las Casas where we arrived.

San Cristóbal is a famous Indian town but what I remember about it were the hippies. It was curious the way they concentrated on each other. If they had come to experience life in an Indian community you would have expected them to spread out more. It seemed a long way to travel merely to meet a group of like-minded North Americans and Europeans. As it was, these hippies, the last remnants of the 1960s, seemed paranoid, mazed by dope, penny-pinching, clannish and untrustworthy.

But that was just a superficial impression acquired from the sight of two or three mumbling, twitching, young people in a café, making one cup of coffee last all morning while they gazed vacantly at the blank postcards they were too befuddled to write. The Indians of San Cristóbal were not going to grow rich serving them, and the Indians knew it. They would cross the road to avoid these mobile *gringo* garbage heaps.

I remembered some of the stories I had heard about these Indians and their attitude to gringos. The Indians believe that men with fair hair are the devil. Recently a fair-haired Englishman walking in a wood in Chiapas came upon two Indian children, asleep. They woke, found him looking at them and fled in terror to their father. When they had told their story their father came to kill the Englishman. Fortunately the Englishman had excellent Spanish and the Indian understood Spanish so the Englishman was able to talk his way out of it. The explanation was that the Englishman had fair hair and was therefore the devil. The Indians had been told that the devil was being fed on the souls of their children. This was the pay he demanded in return for allowing the government to take his oil from the earth.

In the previous year two German agricultural advisers had been murdered in Chiapas. The villagers had killed them and pushed their Volkswagen into a *barranca*. The crime had only been discovered after an alert bank clerk in San Cristóbal had noticed the numbers on some travellers' cheques which the Indians had tried to cash several months after the two Germans had disappeared. The whole village was then tried for murder, but everyone was acquitted because they had genuinely believed that they had killed two devils. First, both the Germans had red hair, another sign of devils. Second, they had been working in a field that the Indians had set aside as a place apart. Then they had done this on a holy day. Finally the villagers had twice offered them food and drink, which they had refused. After the second refusal the villagers killed them. Devils do not eat food or drink.

One can see the inevitability of this tragedy. The Germans, who spoke no Spanish, puzzled by the disused field; their growing conviction that they had found usable ground which the ignorant Indians had failed to put to use; their repeated refusal of food and drink because they did not wish to get food poisoning; this determined concern for their health ensuring their death sentence; the satisfaction of the Indians at the thought of a good job well done; the state's acquiescence in this. I looked at two of the hippies, one English, one German, giggling inanely in a café, under the influence of the mushroom which the Indian witches used so sparingly and so seriously. After one night I was glad to leave San Cristóbal. I took the bus to Comitán.

I had time on the bus to wonder about the Indian religion. We were now deep into the state of Chiapas, the lost state of Guatemala, and the state towards which Graham Greene headed in the journey he described in *The Lawless Roads*. There has always been a mystery about the Indian's Christianity. It is heavily tainted with pre Christian features. One famous Indian carver's daughter died and he put her ribs into his next crucifixion. One mission church became a very popular centre of pilgrimage and the priest was uncertain why his crucifix should attract so much devotion. Then the church roof started to leak. In order to mend it the priest had to move the cross and within the rather exaggerated rib-cage of the Christ he found that someone had placed a Mayan idol. The carver had made room for the image when he first undertook the work. The priest removed the stone idol and sent it to a museum. When he replaced the crucifix he found that the pilgrimage died away almost at once. In another village the Indians used to place two babies in the crib at Christmas, a boy baby, Tío Jesus, and a girl baby, Natividad. Natividad was there to support the villagers' belief that they were themselves descended from Jesus, just as the old Aztec kings were descendants of the Gods. If the priest removed Natividad from the crib, the Indians stopped coming to his church. Another village could not even be satisfied with this. It did not want to share Christ with anyone. It wanted its own. One day an unmarried girl became pregnant. She was declared to be a virgin. In due course she gave birth to a boy. The villagers called him Jesus and treated him like a prince until he was fifteen. Then they crucified him. There was no resurrection in this case, but the villagers have been the best Christians for miles around ever since. A friend told me how he had once encountered an old Indian in Chiapas who had explained to him the doctrine of the Trinity. There was God the Father who lived in a nearby cave and sometimes made the earth tremble. Then there was God the Son, who was the sun, and then there was God the Mother, who was the Moon. It was quite simple. Such men blasphemed, and stated a cast-iron faith. My reverie about the Indian Christianity was interrupted when the bus stopped and two gnarled *federales* boarded it. They were short men who had long since missed promotion; their technical skills were not cerebral. They wore rather ornate pearl-handled revolvers buckled to the waist and both were memorable for their dreadful, rasping laughs.

Comitán was the last town before the Guatemalan border, the opposite number of Tijuana but in this case – harsh judgment on the land to the south – it was fifty kilometres to the north of the line. It was an unpretentious place, though it had whores and *mariachis* in abundance, and did a reasonable trade out of the hardships of Central America. It was a rest town for the Mexican workers in the relief camps set up for refugees from Guatemala. I went to the parish church of San Domingo, again. It was a tumbledown, whitewashed church of Chiapas, still looking as it must have done in the days of the persecution, when it was closed by the revolutionary government. Only the bright red plastic-and-neon cross on the blistered wall outside served as triumphant reminder that the persecution was over and the church open again. Inside it was very dark. As I entered a drunken Indian was being led quietly down the nave by a frightened-looking boy. I wondered why I went to these churches and decided that it was because they were sure to contain the only entirely familiar objects in town. Here was a font, empty of water, there a window to Santa Rosa of Lima, the first saint of the Americas, canonised for her love of the Indians. A peasant woman genuflected, stiffly and only half-way and on the wrong knee. Another absentmindedly ran her hands up and down the satin robes of the dead Christ – always present this figure, matted, twisted and scabbed, and lying at a convenient height for those who wished to touch him. There was a pool of water on the floor by the high altar. Outside the drunk was lying full-length and face down in the road, blood on his hands. There was another pool of water beside him. Within five minutes he had been dragged off by two policemen, one lashing his back with a switch to make him rise.

It began to rain, at least one month early. I started to write my notebook in the square and a girl in orange trousers and a mustard-coloured shirt sat down on the bench and asked me what I was doing. 'I am writing.' 'Write, then,' she said. I did. I could not decide whether she was a whore or a half-wit or just untypically friendly. She had nothing more to say. Neither did I. 'Does it rain here much in summer?' I asked. She did not reply '*no hay reglas fixtas*'; she did not reply at all. So I wished her well and left. As I did so it occurred to me that I had never heard anyone but myself say '*Adios*' in Mexico.

I went to a news-stand. In Oaxaca I found a local paper, *La Protesta*, which had a front page headline, 'Sadismo Oficial'. This turned out to be a story about rising prices. In Comitán I found a little book called *Denuncia*, a comic-strip story about vice. There were dozens of these little comic-strip books for adults published in weekly instalments. They were extremely popular, everybody read them. I had seen one in the hands of a senior Mexican bureaucrat. All over Mexico people were struggling for literacy in order to be able to read such books. My issue of *Denuncia* started off with a violent argument between a ponce and his scantily-clad whore. By page three, by which point the reader had had to absorb twenty-eight words, he hit her for the first time – 'PLAFF PLAFF'. On page four she was clinging to his arm and calling him a savage. And by page six she was hard at work with her first client of the day. But *Denuncia* is a moral publication and on page 127 her sister stabbed the ponce to death with a blade looking wicked enough to satisfy even a Mexican readership. 'SPLASHHH. AUGHHH.' Next week, *Abuso*, someone else would be taking unfair advantage of someone else. How perverse it seems, to be imposing literacy on an underdeveloped world, just when there was less need of it than there had been for several centuries. V. S. Pritchett has noticed this change between the England of today and that of the 1930s. Of tradesmen in small towns in England before the Second World War he wrote, 'These people talked clear English . . . They read the most . . . They had seen the word printed. They belonged to a time and culture based on printing, and not to the oral or pictorial culture which is rapidly destroying the word today.'

I knew of a story in Comitán and it finally broke the trance I had fallen into in Mexico City. Outside the town the Mexican government had established various camps for the Indians from Guatemala who had fled across the border. In the correct manner I had tried to get permission to visit these camps while I was in Mexico City but had been defeated by the telephone system and the need to approach an ever-lengthening list of officials in order to get permission to approach the one I was already talking to. It seemed simpler just to ignore the rules and drive out to see the camps. In Mexico City I had been told that there were unreported riots in Chiapas. Two politicians had been shot. One of the causes of the troubles was the presence of these Guatemalan refugees. The simple people believed that they were the advance guard of a Guatemalan invasion; Chiapas had been part of Guatemala until 1821. At a different level, the Foreign Ministry, expressing Mexico's traditional dislike of Guatemala, wanted to shelter the refugees. The Interior Ministry, which was suspicious of any subversive elements, wanted the refugees to be returned; it took the view that Mexico had quite enough communists of its own. And the governor of Chiapas wanted them to be expelled because they were a financial burden on his state and needed work. There was no work to spare in Chiapas. The Mexican army seemed to be in unofficial league with the Guatemalan army, which hunted the refugees even across the border into Mexico, if it thought it could get away with this.

My contact with the refugees was Rafael Bracomontes, a young man who, following an air crash involving his superiors, had been put in charge of all the refugee camps. They used aeroplanes all the time because the camps had been placed well away from everyone else in remote areas of jungle near the border. Before going out there Rafael insisted that I got a pass and drove me to the police station for this purpose. There was little to see in the police office, apart from a measuring board on the wall marked up to 160 cms (5′3″); perhaps they only measured Indians. No decisions could be taken until the *jefe* appeared and no one knew when that would be. The policemen stood around, their guns dangling enticingly from their belts, making jokes about whores, pulling each other about reassuringly and giving out their strangled coughs and laughs, which were sometimes hard to distinguish. One imagined they had throats made of iron and lungs reduced to kapok. Whatever it was the *jefe* was doing that evening it took too long and so, after another round of jokes about whores made to an accompaniment of choking sounds, I left the police station and decided to approach the only people who actually controlled access to the camps – the pilots of the planes.

I found the pilots eating steaks in a restaurant. They were led by the *capitán de los pilotos*, a large, hostile and offensive man with a Castilian lisp. This turned out to be due to the arrangement of his teeth rather than recent Spanish ancestry. He held court at his restaurant table, wore a chunk of solid gold around his neck and amused himself by making offensive remarks to Carolina, a student from Colorado who was also keen to see conditions in the camps. The *capitán* said that in Mexico a man needed a wife for children, a mistress for passion and a friend for his soul, three different women. Which position he was offering Carolina was not immediately clear. She responded with a defence of the North American practice of allowing lesbian couples to adopt children. This promised to be quite a comical conversation but the mention of lesbians threw a deep gloom over the party. One of the pilots said that a friend of theirs, also a pilot, had suffered the tragedy of losing his wife to another woman. The tension was affecting his work. It was driving him mad. He was being cuckolded by a woman. There was no acceptable way of dealing with this insult. It was clear from everyone's expression that there could hardly be a worse fate. Eventually it was arranged that I could fly on the following day provided that I gave the *capitán* my blood group.

Next morning at 6.45 Corso, the dashing young pilot with a distressingly scarred and burnt face, and something of a limp when he walked, was impatiently hooting outside the hotel. It was cold and according to Corso rather cloudy. Not many clouds were visible from the town but he said that over the forest they were building up. He was anxious to start. We drove for about half an hour to the *capitán*'s airfield, which turned out to be a grass strip, beside which six planes were parked, half of them in pieces. I recalled Rafael's remark on the previous day about the *capitán*'s poor maintenance. The previous month there had been a crash in which five people working for the refugee project had been seriously injured. Slowly two of the planes were assembled. They were loaded with the supplies essential to life in the camp and took off despite the gathering clouds low over the forest.

Bored, I started to play a game of flicking marbles with a coffee inspector. The inspector said he was waiting for the coffee to be flown in. This was the *capitán*'s normal work. The refugee contract was no more than an additional source of income. His planes now had refugee supplies as a cargo for the outward flight. Then they would hop over to a coffee *finca* and pick up a commercial cargo on their way back. Waiting for the first plane to return I read a notice pinned up by the pilot's office. 'Missing. A student of anthropology, 21–22 years, 170 cms, swarthy, thin, curly hair.' His name was not given, nor did it say how long it was since he had disappeared into the forest. Judging by the state of the notice he must have been long dead.

Our plane was ready when suddenly the *capitán* raised the question of payment. He wanted $50 American dollars for two twenty-minute flights. Nothing about this had been mentioned before. I also discovered that if a passenger was taken supplies had to be left behind, that there were no Indian interpreters at the camps, and that it would be necessary to return after two hours. The opportunity *not* to fly was too good to miss. I would find some other way to get there. For the rest of the morning the *capitán* refused to speak to me. Later Corso flew in with a load of coffee and one sick Indian. The man had severe asthma. In his struggle to breathe he had gone a delicate shade of green. His elderly father humped him out of the plane like a sack of coffee and laid him in the back of a truck. Then Rafael arrived to check that the *capitán* was moving supplies out to the camps. Apparently, despite the state of the people dependent on his planes, he could not be trusted to carry out his contract. As it was, the asthmatic Indian had not been flown straight back. Even with a sick man on board a load of coffee had to be picked up. Rafael took the asthmatic to hospital then drove me out to the only camp which could be reached by road.

Rafael and I drove towards the border for half an hour, then branched off up a rocky road that led into an area of thin soil and boulders. The governor of the state of Chiapas had placed the refugees in this area because 'nobody lived there'. One could see why. The camp we were going to contained 3,000 people. It was new, formed when two of the original camps, placed even closer to the border, had been attacked by the Guatemalan army. At this point the frontier was a shallow river only four kilometres away. The huts, built of bamboo cane, with reed roofs, were placed on a stony hillside near the only village in the area. We were escorted round by 'the Representative', a lucid and intelligent character. When I asked him how long the people had been fugitives he gave me four separate dates over the two previous years, which applied to each of the various groups within the camps. All his answers were precise. All the refugees had come from the Guatemalan departments of Quiché and Huehuetenango. They had walked for 150 or 200 miles across very mountainous country to find safety in this camp. When they arrived they were generally half-starved and sometimes carried nothing but their beloved *marimbas*, their musical instruments. They were all people of the highlands who had no resistance to the low-altitude diseases of the forest. They were riddled with asthma and fevers and T.B. and parasites. Malaria was so common that only the more severe cases were treated. Since the camps were first set up, 200 children had been born there and lived. Rafael was startled by this figure, but the Representative looked rather proud of it. Some of the mothers were still feeding babies aged eighteen months, although they had been told that their milk was no longer sufficient.

In appearance the camp, perhaps because it had been built by the Indians, looked much more like a village than a refugee camp. The women sat outside their huts overseeing the children, carrying water and wood and making bread in the communal *adobe* oven. Only the men looked at a loss. Under the laws of Chiapas they were not allowed to work for money. They had to remain refugees. Unofficially, they earned a little by helping the Mexicans in the village. The minimum rural wage in Mexico was 240 pesos a day, although many Mexican peasants worked for 150. The Guatemalans were paid between fifty and seventy-five pesos a day. They were allowed to sell their own produce and their parish priest had erected a large hut for them and equipped it with four looms. Guatemalan Indian weaving is famous and it is always done by the women, but in the camps it was the men who did it. They had nothing else to do, and they had taken to this potential source of income with spirit. They were not allowed to travel more than fifty kilometres from the border, which meant that they could not go to the only available market in Comitán, but they had so far broken this law without punishment. *No hay reglas fixtas*. The local Mexicans were forbidden to sell them liquor, and Comitán was also the place where they went to get drunk. So trade became, in the Indian tradition, a social occasion once more.

I asked the Representative whether they felt safe in this camp. He said that one month earlier a three-man patrol of the Guatemalan army had been seen two kilometres from the camp, that is over a mile inside the border. There were only two Mexican army units in the neighbourhood and so they did not feel very safe. At night they could pick up Guatemalan radio stations and listen to broadcasts which told them that everything was now quiet. And they had been invited by the Guatemalan Red Cross to return home. But they did not believe the assurances they had been given. Refugees recently arrived from Guatemala contradicted them.

On the drive back to Comitán, Rafael described the problems he faced with the local churches. Both Catholic and Evangelical churches, but especially the Evangelicals, refused to help those refugees who were not church members. The priests and ministers also accused Rafael and other U.N. officials of being rich men from the city who stole money and supplies for themselves. Whenever they could the church leaders interfered in his work, but at least they refrained from getting involved in local politics. The Mexican doctors, on the other hand, who were generally young and idealistic, frequently suggested political action to the refugees. So far the refugees had refused to respond. They had had enough of politics for the time being and asked to be excused from such activities in the future. As a community they were much better behaved than the local Mexicans. They never fought over women, they observed their religious feast days religiously. While in the camps they remained sober. Whenever they could they worked hard. They wanted to go home, but only when it was safe.

We drove back through the mountain passes to Comitán. It was a fine still evening. Eagles circled high over the *barrancas*, the wheels of the car threw up a soft dust, there was water in the streams and dappled shades on either bank of the occasional river crossing. As we reached the road I read again the passing signs of Mexico, official and otherwise. '*Ceda El Paso*', '*Se vende esta casa*', '*Fuera Corruptos*!' Spanish is a beautiful language for phrases and slogans; Spanish slogans sing. What could be more beguiling than the construction of '*Se vende esta casa*' – 'It is for *sale*, this house' – on a dying fall? Rafael began to talk about the national obsession, Mexican politics. He said that in Mexico there was a pun to describe their form of government. Central America was ruled by dictators, *dictaturas*. *Tura* means strength. People said that in Mexico there were no *dictaturas*, only *dictablandas*, they were ruled by *dictablandas*. The meaning of *blanda* was clear enough, but later I looked it up in a dictionary. '*Blanda* – soft, mild, gentle, yielding.' I liked this pun. I thought of the state of Mexico; the corrupt pilots, the brutal police, the censored press, the unreported riots; a government that robbed the people of hundreds of millions of pounds. '*Dictablandas*' was a kindly judgment.

Rafael began to talk about himself. He told me that his name, Bracomontes, was most unusual in Spain and that it was in fact of French origin, it was the name of a town in Castile. This, with his blue eyes, made him *criollo*, white, a word not to be found in the Mexican political dictionary. In fact *criollo* has two meanings in Spanish: one is 'creole', a person of mixed birth, the other is 'a Spaniard born in America'. One of the main reasons why Spain lost its American empire was its refusal to allow even pure-bred Spaniards born in America to govern its colonies. Rafael Bracomontes was a descendant of the natural governing class of Mexico who had had to revolt before they were able to rule.

Bracomontes said that his was also a notable name in Mexico, an uncle had been a bishop in Guadalajara during the religious persecution. He told me that if I wished to understand Mexican politics I should understand that the *criollos* had always ruled Mexico. I would not find this stated in any history books, but it was none the less true. I asked him about Juarez, the Indian president. Was he not an exception? Not at all, said Rafael. In fact under Juarez the *criollos* had been more powerful than ever, because Juarez was a democratic president who had ceded far more power than usual to an elected national assembly, which was packed with *criollos*. Juarez, as an Indian, had been the perfect figure to lead a national uprising against the imposed French emperor Maximilian. But the *criollos* had never lost their grip on the country since they had first imposed it. Bracomontes said it had been a successful rule because it had been such a subtle one. There was, for instance, an official history of the country and a true history. The official history accounted for the public position of Cortés. He told me that the previous president had actually unveiled a new bust of Cortés, the only one in Mexico City. But it was still a rather surreptitious form of approval. It stood in the hospital, Jesus Nazareno, the first hospital in the Americas, founded by Cortés. You had to ask to see it. Nobody could be offended by it by mistake. Throughout our conversation Rafael's driver sat alert and listening. He was not *criollo*.

On Sunday, 17 April, I took the bus from Comitán to the Guatemalan border. It was a two-hour ride and there were no towns on either side of the frontier ahead. Apart from the refugees there was no urgent necessity among the people of either country to cross the line. To cross from the state of Chiapas to the department of Huehuetenango is to move from an obscure part of the world to one more obscure.

I arrived at the bus station early. I had been encouraged to do so by the notices displayed there. Even now, after five weeks in Mexico, I had not learned my lesson. I still believed the official notices. 'Buy your ticket four days ahead,' they said. 'Check your baggage half an hour in advance.' '*Evite contratiempos*.' It was all nonsense. A sullen boy refused to sell me a ticket. He had no tickets for sale, it was all done when the bus arrived, by the bus driver, for cash. Nor would he take my suitcase. So I sat on it on the pavement outside his office, in the watery sunshine, and read *Scarlet and Black*. It seemed to me that Stendhal was not much of a naturalist. On one page he described 'huge naked boulders which had fallen long ago from the mountain down into the middle of the forest'. But surely the fall of the boulders would have preceded the arrival of the trees? On the next page he described 'a sparrow hawk . . . high above his head . . . tracing huge circles in its flight'. I was wondering why

Stendhal knew so little about the names of birds when a shadow crossed the page. One of the border police, last seen in the police station, was looking down at me. The man was smiling. He wanted to know where I was going and he wanted to know why I had not returned to see the *jefe* and he wanted to know whether I had been to the refugee camps. I decided to say 'no'. If he already knew I had been out with Rafael then I was already in trouble; a lie would make no difference. If he did not know he was unlikely to enquire further before the departure of my bus. When I answered his questions he departed, I thought with untypical speed, in the direction of the border police station.

The 9.30 bus eventually left at 10.30, the driver having retired on arrival to eat a full, cooked breakfast at a nearby café. There was nothing to be done while we waited except to keep glancing down the road towards the police station and then at the sullen office boy answering the telephone, which he did by saying, 'Cristóbal Colón', the name of his bus company. Then, after a very uncomfortable wait, our driver appeared and the bus, almost empty, departed.

I dozed most of the way to the Guatemalan border. The road was already familiar to me; it was the road to the refugee camp and it was pleasantly warm in the bus. I woke once to find the assistant driver, an odd man, just avoiding a collision with a farmer's truck. After that whenever I opened my eyes it was to see his anxious face in the mirror. He drove rather slowly, the chief driver was asleep on the back seat of the coach, and he played constantly with the pedals and switches. He had all the nervous indecision of a passenger left alone at the controls of an aeroplane. He pulled the most extraordinary faces at himself in the mirror, and he kept glancing fearfully over his shoulder at an invisible pursuer. He was the least reassuring bus driver I could remember. But it made no difference; for most of the journey I dozed on. Mexico had taught me that at least. When I entered the country I had been in a state of over-organised irritation, eager at every opportunity to shortcircuit Latin inefficiency. Leaving it I was in a state of torpor, too relaxed to do more than look on at a coach driver who was suffering from hallucinations. Needless to say we reached the frontier without mishap. I carried my cases over the line in the company of two hippies, a French boy and a German girl. I did not know it then but these two were to haunt the rest of my journey. She was taller than him by some inches and the two Mexican drivers could not resist it. The Frenchman struggled, eventually successfully, to lift a pack of eighteen kilos on to his back. She swung a pack of fifteen kilos on to her shoulders without effort. 'Why don't you carry them both?' one of the drivers asked the boy, then both men erupted in a fit of harsh laughter, delighted with their subtle wit. As I walked up the hill to the Guatemalan police post that laughter was the last I heard of Mexico. It could have burst through the doors of Tenampa.

7

Into the Barranca

> 'For anyone who has lived in Guatemala other countries, by contrast, are lacking in savour.'
>
> Norman Lewis, *The Volcanoes Above Us*

There had been an idea around in Comitán that if one took the 9.30 Cristóbal Colón service to the frontier one would be able to connect with the midday direct service to Guatemala City offered by El Condór. This was not the case. Emerging from the Guatemalan police post I saw that the frontier was established on a road that ran down a deep, narrow valley. Thickly wooded cliffs rose on each side. There was a *cantina* to one side, and nothing else in sight except a beaten-up old rattletrap bus with wooden benches, both front wheels jacked up on bricks and the tyres off. This was the only bus available and it was not going to reach Guatemala City that night.

I had already waved goodbye to the hippies, Philippe and Manuela; the first of many farewells. They had reached the Guatemala frontier without realising that they needed visas and they had been turned back. Up went the eighteen kilos again, up went the fifteen kilos, and back they went into Mexico, probably as far as Comitán. Feeling a rather superior type of traveller I pushed on to the *cantina* and started to make encouraging remarks about a bus.

There were a couple seated in there who looked prosperous. They said, in response to the enquiries of the cook, that they were not Mexican but Guatemalan. They had reached the border in their own car but they had left this in Mexico. They were continuing their journey by bus. I began to wonder what they were doing. If they were as rich as they looked they could certainly have afforded an air ticket. If they merely wanted to save money they should not have crossed the frontier at this point. The usual crossing place was on the coast at Tapachula. Things were quiet down there. The road we were on ran through Huehuetenango and there had been a lot of trouble in this department. At least four large river bridges had been blown up in the last year on this road. The prosperous couple did not enjoy being questioned and the cook left them alone.

The interruption ended, as they frequently do when one is travelling, without notice. One moment there was nothing, no wheels, no driver, no hope. The next, a grubby fellow in a greyish vest was scratching out the bits of food that had worked their way into his stubble – he had been eating in the kitchen with the chickens. He said that we would leave at once. I looked over my shoulder towards the shadows where the crippled bus lurked and, sure enough, its wheels had been soundlessly replaced. Stranger still, the hippies were standing beside it. They had conjured up a visa without having to return to Comitán, and on a Sunday afternoon too.

It was a slow business, that bus journey from the Mexican border towards Guatemala City through the disturbed department of Huehuetenango. In the first place there were the interruptions caused by the terrorists. At each of the four fallen bridges the bus had to make a detour down a dirt track beside the crumpled girders and shattered arches and across the boulders at the bottom of the dried-up *barranca*. On the stonework of one of the shattered bridges an army officer had caused to be painted a fiercely sarcastic response: 'Another contribution to progress made by our subversive elements.' The black painted capitals blazed out, over the extensive concrete wreckage, visible as far away as the high crags where the guerrillas lived. The woman in the seat beside me produced an Old Testament and began to read the psalms. She was, I realised, an Evangelical Christian, one of the recent converts from Hispanic Catholicism to North American Protestantism, and she had recognised another in the adjoining row. They murmured the psalms to each other. You could see they felt special. They had the Word and the Book now, without priestly mediation.

The second, and far more frequent, type of interruption was caused by those opposed to the terrorists. Our bus was stopped about every fifteen minutes at road-blocks. On three occasions these barriers were manned by well-equipped units of the Guatemalan army. The rest of the road-blocks were erected by the *Guardia Civil*. The formation of this raggle-taggle peasant army was the latest development in the guerrilla war which had lasted since 1967 and claimed 40,000 dead. These peasants were armed with *machetes*, percussion-cap rifles, airguns and other tat. Some of them looked about twelve years old, occasionally there was a professional soldier in their midst, but, poorly armed as they were, there was no question about their determination.

'*Todos los hombres*! *Papeles, papeles*' . . . On and on, through the afternoon went the cry and yet again the men in the bus would have to disembark and produce their papers and be searched. At one of the army-blocks there was a chilling sight, a man in a hood, carefully guarded, was taken down the line of passengers, peering into each face, only his eyes glinting out. He was a *subversivo*, a guerrilla who had surrendered. Now he was trying to identify any of his former comrades who were travelling on our bus. He paused before the prosperous-looking man, then moved on without comment. People identified by such denunciation were usually taken a short distance away from the road, questioned, tortured and shot. This was called execution by military tribunal. No one was taken from our bus.

At another of these stops I bought three oranges from a little Indian girl who had a basket full of them. They cost five centavos (about 2½ pence). I gave one to the delicate-handed French boy. He was by this time trapped in his seat by his Manuela who had collapsed enormously across his knees. He looked up at me rather helplessly like a man who is pinned to the ground by an elephant he has just shot. 'Has there been some trouble in this region?' he asked, after one of the road-blocks. It was hard to say whether or not it was an advantage to travel across Central America with so little information. Eventually our bus reached Huehuetenango and I said goodbye to the hippies for the second time. They were going to spend a few days by Lake Atitlan, 'the most beautiful lake in the world'. Then they were going to continue 'as far as Chile'. They had a year before they had to be back in Mexico.

It was now late afternoon and I was still a very long way from

Guatemala City. I became infected at this point with traveller's panic. Whatever it cost me I decided I would get to my destination that night. I had promises to keep, a telegram to be sent, an appointment to be kept. I forced a tiny man who called himself Al Caponé to carry my two heavy bags across the town to the depot of the El Condór express bus company. I felt rather stiff after a day in the bus and did not want to strain my back. There was a clerk at the bus depot dozing in the shade. Al Caponé told me that the next bus from this depot to the capital did not leave until tomorrow. I made him wake the sleeping clerk in order to confirm this information. Then I made the little fellow run back to where he had started from and find me a local bus to Quezaltenango, the destination of the bus I had just abandoned. After much panting, and several frantic redirections – one bus actually started off as we were running towards it – Al Caponé succeeded in his mission. We were just in time. His legs had become more and more bowed as his task wore on. I climbed into the bus and gave him one and a half quetzals (about 75 pence). He protested vigorously about this but it seemed generous to me. The bus started up and I sat down rather heavily in an empty seat. Too late I realised that a steel spike was sticking out of it.

At Cuatro Caminos, a crossroad in the middle of nowhere, I repeated the performance. A fellow passenger had told me that our bus was going to 'Shayla', not Quezaltenango after all, I was irritated by the hole ripped in my trousers and sickened by the diesel fumes that poured into the bus from an open engine cover. It seemed that at this crossroad there was bound to be a direct bus to the city. It was dark by now, and as once more I saw the bus which I had just abandoned disappear up the road I realised that 'Shayla' was spelt 'Xela' and was the local name for Quezaltenango. Furthermore there were no buses from Cuatro Caminos to the capital. There were buses destined for villages all over western Guatemala, but none it seemed to the City. I was eventually rescued by a friendly bus driver. Looking at a pair of approaching headlights, indistinguishable to me from all the others, he said, '*That* bus is going to Xela. From there you can get a night bus to the City, via the coast.' He was right. And so, on the third bus destined for Quezaltenango I actually reached it. Once there I lost my head again.

It seemed to me by now that fate, time, night and various other powerful malignities were in conspiracy against the success of my plans. At the office of the 'America' bus company I asked if there was a night bus to Guatemala City. They denied it. I pressed the girl on this point. Was there not one via the coast road? Oh yes, so there was. It left in one hour. It would arrive at midnight. I asked for a ticket. There were no seats left. I said I would stand. The girl was amazed. It was a three and a half hour journey. I purchased a ticket. I then went to the office of a rival company and made similar enquiries. They had a bus and they had seats. But instead of getting a refund and transferring my luggage across the square I stayed with 'America' *because they claimed their bus would arrive half an hour earlier*. I did not intend to give the conspirators even that much chance. I had risen that morning at 7.30, in another country and as it now seemed another incarnation, confident of being in Guatemala City by 6 p.m. It was now 8.30 and there was a three and a half hour journey ahead, but for the sake of half an hour I had turned down a comfortable seat in which I could have slept.

The journey started in chaotic fashion. Even as we drove out of town a ferocious argument broke out between two drunks and the conductor. The first drunk, a woman, was turned out of her seat. She was supposed to be standing. I, who was also supposed to be standing, was then placed in the seat she had been evicted from because its rightful occupant was a friend of the driver and was crouched on a stool beside him, deep in conversation. The female drunk went on interminably about this situation. It turned out that the woman in the seat beside me was of her party, but *she* was sober and had no intention of moving. The drunken woman resented this. She discussed it in a loud voice with the other drunk, a man seated on my other side, across the aisle. Sometimes one drunk stood, sometimes the other, sometimes both at once in drunken affection swayed in the corridor of the bus, lurching and pressing themselves against their fellow passengers. 'Why did we come on this bus?' asked the woman. 'Why did we not take the normal route in the *camionetta*? It is all her fault.' She was speaking of the woman beside me. '*She* made us come on the coast road because the view was so beautiful. Did she not realise it was going to be pitch-dark, to say nothing of the pouring rain? Look at her. It is all right for her. She is as cosy as a *novia*, a bride tucked up with her *gringo*.' She pronounced it, with great emphasis GREEENGO. 'Look at her, a married woman, shameless in her comfort, heedless of being compromised by this cosy situation. With a *stranger*. And a *gringo*.' My companion merely chuckled at this recital. Then she went to sleep, quite cosily enough, at my side.

After half an hour, the talkative passenger reclaimed his seat from me. Making for his stool I was instructed instead to stand in the corridor, which I did for the next three hours. And so we arrived eventually in Guatemala City. I had been travelling for sixteen hours. You can spend many days like that on a bus in Central America.

In Guatemala City in 1984 it was said that for fifty American dollars you could hire an assassin who would ask no questions. The price had not changed for two years, a tribute to the stability of the currency. That would buy you one murder. There were at that time at least five groups of people generally suspected of killing their fellow citizens. There was firstly the army. In its battle against the guerrillas the army killed a lot of people who were neutral, or who were on their side, mainly peasants. It was regarded as careless by city-dwellers to be killed by men in uniform because there were rules for avoiding them when they were shooting in the city. You did not walk in the streets for long after the cinemas had closed. If you heard trouble near by you avoided it.

Then there were the guerrillas. They killed soldiers. They killed people who they suspected to be police informers. They also killed people who resisted abduction. And some said they killed people who were humble supporters of their own cause, again the peasants, if they could make those deaths look as though they were the work of the army. There were four or five guerrilla organisations at work.

The third group of killers, the death squads, were the most feared. Guatemala has this distinction; it is the country which invented death squads. They were first heard of in the 1950s and are manned by plain-clothes soldiers or policemen. The headquarters are in a building behind the Palacio Nacional, which is prettily painted the colour of pistachio ice cream. There used to be a permanent liaison officer from the office of the president attached to the office of the death squads. This was known because one of the holders of that responsible position turned out to be working for the guerrillas.

Fourthly there were the organised criminals. The criminals were enjoying a boom. Very few violent crimes were ever solved by the police. The criminals were adept at making their activities appear to be political, and if this disguise was successful the police did not even bother to investigate. If you were shot you were of little interest to the police, but if your car was stolen they *would* try to help. They would certainly start an investigation. This was not necessarily a help if the stolen car was a Mercedes. In 1982 the stolen Mercedes racket was booming. Then there was a change of government, someone denounced the outgoing Minister of the Interior, and investigation showed that he had twelve stolen Mercedes in his garden.

Of course none of the above groups could be hired to kill a man for $50. That was done by a fifth group, the enthusiastic amateurs. There were plenty of guns in Guatemala City, and plenty of poor men who could use them. They too escaped investigation by disguising their crimes as political. This was not hard to do. One evening I chose to dine in a restaurant noted for its pasta. Two days later I opened the paper and found a photograph of a man who had been dining alone in the same restaurant. My spaghetti had been over-cooked. His spaghetti was over-his-face. More precisely, his face was deep in his spaghetti. He had been shot by an 'unknown assailant'. A left-wing leaflet was found by the body. The police concluded that this was a political crime, but it could have been a jealous husband.

I liked Guatemala City in 1982 when it cost $50 to hire an assassin, and liked it again, though rather less, in 1983 when the death squads were in temporary retirement and the general murder rate was much lower. The place I enjoyed most in the evening was called *El Gallito*. It was a clip-joint which employed a famous band of *marimba* musicians. I went there on the Monday evening, the day after my arrival. There were whores at work but if you explained you had come for the music they tried someone else. It was understood that the band was quite good enough to attract its own enthusiasts. I sat in the dark, by the deserted dance floor, in the forlorn little club, and heard again after a year the *marimbas*. The seven men in the band had not changed. A *marimba* is like a large xylophone, and this band had two of them. The 'leader', the man I always took to be the leader, chose the melody. Every darting movement he made with his hammer was followed by the man at his side. On his other side two more players, the rhythm section, each held three hammers. A fifth player had an entire *marimba* to himself. In addition there were a drummer and a bass. The 'leader' resembled an elderly, albino chimpanzee. Of these seven, only the drummer was not old. *Marimba* music is music for old men. As you get older and older you seem to play it better and better. It is the music of the Indians, and the music of Guatemala in a way which not even the *mariachis* can quite manage to be the music of Mexico. There is something about *marimba* music that affects the personality of its practitioners. This was most apparent, in this band, from the behaviour of the bass player. He stood with his back to the band and to the world, in the corner, like a child in disgrace. He may have done this to catch some acoustical effect. But as a tune progressed his original purpose, whether musical or emotional, was lost. Gradually he screwed himself round, away from the corner, until he was full profile to the room. He always moved anti-clockwise. He never quite faced the audience.

Marimba music can be just silly, but when it is at its best it is both silly and sad. Bouncy little tunes succeed one another cheerfully enough though few of them progress very far from their first theme. A tune will set off, with frequent high notes, it will be repeated with mild variations, then it will stop, abruptly. When the evening is going badly or the musicians are distracted one can watch them without knowing whether they feel anything or not. They will abandon a strict tempo, get ahead of each other, lose concentration. But when, as in *El Gallito*, the musicians become involved in their own music it is magical. *El jefe*, on this night, looked sad and anguished, the oldest rhythm man looked sad and tranquil, the bass player looked sad and ashamed. The music took each of them quite differently; although they had been playing it all their lives they could still be surprised by it, and their subconscious reaction was vividly displayed on their faces.

The *marimbistas* played in short bursts with frequent long breaks for beer. During one of these I talked to the fifth man who played alone. He said that 'the leader' was not the leader of the group, he just led the tune. He asked me why I liked the music and after listening for some time to my attempts to express myself he said, politely, that I meant that the music was *melancólico y ligeronde*, sad and light-hearted at once. He said that it expressed his culture, the Indian culture. He was not in fact Indian but *mestizo*. It was a tribute to the power of the *marimbas* that a Guatemalan *mestizo* should thus have acknowledged his Indian heritage.

After a while other customers found their way to *El Gallito* through the deserted streets. Some began to dance contentedly in the near-darkness. A woman with a straight back, motionless from the waist up, wriggling violently below, allowed herself to be pursued across the dance floor by her partner. Her expression was entirely decorous and modest; her movements entirely abandoned. Her partner pursued her, hunched forward eagerly. His tie was straight, his jacket buttoned. They never touched.

Contrasted with the expectant dancers the anxious preoccupation of the *marimbistas* with their carefree music seemed even sillier and sadder. There was the leader's twisted expression when he reached an intricate passage, and the heartrending increase in his stoop. One remembered the middle-aged men who strode on to the stage at the beginning of the set, refreshed by their beer. After only three numbers a troop of exhausted ancients shambled off. Looking at them as they collapsed back into their chairs one asked oneself, who were these wrecks? Certainly not the band. Behind them on the stage the bass player remained, still perched on his stool, still in self-imposed disgrace, dozing gloomily, abandoned by the vitality of his music.

The performance of this band was capable of reaching a level of pathos reminiscent of a chimpanzees' tea-party. At one moment the older rhythm man lost the knob at the end of his stick. One almost rose to one's feet in horror. *Mein Gott*! His knob had flown across the room. The rhythm man, reduced to two knobs, leant forward over his *marimbas*, peering and groping in disbelief. After a prehensile swoop towards the floor, his lips parted in concentration, he retrieved his knob and resumed his work. This performance was watched impassively by the club bouncer, sitting in a distant corner, a luminous figure with his white shirt, tight blue trousers and gleaming black hair. His stomach was impressive in the half-light from a distance of twenty yards, his thighs, each of them, much more so. I was not able to discover, in conversation, whether a club bouncer in Guatemala City carried a gun; it would be reasonable to assume that he did. Merely to 'bounce' someone would seem in that place to be such an understated threat. He too corrected me when I referred to '*el jefe*' of the band. 'There is no chief in that band,' he said. The man I called the chief had been playing *marimbas* all his life. It was almost unbearable to think of this yellowing genius spending his entire life bent over his hammers, for much of that time confined to this dusty and deserted club.

When *marimbistas* stop playing they form intimate groups and talk furiously about the music. Alternatively they sit, solitary, morose, collapsed. One often sees, in a crowded restaurant, old men in silly uniforms, like bellboys, dozing off between sets. Later that week I dined in a restaurant which had been selected for a reunion of a Guatemalan-German Friendship Society. Nothing that band could do would make the Germans dance. Eventually a very small Guatemaltéco invited a very tall blonde woman on to the floor. They danced with determination. It fell to the German woman's husband to invite the wife of the Guatemalan to dance. He refused to do so. That was the end of the dancing. Those attending the reunion did not even clap. Eventually the band began to laugh about it, but you could see their feelings were hurt. Behind them a Diners Club sticker had been attached to the wall, next to a picture of the Pope. Beneath that a shadow moved, rustled, then flapped. In a cage the size of a missile cone, a horned owl as big as a corgi, with its wings folded, was confined. It gave the usual basilisk glare from its yellow eyes but the beak, claws and wingspan were less routine. The bird looked as though it might take a child a night. Behind my chair a Canada goose began to peck at the plate glass. When it hissed the glass filmed over.

I went to interview a German businessman who knew the

country well. 'I like Guatemala,' he began. 'It could be a paradise except for the Guatemalans.' He had some excuse for this unenthusiastic view. 'I even like the Guatemalans,' he continued. 'But there is no doubt they are rather dangerous people. My wife and I are living in a fortress. Everywhere I go I have bodyguards and I am driven to work in an armoured car.

'These people are unevolved. I don't know where they are on a European timescale but the Indians are unchanged since Cortés. They won't change as Indians. If they decide to join the modern world they cease to be *indigenos* and call themselves *ladinos*. That just means they wear European clothes. My driver is pure Indian but he always points out *indigenos* in the streets. They are quite different people to him. There is a small group of European descent but they wield little power. All the power in this country is held by the army, and that means by *ladinos*. The army is an education and a career. Oddly enough the guerrillas are also run by *ladinos*. Their leaders are people who went to university, picked up Marxism and never grew up. They actually believe it does good. They remind me of the French intellectuals of the 1940s and 1950s. Of course, as a German, I find their views surprising. The point to understand about politics here is that the struggle is between two groups of educated *ladinos*. A lot of journalists come out here and decide it is a battle between colonels and *peones* who are defending their land. That is not the case.'

The German, I will call him Dr Blitzer, was not impressed with American policy in Guatemala. 'This place is supposed to be run by the U.S.,' he said. He repeated this humorously. As a general statement it was true, though hardly one to be found in an Embassy communiqué. However, Dr Blitzer concluded, the U.S. had no particular policy in Guatemala. This made their self-appointed task more difficult to achieve.

'A hundred years ago,' he said, 'most of the world was run by the British. There were a few French or German or Portuguese, funny people like that, around the place. But most of the world was run by the British. What was produced in Central America went to London. What would happen in Africa, or India or Asia, was decided in London. Now it is the Americans who are meant to do that, and it seems that they cannot do it. They are a people troubled by religious scruples and by moral considerations. *That never troubled the British*. The British had no morals but they could run the world. The Americans are a moral people so they have no imperial policy.'

Dr Blitzer's analysis had a wonderful simplicity. It also held a perceptive truth. The U.S. does not have a policy in Central America. A distaste for communism does not amount to a policy. A policy suggests a preference: a distinct national interest and a preferred means of serving it. The reason why the United States has no distinct national interest went deeper, it seemed to me, than Dr Blitzer's observation about morality. There is no distinct U.S. national interest in Central America because there is no distinct U.S. nation. Too much U.S. energy and ability spends itself in attempting to decide what sort of nation the U.S. should be.

Despite Dr Blitzer's strictures, most of the Guatemalans you meet in positions of authority are not *ladino* but European. I read in the newspaper *La Prensa Libre* that its offices had been machine-gunned on the previous night and went to interview one of its staff about the matter. It was this person who told me how much it cost to get a man killed in Guatemala City. He said that the situation of the press was very difficult. Journalists were in danger from both the government and its enemies. Some years previously a director of the paper had been killed by guerrillas on his way home. Then another director was kidnapped by leftists, and was still held. In the previous fifteen years, thirty-seven journalists had been murdered by rightists and 'elements supporting the government'. This imposed an effective system of self-censorship on the newspapers since the result of criticising the government was generally a shooting. In the case of the recent event outside *La Prensa* he could only say that at 1 a.m. a car had passed the building, a machine-gun opened fire and a grenade had been thrown. No one had been killed. It was a warning. The paper had recently been critical of the government and had been under attack for several days from government spokesmen. I asked him what conclusions he drew from that. He said he drew no conclusions, he was just reporting it. He asked that his name be withheld because he was still interested in living.

8

The Indian Highlands

'Long live religion! And death to foreigners!'
Battle cry of Rafael Carrera, Guatemalan Indian War Leader

The Indian Highlands of Guatemala provide some of the most beautiful scenery in the world. The first time I went there I took the road from Guatemala City to Antigua, the former colonial capital and seat of the Spanish captains-general. The town is surrounded by volcanoes. The road to it descends through thick woods. That first night there were electrical storms lighting up the skyline constantly but silently; I convinced myself that I was looking at the flaring cones of live volcanoes. When the Spaniards first built a city here it was destroyed by Agua, the volcano to the south, which rained down stones and water. Beatrix, the widow of Alvarado, the most brutal of the conquistadors, was left to rule the entire country with only 100 Spaniards. Even then the Indians did not rise. Opposed by 100 frightened and ill-led Spaniards they chose to remain subdued. Of Alvarado, Bernal Diaz wrote, 'I recall so well his winning smile. He was such a handsome man, so frank, such a good horseman, so dashing a fighter . . .' He was also the man who nearly threw away the conquest of Mexico when he lost his head and butchered a peaceful Aztec dance. Then it was he who accomplished the conquest of Guatemala by slaying in single combat the Indian king Tecún Umán during a battle by a river still known by the Indians as the River of Blood. The Indians accept the verdict of such great events. They did not challenge fate on a later occasion merely because Alvarado was dead and their new rulers were reduced to 100 men led by a woman known as *la sin ventura*, 'the unadventurous'. That was no reason to rise. The matter had been decided at the River of Blood.

Something had broken in the Mayan civilisation, the scholars are still uncertain what. But it is clear that the Indians had little understanding of what was happening to them. The Indians of the Bahamas, who were kidnapped by the Spanish of Hispaniola to work in the gold mines, boarded the slave ships trustingly, in the firm belief that they were being taken to Paradise where they would grow young again.

Much of the city of Antigua has, at one time or another, been damaged by earthquake. It is kept, as it was planned, a Spanish colonial city, laid out on a grid, few of the stone houses having an upper storey. Here at last, most beautifully preserved, was the city of the *Archivo de los Indias* come to life, the city which I had first seen in the map room in Seville. In Antigua I stayed in a convent and slept in a tall room with a stone-flagged floor, a painted wooden ceiling supported by beams, and an open fireplace. The high barred window looked out on to an enclosed inner courtyard where a water garden was fed from deep, stone cisterns. Next morning I had breakfast sitting in the sunlight on the broad window-sill, watching the parrots.

On the previous evening one of these large and gaudy birds had been placed on a perch beneath which a *marimba* band started to play. As usual the bouncy little tunes soon skipped beyond the control of the players. In attempting to recapture them very little harmonic progress was made. The cheerful, high notes leapt around the courtyard, taking refuge in the echoes which flooded out of the stones to welcome them. And the source of the tumult was just a foot or so beneath the perch of the parrot. It seemed rather hard on her. She sat bolt upright, wearing a nervous air, looking down her beak at the noise, not at all sure that she wanted all these men to be playing, apparently to her alone. After dark two servants carried her away for the night, on a long pole which she shared with another parrot. Both birds as they swayed through the gloom made a contented noise, like the cluckings from a drowsy hen-house.

Antigua used to be a popular attraction for tourists to Guatemala, but few tourists go there now, just as the Indian textile market in Guatemala City is nearly deserted for days on end. In *The Volcanoes Above Us* Norman Lewis, having commented on the savour of Guatemalan life, wrote, 'the problem confronting the people who want to promote a prosperous tourist industry is how to take out this over-strong flavour so that only the safely picturesque remains.' The state of Antigua today is a fair indication of how they have failed.

The beautiful old buildings, converted to hotels, remain welcoming but empty. I and the parrots formed the entire audience for the *marimba* band. Outside in the streets the Indians who had travelled down from the hill villages could still be seen, but they did little business. As I stood admiring the neat, abandoned, old colonial town the sound of church bells died away and was succeeded by that of pipes. Then a procession of dancers rounded a corner and approached the entrance to the *convento*. They paused at each street corner to perform, a thinly-scattered crowd at their heels. There were four men, each hidden by a tall wooden frame draped in flowing robes and surmounted by a grotesquely carved and painted human head. Their dance looked like a variation of the original *Moros y Cristianos*, inspired by the conquistadors' stories of the fall of Granada. Two of the carved faces were European, two were dark. Other men were dressed in female clothing and face masks.

At each street corner the crowd formed a circle, a *marimba* band struck up and the dancers danced. The men inside the tall frames were obviously under strain but they jogged and whirled around, moving the rigid figures above them in a manner both graceful and ridiculous. The unencumbered masked men were free to carry out their more clownish movements; they jerked together and apart, simulating drunkenness. So lifelike was the impression they made that one found oneself responding to the fixed expressions of the masks, some laughing, some grim. The audience smiled back at the jolly, drunken women or froze beneath the stare of the cruel-faced men. A comical effect was produced by the grave heads on the frames and the jerky movements taking place so far beneath them. Occasionally the robes would swirl apart, and we in the audience, still responding to the fixed expression of the mask, would find ourselves face to face, confronted by the gaze of the real dancer, the laboured, grunting human on our own level, peeping from behind the robes, and we would feel foolish. The Indians and *ladinos* who followed the dancers faithfully from corner to corner and right up to the steps of the *Convento de la Merced* were, though they took much from the performance, very sparing with their pennies.

The next day was Sunday, and was celebrated at the *convento* as Corpus Christi. Once again the dancers and their band were on the church steps. There were several other bands there as well, and a small fair, and a man firing mortars, and a shower of flower petals and bunting. After mass the women of the congregation, dressed as the members of a sodality, led a procession from the church. They wore black skirts and white blouses, and yellow and white ribbons from which hung their sodality medals. Then came more banner bearers, then the canopy beneath which walked the bishop holding the monstrance, finally the rest of the congregation.

As they stepped from the church the organ music, which filled the building effortlessly, was succeeded in their ears by the considerable noise of the town band, perpetuated by the ferocious explosions of the mortar. The change was so abrupt it was like passing through a curtain of sound. Later even the noise of the band was to be drowned by the bells. It was a triumphant mixture of faith and theatre, and a dramatic surprise, that all this rude life could burst out of the old building still. Then the procession set off through the streets of the town, which were decorated with palm fronds and paper streamers and confetti, the people kneeling in the streets as the Host was carried past, and the mortars continuing to explode through the morning.

On the other side of the town, in the cathedral long since wrecked by earthquakes, there was no celebration of Corpus Christi. Instead mass was said in English before a sparse, chiefly North American congregation. It was a curious occasion. On the altar, beside the priest, a self-conscious, blond youth in jeans and a yellow T-shirt mumbled and giggled his way through the responses. At the back of the church a large number of Indians, eager to observe the mysteries but baffled by the irreverence, first joined then left the service.

The sermon was on Job and Faith. The priest, speaking in English, said, in his thick German accent, that the Church was being tested today, sometimes it seemed to the point of destruction. But we in the Church were a kingly people, we were a priestly people and we were a chosen people, and we knew that however hard the storm raged there was a man in the boat who would say 'Be still'. And it was the duty of the Church to preach love of each other and of God to all men. It was not the duty of the Church to preach violence.

After mass he stood on the cathedral step to greet his small but smartly-dressed congregation. They had not apparently met each other before. They showed little interest in talking to him.

Later that day I drove out of Antigua and took the winding country road to Chimaltenango. The road to Chimaltenango is very beautiful; shaded by tall trees, surrounded by green fields, it dips into hollows and twists between high-banked lanes. But Chimaltenango is a centre of guerrilla activity, and outside the town a long column of troops was marching at a fast pace down a leafy avenue. They were singing one of the Guatemalan army marching songs which, roughly translated, means something like, 'Give yourself a treat, kill a Commie this afternoon.' At Chimaltenango the road-blocks started. This is the edge of the Indian Highlands and a centre of armed resistance by more than one of Guatemala's five terrorist groups.

The country beyond the town opens up and then becomes mountainous. At the road-blocks regular soldiers stopped every bus and turned out the passengers. '*Todos los hombres*!' rang out again, and at one block another figure in a black hood peered into every face.

My intended destination was Chichicastenango. At Los Encuentros I turned off the highway. From here on it was impossible to ignore the presence of guerrillas. At regular intervals mills and farm buildings had been burnt out by the army, determined to prevent the Indians from harbouring insurgents. The wreckage was covered in painted revolutionary slogans. Every few miles one passed the incinerated wreck of a bus destroyed by the guerrillas, part of their 'economic war' against the government. As a tactic it was not very subtle. The destruction of a bus merely ruined the economy of some insignificant bus driver.

Round one corner, on a heavily-wooded stretch of road, two men in civilian clothes stood in my path and waved the car to a halt. They said they were teachers hitching a lift to town. How were things? '*Very* good, señor.' Oh really, no problems? '*No* señor, no problems. *Tranquilo.*' We passed the wreckage of yet another burnt-out bus.

Before the guerrilla war made it slightly dangerous, Chichicastenango was another popular tourist centre. It is far enough into the Highlands to be an important Indian town, but not so far up that the paved road runs out. It contains a famous Indian market, an accessible pagan idol in the forest near by and two famous Indian churches, Santo Tomás and Calvario. It is unusual today, in no matter what part of the world, to find Christians worshipping their God with fire, but that undoubtedly is the practice of the Catholic Indians of Chichicastenango. Here it was, at last, right out in the open, the ancient, furtive and shameful habit of paganism, the worship which Cortés tried to persuade Montezuma to renounce. As far as Chichicastenango is concerned, the Inquisition laboured in vain.

Tourists used to be warned not to take photographs in front of these churches for the Indians did once kill a tourist who photographed their rites. But what is to be seen there is not, on the face of it, so remarkable. In the market there arc stalls cluttered with used Nestlé milk tins which have been perforated with a skewer and threaded with a wire handle. They are then put on sale as incense containers. Fire played a fundamental part of the old Mayan religion and it continues to play its part in the Christian religion of the Mayan Indians today, even though the present religion is supposed to be in direct opposition to the former one. One of Cortés's first policies in Mexico was to turn Aztec priests into Christian acolytes, and to convert sacrificial altars into shrines to the Virgin. But a strong faith is fed by persecution.

On either side of the market square the two white churches stand, each approached by a considerable flight of steps. Here, on these steps, the Mayans made their first incongruous intervention. The sacrificial altars, placed on top of the pyramids, were approached by steps, and the present-day worshippers have made the church steps into the holiest part of the church. Here fires are kept burning, the Nestlé thuribles are swung and a sticky blackened wax is smeared over the stones. Prevented by the missionaries from bringing their fires into the church, the Indians have simply erected stone fireplaces as close to the doors of the church as they could and then made that place more precious than the altar. There is a wild and dangerous look about those who tend the fires. Rapt in their mysteries, bundled in their ragged clothes, they seem so out of time and place that I thought the weathervane on the church roof struck a jarringly modern note before I realised that it was of seventeenth-century Spanish wrought-iron.

Inside Calvario a large tray covered with candles had been placed on the floor and an old lady holding a Nestlé tin was kneeling beside it and tending the candles. All the benches had been removed from the church, which was almost bare. There were a few images on the walls, the altar was still there – covered with dead flowers, beyond it, in the vestry, some sort of shrine had been set up in the darkness. The tabernacle was empty.

A man, whom I took to be the verger, offered to show me the little church. As we walked round he seemed to me to be acting more as a priest. He sprinkled water over the tray of candles and then over the bare altar in a precise, preordained way as though he were following a rite, though this was no Christian rite known in other parts of the world. Water and candles are familiar to a Catholic, but not as an end in themselves, only as symbols. Here, under the guidance of this verger-priest, the natural elements had become the objects of worship.

I crossed the square to the much bigger church of Santo Tomás. Again there were the stone fireplaces on the steps of the church, the wooden slabs set into the floor of the nave to support the blaze of candles, the same huddled, ragged, figures stooped over the flames. In this church my guide was a smart little boy, one of a gang who had attached themselves to me in the square. According to this boy, one worshipper, a man who had lit fifty-six candles on a single tray, was praying for several *matrimonios, todos muertos*, killed by *guerrilleros*, two señoras, one hombre. I don't know whether my guide was telling the truth or making it up as he went along. There were no reports of such murders but they were not uncommon, and the imagination of Indians generally takes less romantic forms. Nor was there any reason for him to be dishonest.

On the wall, almost the only adornment, was a large notice warning visitors not to take pictures of 'the religious rites of the

Indians', a tactful piece of phrasing. Again the church was almost bare, a few benches, one or two images dressed in gaudy costumes like large dolls, but, again, a deserted altar. Beside the candles ranged along the floor some of the Indians were heaping piles of maize cobs and black beans as an offering to the saint. I asked where the priest was and the child told me that no priest lived in the town but that one came up occasionally from Antigua. I could see why he did not leave the Blessed Sacrament in the tabernacle when he left.

Beside the church there is a large cloister, for this was, in its days of certainty, a Dominican priory. The priests who came here originally gathered a famous collection of jade and made themselves scholars of Mayan mythology. Today there is just the bougainvillaea on the walls, and the doors of abandoned classrooms swinging in the wind. Such a peaceful place, but only a few years ago this cloister was the scene of a violent commotion. For there is a story about the Indian parish of Santo Tomás, and it is not one the diocese wishes to publicise.

Some years ago a new parish priest was sent up to Chichicastenango from Antigua. He was a young missionary from Spain called Padre Casas, and he was very zealous. When he saw Santo Tomás he was very shocked. Perhaps the bishop, despairing of the persistence of the Indians, thought that some fresh missionary blood, untainted by the ancient realities of evangelism, would work the trick. On his first night in town Padre Casas hired two *ladino* masons and broke up the Indian shrines and altars which had been set up on the steps and platform of Santo Tomás. Next morning he was woken by the noise of an enraged crowd of Indians armed with clubs. When he tried to calm them they abused him and started to surround him. Suddenly he realised he was in real danger. He retreated into the church but the crowd broke in after him. Padre Casas had to run for his life. His congregation chased him out of the side door, through the cloister and into the convent. If they had caught him they would have killed him. But he managed to climb out of a window of the convent and hide in the house of an old Indian woman who gave him shelter.

Padre Casas was not seen in Chichicastenango for about six months. When he came back he was a changed man. The fireplaces had been reconstructed and they remained undisturbed. He seemed less interested in the sites of worship. Instead he busied himself with social work. He concentrated on the school, he opened a clinic and a soup kitchen. He became involved in matters of state and taught his flock that Christ took sides in the political arguments of Guatemala and that the Lord was not a government supporter. He worked in this way for more than fifteen years. Then one day he received a warning, unofficially, 'Get out. They've had enough of you.' For the second time he had to leave Chichicastenango in a hurry. He was put on a flight to Spain. He has not been seen since. That is why the children of Chichicastenango are taught nothing about their religion, and the altars are bare. The Church has proved itself, for the time at least, to be incapable of offering either spiritual or material comfort.

The Catholic Church in Guatemala was once in an enviable position. It had a monopoly of faith in that country. Today it is divided and ineffective. In Antigua a priest, a good man, will preach against violence. In the Highlands another will support the guerrillas. Other denominations have profited from this indecision. Evangelical missionaries from the United States have poured into the country. Many of the Indians, attracted by their old-fashioned liturgy and authoritarian certainty, have abandoned Catholicism in their favour. And in Chichicastenango I found another missionary, not even a Christian, who had also profited from Catholic divisions. When I went to look for her I did not realise that she was even a missionary. She attracted me because I thought she was English, Señora Jenny Taylor, and she lived alone in bandit country and ran a guest house.

Jenny Taylor was born in Costa Rica. Her father was a 'sea captain', her mother was English. Her first language was Spanish, but she spoke good English as well. In adult life she had embraced the Bihai Faith and was now one of their few missionaries in Guatemala. She was an experienced nurse, she ran a clinic and a coffee shop. She was modest about her achievements as a missionary. She said that she had not made many converts but she had many friends. She had spent her life working among the Indians. She gave me the secret of her small success. 'I always treated them like I treated everyone else. When I visited them I sat on the floor with them and ate their food. When they came to my coffee shop I served them like Europeans. They paid the same price for their coffee. So why not?'

She did not say so but she gave the impression that this was not how Padre Casas had behaved. She did say that when he had returned to Chichicastenango, burning with ideals of social justice, he had told her that he would drive her clinic and her shop out of business. Later they became friends. And it was she who remained; alone, old, 'I am so tired,' she said, very isolated; but still in Chichicastenango, and still in work. She saw very few English people, and seldom spoke English nowadays. But she had called her son Herbert. He was an architect in Mexico. She was proud of him.

I had lunch in the Santo Tomás Hotel. It is a beautiful building, yet another former convent. When I first tried to get into it I thought it was closed. Continual hammering at the door brought a frightened waiter to the grille and he admitted me. There was no one staying at the hotel and no one expected. Over lunch I was told that the manager of the other hotel in town had been shot by guerrillas six months earlier. He was a man who went everywhere with his gun. One day as he approached the hotel entrance he saw someone standing in the doorway who fell to the ground. Inside he found one of his staff lying dead. He ran into his office and exchanged shots with an armed stranger. The manager was wounded in the leg and had not been seen in Chichicastenango subsequently. This incident explained why the door to the Santo Tomás Hotel was always locked, and why I had the town to myself.

In the empty dining room a beautifully-bound Roman missal, printed in Spain in the nineteenth century, stood with its silk ribbons and brass clips on a carved lectern, gleaming and unread. It had been a present to the mission from the Archbishop of Barcelona. The poor man probably thought that it would be used for centuries. The hotel was run by a courteous woman, who looked surprised to see a guest. The floors were highly polished, the flowers bloomed, the kitchen was full of food. But, judging by the visitors' book, nobody else had been there.

After lunch I went for a walk. The clerk in the post office was tapping out telegrams on a morse transmitter. Down the cobbled street outside passed an Indian wedding procession. It looked more like a funeral. At the centre of the slowly-moving crowd walked the bride, in white and carrying a bouquet. Her companions wore their smartest costumes and their gravest expressions. There was no music and no conversation. I thought at first that this wedding had been marred by some tragedy but was later told that all Indian weddings are executed in this manner in public. The party were returning from some ceremony at the church, not one requiring a priest for there were no priests in town that day. When they reached the bride's house they would be expected to cheer up.

I filled the car with petrol and set out deeper into the Highlands. I intended to spend the night at Santa Cruz del Quiché, where the Guatemalan army has established its regional headquarters. Quiché is the department where some of the fiercest fighting of recent years has taken place, although in 1983 during the brief presidency of Rios Montt the army had been scoring some major successes. As I drove northwards, through the archway that marked the town limit, a group of smartly-dressed women of nearly identical appearance signalled me to stop and when I had done so pushed one of their number into my car. She was shy but quite happy to be drawn out. As we drove along she started to tell me about the local beauty spots.

'This lake is the source of the Rio Negro,' she said. 'It flows all the way to Mexico and then to the Atlantic. In this beautiful lake we have very fat fish.' She beamed. Then another thought occurred.

'In that lake last year there were also five severed heads. They were too decomposed to know the sex.'

She explained to me that she had hitched a ride because there was an early curfew. It was still some hours before dark but she wanted to be absolutely sure not to miss it. The curfew was very strict and her husband had warned her not to rely on the last bus. Then she resumed the topic she could not forget. 'Many dead around here,' she said. 'One morning we had sixty corpses. On that day I left for the capital. On that same afternoon.'

When she discussed the darker side of life in these beautiful hills she spoke very quickly, glancing frequently at my face to see the effect of her words. She thought I was a tourist and she was not happy about letting her country down.

We turned a corner of the road. 'Here, just here, there was the corpse of a man run over. He had been machine-gunned afterwards. *They* really like their machine-guns.' I thought it was about time to find out who *They* were and which side the corpses had been on. I was about to ask whether *They* were soldiers or guerrillas when, in the nick of time, she told me that at 5 p.m. her husband would be getting hungry. 'He is a military man,' she said. I looked at her and her clothes. If her husband was a military man he must be an officer. 'He is a *Coronel*,' she said. I had been about to ask the wife of the colonel commanding in Quiché whether her husband's men were doing all the killing in these parts. In fact her husband turned out to be the previous commander. Still, it would not have been a very tactful question.

Throughout our trip the *Coronel*'s lady continued to point out the sights of the atrocities. And so I steered this sweetly-scented dumpling along the road and listened to her politics. She wore a white silk dress with black polka dots, tightly cut, and a grey scarf around her throat. She also wore a large wooden crucifix. She would have looked more at home in a cake shop talking about her grandchildren than in my passenger seat describing the depths of blade wounds in the chest.

When we reached Quiché we had to navigate numerous road-blocks and road-humps, all of which she knew by heart. She guided me to a hotel, the *San Pascual*, but would not let me drive her to her door. She managed to suggest that if she were to arrive in the passenger seat of my car it would spoil whatever excuse she had dreamt up for her late arrival and would not improve the *Coronel*'s digestion. And so she disappeared, with a wave of her lace handkerchief and a clatter of high heels, trotting along the cobbles to cook his supper.

I walked round Quiché before the curfew fell. This was now beyond the tourist country and in a district where there had been heavy fighting until quite recently. It was also an important garrison town. Eager to inspect it I headed for a handsome stone gateway to the side of the plaza. Inside, the building looked rather drab but there was a notice about visiting hours and I pressed on. I was in the mood to visit anything by then.

There were armed men at the gate. They gave me a warm welcome, and I soon found that my difficulty was in getting out. It was the town jail.

Beside it there was a run-down café, the haunt of the prison guards. Despite its condition a notice on the wall said, *En este establacimiento velamos por su salud*, 'In this establishment we are concerned for your health.' Another read, *Agradecemos su cultura al no escupir en el suelo*, 'We thank-you for your good breeding in not spitting on the floor.' Beneath these signs the prison guards and policemen undid their guns and the flies buzzed on and off the food. When the policemen took off their hats you could see how young they were. The girls crowded out of the kitchen to stare at them. The policemen continued to look shyly into their soup, guns always to hand. Close up, the bullets in their belts looked uncomfortably large.

Sitting at a table near mine a small boy ignored the noise all around him and bent over his school copy-book. We sat there side by side writing. I wondered if this child had any idea how long this writing business could go on for? I wondered really, should he start it at all? His writing was certainly much better than mine. That was another thing he should know. The longer you did writing the worse your writing became. He reached the bottom of the page and was rewarded by one of the girls with a Pepsi. So he even got paid quicker than me. I examined his book to see what he had written, '*Loma, Lola, Luna.*' He sat back, sucked his Pepsi, and regarded me with a satisfied air.

That evening I looked for a meal and found the Musi-Café. The menu was painted up on the wall. There were drawings of hot dogs and hamburgers and pies, between more complicated examples of the proprietor's art. In one picture three buck, silhouetted in moonlight, gambolled away. Behind them, in the forest, a lion pulled down a fourth. The next panel said 'Hamburguesas 0·50' and was by the same artist. Then a gringo hippy was to be seen crucified on a hypodermic syringe. The caption was '*La Moderna Crucifixion*'. Then 'Domingos-Chow Mien Plato 1·00'. Then a skeleton leaning thoughtfully on a tombstone. Then a naked woman with a severed arm knelt on a block, her neck stretched out, thin and waiting. Then '*El hombre y la Bestia*', a study of a face split into two personalities and a number of pills.

While I was waiting for my meal the proprietor showed me round his art collection. We started with the buck and the lion. 'This one has two symbolisms. Do you know what they are?' This seemed more ambitious than Diego Rivera. 'No,' I said. He explained something to me at length. We moved on to the thoughtful skeleton. I noticed that the skeleton was clutching a shapeless grey lump, and asked what it was.

'It is hard to say. It is his thoughts. Or even I do not know what it is.' As we talked there was a rattling noise in the passage, a dog shot into the room closely followed by the rattling object, a burning brand of wood. The dog sat down and began to bark, apparently at its own fleas. The food, when it came, was unusually bad.

Later that night I walked back to my hotel through the streets of Quiché. There were few people about because of the curfew. One shop, a late-night chemist or grocer, was still open. From the wooden doorway a pale light spilled out on to the quiet streets. Then from out of the darkness a Jeep roared past and pulled up beside the shop. An officer and a soldier got out, both well-armed. The officer walked quickly through the shop and into a back room. The soldier remained in the shop with the customers. From the street I could hear some of his questions. He was asking where a certain man was. There were two women behind the counter of the shop, both very pale. One said, 'He went to Antigua.' The other said, 'We have not seen him.' A man standing in the shop made a joke. There was not much laughter. The officer came out of the back room and the two of them drove away. This was my first sight of the Guatemalan army at work in the Highlands.

When the army carried out its pacification programme in towns such as Quiché, no one felt safe. In those days, just a few months before, the towns were a battleground for both government and guerrillas. At Todos Santos in 1981 the E.G.P., the Guerrilla Army of the Poor, walked in one night although the town was officially a government town. They did not throw their weight around. They just called a meeting in the plaza and hoisted a Che Guevara flag. After their speeches they left with about ten recruits. Nobody took the flag down. Shortly afterwards the army drove in and took the flag down. About twenty townspeople were killed that night. Then the army left. The

E.G.P. came back. There was another flag, another meeting, and this time they left with thirty recruits. It was wise to get out of town before the army returned to Todos Santos. Of the people who did, some would have ended up as refugees in Mexico.

In Comolapa at the same time the army killed six people in one night. Their bodies were found in the square in the morning. There were six more on the following night. One night there were 200 people sleeping in the church, too frightened to sleep in their own houses. All those murdered were involved in farming co-operatives which had been installed after the earthquake of 1976. Things were quieter after that in Comolapa until the stink from the *barranca* became insupportable. Everyone in town knew about the *barranca*. When they cleared it out they found that all the identifiable bodies had been people of liberal or left wing views.

In Huehuetenango six months earlier, there were a lot of guerrillas in the neighbourhood and they were known to have strong political support in the town. The army moved in, in force, and the killings started. Every morning people came out of their houses after the curfew to find bodies in the street. Ten feet above the rooftops helicopters flew all day. Every time a lorry passed a house and changed gear people inside unconsciously paused and waited for it to go on. They were very frightened. This was what life had been like in El Quiché until very recently.

I left the chemist's shop and continued back through the moonlight to my hotel. The church was closed but in the dark a man was kneeling in front of the barred door, on the steps high above the square, his bundle beside him, as close to the saints as he could get. In the square all the booths and stalls of an Indian fun-fair were closed. Walking between them one could hear the sound of a baby crying and muffled breathing and coughing. Whole families lived in these small tents, and were now sleeping in their daytime booths and shooting galleries.

The next day I continued to drive north, heading this time for Sacapulas. On the edge of Quiché, where the paved road stopped, I was waved down by an old man in a trilby hat. He climbed in and after a period of courteous silence he started to talk. I asked him where he was going.

– Huehuetenango.

Where did he live?

– Huehuetenango.

How was it there?

– *Muchas problemas*.

Worse than here?

– Egaaaaal!

He drawled the last word with a resigned shrug and on a descending note. It was the same everywhere. Bad. Many people had been killed. He did not look at me as he spoke, but stared dreamily ahead.

It was an unusually hot day. We were driving across a dry plain, leaving an immense cloud of dust in our path. One could pick out the undulating track for a mile or so away by the occasional cloud of dust from a distant lorry. As we descended from the plateau of Quiché towards the river valley of Sacapulas the heat increased even more. Every time we braked or checked our dust cloud caught up with us and poured in through the open windows of the car. As our conversation continued the old man became whiter and whiter. The dust clung to his hat, his face, his moustache, his eyelashes and his hands. He did not complain.

Who was doing all the killing?

– Oh, the guerrillas of course. If the guerrillas see you and do not know you they kill you.

– And what about the army?

– The army are all right, if you greet them and have papers.

– Was there enough food?

– There is enough food, but there is no business. Either in Huehue or in Quiché.

He was a trader, which meant that he was a traveller like all the Indian traders and he was very good company. All his life he had lived in Quiché, but his children had settled in Huehue, and for the last three years he had lived with them there. He preferred Quiché, he said it was cooler, and he had come back to visit his friends. There had been one of them, the same age as him, by the road to see him off. He intended to get back to Huehue that night and since there was no bus service between the two towns I thought it was rather optimistic. What would he have done if I had not chanced along? Not for the first time I wondered what people like him would do if I had not been there to drive them around in my car. The answer of course was that they would have waited happily enough by the side of the road. Even in the highlands, there was always 'another one behind'. Perhaps he found six vehicles a day a very busy road. Perhaps he found so much traffic disturbing. I thought of the other old man, his friend, standing by the road, not waving but gazing after him; the two of them having grown up in the same town, spent their lives there, separated now; the occasional reunion, haphazard like all Indian appointments; the other man watching the cloud of dust, wondering whether that would be the last sign of his friend.

The road was too pitted to allow the car to travel fast enough for a breeze, and inside it grew steadily hotter and dirtier. There was no sign of water on that plain. The river beds were dried up. There was plenty of grass around but no sign of what nourished it.

The old man asked me how old I was. The purpose of this question became clear when he told me how old he was. He said it with some ceremony. We remarked that he was exactly twice my age. Then he said, 'Do you have guerrillas in England?'

'No, it is a country of peace.'

'Gracias a Dios.'

'Gracias a Dios.'

His next question caused him to hesitate.

'Are you *Catolico*? or [pause] . . . *Evangelico*?'

'I am *Catolico*.'

'Ah,' he said. *'Gracias a Dios.'*

'Gracias a Dios.'

'I too am *Catolico*.' He paused.

I appreciated this emphasis of the obvious.

'What is the name of your patron saint?' he asked.

'Patrizio.'

'Ahhh.'

'Do you know him?' I was surprised.

'Oh yes. He is in the Bible.'

'Really? . . . And who is your patron saint?'

'My patron saint,' and he paused, before saying with tremendous pride, 'is the Apostle Santo Tomás.'

'Ah.'
He continued, 'And the patron saint of the department of Quiché is St Helena of the Cross. All we in the department are under her protection.'

He spoke of the saints, as he spoke of Catholics, as if they were extra-real people. I asked him if the country of Guatemala had a patron and he said, 'Yes. Our patron is the Virgin of the Rosary. She protects all of the *ciudad*.'

So there it was again, the idea, not of a unified national state but of a neighbouring power, the city that rules one's part of the earth; the *ciudad* for the country, the name of the country for its capital, the Indian idea that a country was as distant as a capital, and that both were alien to oneself and one's familiar region.

As the road descended more steeply and the car moved even slower, the temperature rose by several more alarming degrees. We passed a wedding party in all their finery walking along the road. We were no longer travelling fast enough to raise any dust. Then they passed us, by taking a short cut across a dry river bed. We passed them several times. They kept taking short cuts and getting ahead of the car again. This was a strange country where Indians who lived in a dream were able to walk faster than people driving a motor car. I began to wonder how long the springs of this small vehicle would stand up to the Highlands. We drove by several Home Guard positions, a pile of sand-bags, a blue and white flag and no one in sight. Too hot. I asked Tomás about the Pope, who had recently visited Guatemala. He had even visited a town in the Highlands only half a day's journey by slow bus from Huehuetenango. Yes, Tomás had heard of this. Had he seen the Pope? Oh yes. So he had gone down to Quezaltenango? Oh no. Tomás had seen the Pope on a television set in his own town. This seemed inexplicable to me, for Tomás placed the Pope on a level with the Disciples. Was he not worth a day on the bus? Oh no. He had been on the television in Huehuetenango. That was extraordinary enough.

At last we arrived in Sacapulas. The heat by now was bad enough to make one faint. The square was unpaved. Just a tumbled line of buildings on each side of a slope. A church at the end. A clump of tall trees and a large fountain in the middle. I parked the car under the trees and said goodbye to Tomás. He walked happily off into the heat. I bought a mango and peeled it with my penknife and then washed the juice off into the fountain. Then I looked for a *cantina*.

There were no other cars in town, no buses, and only a few lorries. But I was told that if I took the cobbled lane, the only paved road for miles, further down the hill towards the river I would find the *Comedor Gloris*. In fact at the bottom of the hill the road was blocked. A platoon of soldiers had laid an enormous beam of wood across the cobbles and they refused to move it. I was not surprised. It looked terribly heavy. So I left my car in the lane and proceeded on foot.

In the *Comedor Gloris* a sluttish family of young women was serving a heavy-smelling stew to various rascals in overalls. The radio was playing a song I remembered from Tenampa. *Mariachi* music was unusual in Guatemala. It reminded me of *La Plaza Garibaldi*. I fell into a daydream. Then the music stopped and a girl in an unbuttoned dress was demanding my order and I was back with the usual parrot in the usual place, the smell from the kitchen, the flies and even, though why?, traces of old fly-papers hanging from the rafters.

Also on the wall was pinned a cover of *Let It Be* and beside it *Cristo* looking down over Jerusalem. So John Lennon had been only partly right. The Beatles were not more popular than Christ, at least not in the *Comedor Gloris*. This *Cristo* was a gringo *Cristo*. The city was lit up by the halo round his head, he had soft, brown, wavy hair and pink cheeks. In this stinking, steaming little hovel, with its septic food and slatternly women, I decided that I had to choose where to go. Either I could return south to Chichicastenango and all the comforts of the Hotel San Tomás – I thought of its crisp sheets and cool rooms, the servants, the peace, the beauty of that town with its empty streets and mysterious, undescribed religion – or I could go north, still further into the Highlands, right up into the mountains, to the town at the end of the road called Nebaj. No travellers had returned with news of Nebaj for several months. It was still believed to be inhabited by its Indian population, although there had been many reports of killings in that district. And it was of course garrisoned by the army. They were sent up there from the large barracks I had seen in Quiché and via the staging post set up not far from the *Comedor Gloris*. The bridge outside the café marked the beginning of the military area. It was only a short road as the crow flies to Nebaj, but the drive would take all afternoon, the road was so rough and steep, it was really only suitable for jeeps or trucks, that is if it was open at all. If all the *cantinas* in Sacapulas were like the *Comedor Gloris* I dreaded to think what they would be like in Nebaj, cut off as it was from all normal trade, and at the mercy of the military.

I walked back to the car. The soldiers could decide for me. The wooden beam was still in place. The soldiers were as unhelpful as ever. Within two hours I would be back in cool Chichicastenango. I started the car and began to turn it round. One of the soldiers left the guard post and walked towards the beam. He signalled for help and struggled to lift it. The decision was made for me. I would not have clean sheets that night after all.

On the far side of the river the road divided. To the left, the road to Huehuetenango was closed by the army. Whatever was going on up there was not to be witnessed. Poor old Tomás was sitting by the barricade wondering what to do. No one would say how long it would be before the road was open again. I turned to the right and stopped beside an Indian fireplace. Some tables had been set up, there were shelters from the heat made of palm branches taken from the trees that grew by the river. The women were making tortillas. For water they carried buckets up from the river. In this little gathering was the germ of a city. How often one has wondered why a town was in the place it was, rather than two miles to the left. Here was the answer. A road junction, a bridge, water, trees, a few palm shelters and cooking fires, all the essentials for settlement.

As I paused there was a diversion. Down my road, the road from Nebaj, there came a clattering cloud of dust. From it emerged five army trucks, each crowded with soldiers, a company in strength. They were all covered from head to foot in white dust, the colour of the bare hills, and looked tired as well as dirty. The Indian girls sitting by the cooking fires suddenly came to life. They giggled and even waved at some dimly-recognised spectral face. Could these be the men who were killing Indians? In garrison towns there were usually divided loyalties. It was not impossible. Many of the soldiers were

Indians themselves, after all. My interest in the Highlands awoke. In this appalling heat – feeling too weak even to stroll across the road and take a picture of a man with a mule fording the river under the bridge and evading a guard post – surrounded by these frightened people, I set off happily for Nebaj.

The road started in quite a grand manner. It was also the road to the town of Cobán. Buses ran along it through the thick forests to the east. It was unpaved but broad. Then, a few miles out of town, it forked and there were army bulldozers at work, scraping away the powdery soil to make it passable for the army convoys. Ahead of me was a bus. The driver seemed a little careless on the slippery track and eventually succeeded in putting a rear wheel over the edge. Below him there was a sheer drop of thirty feet, then a long steep slope into the trees. The bus pitched over at an ugly angle. The passengers, in some hurry, began to jump out of the back door. The main door was right beside the edge. For a minute it looked as though the bus would slip down the bank and topple into the ravine. Then everyone was out and the emergency was over. Eventually one of the army bulldozers which had carved this ludicrous tilting surface from the fine sand hauled the bus back to safety.

Nebaj is well up into the Cuchumatanes mountains, the highest in Guatemala, and hundreds of feet higher than Sacapulas. As the afternoon wore on the heat drained away. After about two hours the road reached a cool, green plain, with trees on the hillsides instead of sand. At one point in a small scattered village with a surprisingly large military detachment I was stopped at a home guard blockade and a middle-aged lady with her little niece were ushered into my front seat. The name of the village was Chiul.

I began my questions in the usual way. 'Is it peaceful around here?' Her answers were remarkably direct.

– Now, yes. But last December you couldn't get up here there was so much trouble.

Were many people killed?

– *Bastante*. (A dry understatement which was shocking).

Men and women?

– And *chiquitos*. (She pointed at the little girl on her lap.) Many many *chiquitos*.

– And who were killing them? The *guerrilleros*? I wanted to lead her away from the interesting answer. But instead of following my lead she looked at me as if I were mad.

– *Los militares.*

She said that no one in her own family had been killed, making it less likely that she herself had close connections with the guerrillas. She also said that many, many people both in Nebaj and Chiul, her friends and other people she knew, had been killed.

I asked her why she was travelling and she said that her mother lived in Chiul and she had been taking the little girl, her sister's child, to visit the old lady. Both she and the child were Indian but dressed in *ladino* clothes, another indication, slight, of pro-government sympathies. The little girl fell asleep and her aunt removed the bowler hat she had been wearing over her scarf and placed it on the four-and-a-half-year-old's head. Miraculously it fitted the child just as well.

We passed a house which had fallen in. 'It was burnt,' she said. 'By the soldiers.' She knew who had lived there. That particular house stood by itself in a lonely part of the road, the sort of place where the guerrillas might have come to demand food. It was condemned by its situation. There were more solitary ruins along the road, 'burnt by the army' she said. This had been uncontested guerrilla country until December. I noticed how few slogans there were, and no wrecked buses. Where they were truly powerful the guerrillas did not bother with such publicity. Everyone already knew that the E.G.P. were looking down from the hills.

Something was nagging at my memory as we talked, and as she mentioned again the name of Chiul it came back to me. Chiul and Parraxtut – the two sites of one of the most horrible of recent atrocity stories; I had heard the details in Antigua before I set out.

The reason for the strong military presence in Chiul was that it had once been a guerrilla village. Then, a year ago, the army had pacified it in the usual manner. A junior officer, a lieutenant, had been billeted on the village to organise its men into a civil defence unit. There was another village called Parraxtut about five miles and 5,000 feet down the escarpment. One day the lieutenant decided that his men were ready for a training exercise. 'Do you have *cojones*?' he asked the home guard.

'Yes, we have *cojones*,' they all replied.

'Do you have bigger *cojones* than those communists in Parraxtut?' he asked.

'Splutter, splutter,' they said.

'Well prove it,' he said. 'Let's go and fix them now.'

On the night of 22 to 23 December 1982 they went down to their neighbours, surrounded their village and killed every adult they could find. Three hundred and fifty people died. They did not kill any children.

A few days later a woman from Chiul was walking near Parraxtut and saw some children. They asked her for food. She discovered that almost all the children from Parraxtut were living in the woods outside their village, without food or shelter. She called out all the women of Chiul and they rounded up all the children who had been orphaned by their husbands, 125 of them, took them back to Chiul and distributed them round the village. I looked at the grave little girl, asleep on her aunt's knee, and wondered where she had been born.

We reached Nebaj and my new friend directed me to the *Pension de las Tres Hermanas*. This sounded like a romantic name for a hotel but I soon discovered that it was not really a name, more a description. There were in truth three sisters, like enough for triplets, living in the house which was spread in the usual way around a well and a courtyard. Like my guide, the three sisters were *ladino*. They had long, thick hair, grey and black, and wore dresses of faded flowery prints. The *hermana* who greeted me showed me a room. The bedding did not look very clean but it was cheap.

While I was inspecting the *baño* there was an alarming crackling sound and then an amplified voice loud enough to make me jump. It sounded extremely close, as though a soldier on patrol, or in ambush outside the door, had forgotten to switch off his walkie-talkie. One of the sisters became agitated. 'It is him,' she said. 'Listen, it is his voice.' One had no need to listen, one could hear very little else. I looked in the direction of the sound, expecting the bushes in the garden to part and reveal a man in camouflage, but nothing happened. It then became clear that there was no man in the bushes. The voice was coming from the plaza, hundreds of yards away, amplified by a powerful military machine. 'It is Tito,' said the *hermana*. 'It is his farewell.'

She was talking about Major Tito, the garrison commander and the man ultimately responsible for any irregularities in military behaviour, but she did not seem to regard him as a tyrant. On the contrary she said that no one wanted him to go, that he was a good man. 'We shall *die* without Tito,' she murmured, but she meant it humorously and returned to listening, with mock longing, to his voice.

I went up to the *plaza* to listen to Tito's speech and saw there a quite unforgettable sight. The Indian women of Guatemala weave their clothes from brightly dyed cloth, each village has different traditions and styles, usually the clothes and patterns chosen differ from woman to woman. Nothing therefore prepared me for Nebaj, where every woman wore the same costume, a white blouse, a brightly-dyed red skirt and an elaborate red head-cloth. The whole town and district had turned out to say goodbye to Major Tito and the visual effect was extraordinary. In this thin air and soft light the vivid red colour of the women's costumes had dyed the whole square a smudgy, rusty red.

Above the square, in the bell towers of the church, soldiers with machine-guns kept watch against possible attack from the surrounding woods and fields. Tito and his officers were gathered on a platform. Like his men, the Major carried a machine-rifle slung over his shoulder. He was a bearded man in battledress and a red beret, obviously a combat soldier, and he made by far the best speech. He spoke of Guatemala, 'our country, a great country'. 'We are all Guatemaltecans', he said. 'There is no difference between the people of Nebaj and the people of Chichi or Petén or the coast. There is no difference between *ladinos* and *indigenos*, or between *Catolicos* and *Evangelicos*, or between people of different colour, hair and skin. We are all Guatemaltecans. We can make that true. It is a question of courage, no more. That is how we shall defeat the *guerrilleros*.

'I am a soldier,' he said. 'I have to go all over the country. I have been here for eighteen months. Now I must leave. But I shall *always* remember Nebaj.' His speech was greeted with loud applause. For a farewell speech from the commanding officer during a period of persecution it was an enigmatic *tour de force*.

I liked the *Pension de las Tres Hermanas* although I was more severely bitten there by fleas and bedbugs than anywhere in Latin America. That night, there was a small earthquake at 5.30 a.m. but I slept through it. I was charged two quetzals (about £1) for my room, two quetzals for an excellent plate of pasta and two quetzals for porridge and eggs at breakfast. The room was a dusty cupboard without windows or electric light, the *baño* was a zinc tub and a stained stone trough beside a stinking hole in the floor. But Nebaj could do little wrong in my eyes. Next morning I walked around town. In the market pigs were being examined by local experts and making a lot of fuss about it. Nearby a soldier was sitting in front of a chip of mirror having his hair cut. His automatic rifle was propped against the basin, his legs were too short to reach the ground. I found a blacksmith who said he was really a jeweller and whose bellows were driven by a dismantled bicycle. There were *machetes*, the infamous *machetes*, on sale for ten quetzals each. That was cheap. The legal minimum wage is six quetzals a day, and even on the big coffee estates they pay two quetzals. I examined the *machetes*. They were made in El Salvador and bore the guarantee of Collin & Co., Hartford, Connecticut.

I will always remember the crystal-thin air of Nebaj and the way it smudged the red skirts and head-bands of every woman in town as they crowded round the church steps, beneath the protection of the machine-gunners placed in the bell towers, to listen while Major Tito told them they were all 'one people'. I never expected to see an incredible sight like that. After the Major one of the civil guards started an interminable speech and I only remember one of his phrases, because it too was unexpected. 'There is more in life than war, there is more than that. There is love . . .' He was a burly man in a straw hat and he had an automatic rifle slung on his back. Perhaps he was an *Evangelico*. And I can still recall the sound of the *hermana*'s voice, a curious dreamy up and down noise as she said, 'We shall die if Major Tito goes. Ah Tito, Tito!' Her gentle, yearning manner was touching as well as absurd. She spoke of the purity of the local water in rather the same way. As I drove away from Nebaj two young men, dressed only in underpants, were being made to roll around in the dusty road, overseen by two uniformed soldiers. It looked like a military punishment; the soldiers were happy for the occasion to be photographed.

At the top of the pass on the road back to Sacapulas pieces of paper, staked out in a circle, fluttered in the wind. I stopped the car and went to pick one up. It was a leaflet, advertising the amnesty offered to guerrillas who would turn themselves in. It was aimed at the E.G.P.

> Guatemalan –
>
> You have been forced into rebellion, and have endured cold, hunger, exhaustion and the life of a fugitive. You are unable to be with your wife or look after your children. During this month of Amnesty you can Desert. Present yourself to the authorities in the nearest village. If you bring a gun with you we will pay 400 quetzals, and 1,000 quetzals for a machine-gun. We hope that you will return to your family. They need you. Here is your chance.

The amnesty was honoured scrupulously enough but few people took advantage of it. Those who did would live in fear of their former comrades indefinitely. A little further down the road a large group of heavily-armed civilians were waiting by a tall tree, silhouetted against a stormy sky. They carried no flag and did not return a greeting, but they asked if there was an army detachment on the road behind me. I did not ask them why they wanted to know.

In Nebaj I had met James Hardy, a historian from the University of Toronto who has made the recent history of Guatemala his subject. We decided that we would try to find the village of Parraxtut where the massacre had been reported. The road towards the village had been closed for several days, but the army seemed to have lost interest in it when we arrived and after an encounter with a drunken and aggressive N.C.O. at a road-block, who wanted us to line up in military file, we turned off the road and followed a track back up into the hills. We drove for about half an hour, into an increasingly deserted landscape. There was one man at the road junction, then a couple of cows a bit further on, then as we emerged from the woods on to the plateau where the village should have been, nothing, not even a bird. It was an eerie place, a fine day, fertile land, and silence and stillness everywhere. We came to some houses, all deserted, and decided to walk further and eventually did see a small group of Indians with their goats who, on catching sight of us, began to run in the opposite direction. As they did so there came the first sound we had heard on that plateau, the amplified warning from some unseen army post announcing the evening curfew. Some herd boys came out on to the track, looking frightened and refusing to talk. On the horizon the Indians paused to reassure themselves that we were no longer pursuing them. It was a different picture of life in the Highlands to that received the day before in Nebaj: the deserted houses, the people anxious and frightened, running on sight of strangers, the unseen loudspeaker echoing its harsh commands from the distant hills. We decided to give up the search for Parraxtut and were relieved when we regained the main road before it got dark.

I spent that night in Huehuetenango. By the time I got back to Antigua on the following day a new rumour of government atrocities had spread. Indian tradesmen who had travelled up from Lake Atitlán said that the air force had been bombing San Pedro La Laguna. For a week or more this story was repeated more and more frequently. First there were rumours, then a man arrived who had heard the explosions, then another who had seen the houses destroyed on the day after the raid. Finally a man arrived who had actually been in the village on the day in question. San Pedro had indeed been bombed by the air force; with leaflets. Those traders who gave the original version of the story had by this time spread out far and wide with their news.

When I returned to Guatemala City I found that my German friend, Dr Blitzer, had arranged for me to be flown out into the jungle of Petén where his company was prospecting for oil. The promise of Guatemalan oil has teased people for many years. Even in Mexico City I met a man who said he had 'seen the maps'. The geology is the same as it is in Chiapas, where Jorge Serrano made himself so rich. The geology is perfect. Only the oil is missing.

The day I spent in the oilfields was one of the more puzzling days of my journey. We flew in a light aircraft for about an hour, roughly due north from Guatemala City. We were flying over thick jungle disturbed by cliffs and ravines and hill systems that periodically rose into volcanic peaks. It was a clear day which was a comfort since we were not so much higher than the peaks and this was not good country for a forced landing. A year earlier the son of a friend had flown the same route and disappeared. His father assumed he had lost his way and eventually run out of fuel. He may have crash-landed and survived the impact, but the search parties never even found his plane. Looking down at the tangled mass below one could understand why not. Out of this confusion the outline of a small airstrip eventually emerged.

We were met by the Company's field manager, a Frenchman called de la Roche, who drove us very fast along dirt roads to his camp. For the first time in my life I saw 'clouds' of butterflies. They rose from the track in a sinuous yellow column as we passed. In the shade beneath the trees Indian squatters came out of their huts to watch our car; not much traffic on this road, and all of it concerned with the Company. According to the terms of the Company's contract, this part of the forest had been turned into an enormous private estate. Before the oil, the forest had been almost uninhabited. Apart from a few Indians the only visitors were gum tappers, solitary and brutal men who collected *chicle*, the gum used in chewing gum by the North American confectioners. Now the rumours of wealth had attracted the poor from all over Guatemala. They cleared some ground, sowed some seed, grazed a family of pigs and watched the occasional car. There was no work for them after all.

De la Roche took us on a tour of abandoned well-heads. He told the same story each time. A promising field had been mapped out. A well had been sunk. Oil had started to flow. Then the well had run dry. Now the capped wells remained, half-buried by the returning jungle, a half-collapsed hut to one side had become the home of snakes and birds, and butterflies.

We arrived at one rig where drilling was still in progress and climbed up into the undeflected heat of the drill platform. The drill was running, you had to shout to be heard, the heavy steel deck shook and bounced back the burning air. To one side the bulky shape of a half-naked blond youth, a contracted technician, was bent over the long brake lever which controlled the speed of the drill. He was a refreshing sight. Running with sweat, barely contained by his outsize jeans, entirely nourished by cold beer and saturated fat, he was apparently the only Anglo-Saxon for miles. In his hands he held the hopes of all concerned. Somewhere below him, 15,000 feet into the ground, a diamond bit was spinning away and failing to find oil. All eyes were on the brakeman, the five hundred regular and the five hundred casual employees in the oilfield, the prosperous bureaucracy back in Guatemala City, the vast organisation at home in France, and the government of Guatemala, all were watching this shambling youth as he braked the drill and let it gather speed again. And there were others who kept an even closer eye on him, from somewhere among the surrounding trees. What little oil had been found was being pumped to the coast, and a pipeline that runs through 148 miles of remote jungle must be one of the most vulnerable targets in the world.

I asked de la Roche about the guerrillas several times. The first time he told me there was no problem. He had dismissed the armed guards employed by his predecessors, they had just been a provocation. Now and again the guerrillas called at the camp and asked for food. He gave it to them. Later he volunteered the information that the guerrillas had attacked the pipeline. It was very easy to sabotage. One bullet hole necessitated a complete shutdown of production at all well-heads. Later again he said that the guerrillas had also dynamited the pipeline. 'No problem.' De la Roche spoke good English; I couldn't make out whether he was being indiscreet or laconic. Towards the end of the day he showed me round the control room of the pumping station. He pointed out a couple of holes on the control panel of the computer. He said they were bullet holes. The guerrillas had shot up the control room. They had also threatened to blow up the volatile gas tanks outside until he had convinced them that if they did so they would flatten every building and tree for miles around. And there was another story, quite incredible, about one of his men being shot in the forest and the bullet being traced to the gun of a hunter standing about a mile away. De la Roche had a way of producing all these stories *à propos* of nothing at all. Some of them even surprised my friend from head office.

The oilfield is the modern equivalent of the nineteenth-century silver mine, as described by Conrad in *Nostromo*. I was reminded of the speech made by the 'good' capitalist who owns the South American mine and whose subtle corruption by the realities of his position is one of the major strengths of the book.

> What is wanted here is law, good faith, order, security. Anyone can declaim about these things, but I pin my faith to material interests. Only let the material interests once get a firm footing, and they are bound to impose the conditions on which alone they can continue to exist. That's how your money-making is justified here in the face of lawlessness and disorder. It is justified because the security it demands must be shared with an oppressed people. A better justice will come afterwards. That's your ray of hope.

I wondered how much the Company worried about sharing its money-making with an oppressed people. And to what extent the success of its operations was dependent on the law, good faith, order and security of Guatemala.

The more de la Roche showed us of his oilfield, the more abandoned sites we saw, the less oil there seemed to be and the more of a mystery it became as to why the Company was happy to go on chucking good money after bad. So far it had invested nearly £350 million and its partners were growing restive. It occurred to me that the Company must be paying the guerrillas protection money. How else could it go on operating an unguarded oilfield? Governments might come and go, but even Marxist governments needed oil. Could it be that the Company had taken the precaution of establishing secret contacts with the guerrillas? And I also wondered about the vanishing oil. There was a world oil glut. So long as the guerrillas remained in control of the forest, the oil might well be safest underground.

We said goodbye to de la Roche at the airstrip. He remained an enigma: a big, strong, capable man whose manner was unnecessarily deferential and needlessly indiscreet by turns. He was a naturalised Guatemalan, which seemed an eccentric thing for a capable Frenchman to become. There was something yearning or lost in him which could not be explained. At the end he stood by his truck just to watch our plane take off. He did not wave, just looked up at the plane as it passed. And a few minutes later another plane, nothing to do with the Company, took off and he was still there, long after everyone else had gone, looking after the two planes. Then he was enclosed in the darkness and the trees, and drove back to the world of the camp which he ruled with a necessarily harsh discipline: no booze, no women.

After I returned to Guatemala City I heard that Dr Blitzer's house had been machine-gunned while his wife was inside. His wife survived. No one knew who had done it. I thought of making some joke about this; perhaps the Company was giving the guerrillas the wrong food? Shortly after that de la Roche was flown back to the capital with serious head injuries. 'An accident', they said, 'in the forest'; 'always warned him not to drive so fast', they recalled back in the capital. The last I heard he had been unconscious on a life-support machine for six months. Shortly after that the Company, one of the largest in the world, was sued for £137 million by one of its partners on grounds of 'technical incompetence' in failing to produce more oil.

Back in Guatemala City there was another earthquake. This time it did wake me up. I imagine you always remember your first earthquake. At 12.30 a.m. I woke to find my hotel bed shaking. There was no noise, just the bed shaking and the floor, and the walls of the room. The shaking seemed to go on for quite a time and to come in waves. It was an eerie feeling, hard to describe. One knew instinctively, even half-asleep, what it was. There was the shaking, the silence and the knowledge that this force, which was doing no damage, was still strong enough to shake the bed, the room, the building, the entire city as though they were all the branches of a tree, and that there was absolutely nothing anyone could do about it except hope that it would stop. It was clear why the Sicilians had made Santa Rosalia of Palermo the person to turn to in time of earthquake. She could levitate.

When it did stop I got up and went down to reception and found about eight people there. The night manager, behaving like an air hostess when the plane hits an air pocket, carried on typing. Above his head the great steel lampholders hanging down on chains from the tall ceilings were still swinging impressively ten minutes after the tremor. Later I was told that it was the worst tremor in Guatemala since 1976, when 23,000 people were killed.

My hotel was near the presidential palace. After a while I found that so many slightly peculiar things were happening that I stopped asking for explanations. From the window of the hotel room I could see into the large, empty building opposite. Its rooms appeared to be dusty and unfurnished, its windows were closed. But at one window a figure sometimes appeared. It looked like a man, but it could have been a woman. He would stand behind a shutter, and draw back if he thought I was looking. He wore a scarf around his head and his skin was grey as though it was never exposed to sunlight. Perhaps he was a fugitive or a mental patient or just the caretaker. He seemed anxious to be seen but not clearly. In the street below his window another man walked up and down every night of my stay, shouting out a name. He shouted it about every fifteen seconds and he never stopped walking up and down. This went on from about midnight to two in the morning. Sometimes a woman took over, walking up and down and shouting the same name. No one driving past or walking home paid them any attention. Twice I heard gun-fire coming from the direction of the Palacio Nacional, the traditional scene of Guatemala's numerous coups. It sounded like hand-guns and automatic rifles. It lasted for ten minutes while the early morning traffic continued its brisk pace. I decided to break my rule and ask the receptionist about it. After all, if there was a coup I might have to report it or something. 'Are you sure', he said, 'that it wasn't a car backfiring?' 'For ten minutes?' The usual shrug.

I went to see a Counsellor-of-State, an intellectual and a gentle man. He worked in a heavily-guarded building, understandably, because at that time his activities represented one of the country's few hopes for a distant democracy. He sat in an anteroom, beneath a plaster ceiling decorated in the classical manner of the European eighteenth century with 'Homero' painted at one end and 'Pallas Athene' at the other. He confessed to everything. The government was violent and corrupt. The extreme right-wing menaced everyone. They were not criminals but 'semi-criminal'. They plotted assassinations and then repudiated the assassins. He considered that there were differences between the five groups of guerrillas: some, the least dogmatic, were a possibility; some were out of the question. None the less, he said, the Rios Montt government was different in character from its predecessor. It had brought peace to the cities. It was far more effective against the guerrillas, mainly because of its 'Home Guard' policy of 'beans and bullets'; Indians who opposed the guerrillas would be armed and fed. Further, it was the first government for years which was prepared to talk about talking to trade unionists, instead of shooting them. He wanted economic aid from the United States, not guns. Aid could finance a programme of social welfare. He also wanted to build a party of the centre-left that could oppose the government and help to isolate the extreme right. As for the past and the sins of the past, forget the past. There was no point in dividing the army. It was the only buttress against the extreme right.

I asked him about 'the human rights issue', the killing of Indians, and for the first time he showed himself a true Guatemalan. He seemed to lose interest for a moment, then he concentrated and said, 'the concerns of the human rights activists must be met'. For the first time he was in unfamiliar territory, speaking by rote. 'Human rights activists' were generally gringos. What he was really saying was, 'I wish I lived in a country which respected the rights of Indians, but, since I don't, mind your own business.'

There was pathos in the Counsellor-of-State. He tried to end on a light-hearted note. 'This country is like *Fantasy Island*,' he said. 'But who is Tattoo?' I thought he was quoting Molière, but it turned out to be a reference to a T.V. programme. Then he gave me a package for a friend in Washington. *He did not want to trust it to the post*. He was a Counsellor-of-State, and he was smuggling out his correspondence. He was a sympathetic figure. Where he lived the rich and powerful suffered no restraints, if it suited their interests they turned to crime. In Guatemala the poor take up arms and dubious political philosophies in order to eat. But the rich kill merely in order to eat more. The Counsellor-of-State knew all this and found it impossible to defend but he would not therefore repudiate his country. He risked his life in order to make a sophisticated analysis of a political situation which was brutally simple. His country did not just suffer 'bad' government. It was, literally, governed by criminals. The Minister of the Interior stole Mercedes and kept them in his garden. Such men would never be submitted to justice. They were perfectly safe. The lesson of Guatemala was that a nation does not disintegrate merely because it has a criminal government. It learns to ignore the government in so far as it can and to govern itself. It needs a municipal council, and a few hospitals and more schools, but it does not need 'a government'. They still clean the streets in Guatemala City, even if the police force drives around murdering people. I thought the counsellor-of-state was a remarkable man, to go on working for democratic government in a society so clearly unsuited for it.

Shortly after I left his work suffered a setback. The government of Rios Montt was abruptly replaced by a military regime of a more predictable sort. Various forces had organised this. The extreme right, the U.S. embassy, and, above all, the Catholic hierarchy. The bishops were unable to conceal their jubilation when Rios Montt went. They tried to hide their motives. They said that the Rios Montt regime was 'brutal', although it had done more to control the lawlessness of the rich than any government for twenty-five years. They said that Rios Montt was 'militarising' the country; whereas the Civil Guard movement was the first attempt to build a bridge between the army and the Indians and the most effective blow ever struck against the guerrillas. They said that Rios Montt had abused his power to assist 'an aggressive and fanatical' religious group. And here was the real cause for the bishops' jubilation. Rios Montt had converted to an Evangelical church. So had nearly a quarter of the population. The bishops had become so worried by their failure that they began to prophesy 'a war of religions'.

After Rios Montt's downfall the vicar-capitular of the Archdiocese of Guatemala City called on the new, Catholic, general who had become president and announced that he was 'a man of goodwill'. Shortly after that, Rios Montt's programme of land reform was abandoned by the new regime. Then the death squads were seen again in the streets of the capital and the rate of murders and disappearances rose to 200 a month. It was to be a year before the bishops voiced any criticism.

I had a haircut before I left Guatemala City. It was impossible to resist any longer the appeal of the barber's shop sign, *Estetica Masculina*. A shoe shop nearby advertised *cuñas elevadores*, four and a half quetzals a pair, 1·45 centimetres guaranteed, 'Increase your height and improve your personality'; quite a lot to claim for elevator heels. And one of the last things I noticed was a brass plaque set into the pavement on Sixth Avenue. It read, 'Guatemalan . . . Here on the 25th of June, 1956, the following five students died fighting for liberty and democracy and in defence of the autonomy of the university.' That was just two years after the United States had arranged the overthrow of Guatemala's last elected government, which was attempting a programme of land reform.

On the bus to the El Salvador border I sat beside a young woman who, poker-faced, pressed herself against me throughout the journey. There was nothing sensual in the contact, it was not even friendly; it was a fierce demand for physical contact with a stranger in circumstances that would not cause comment. Her sister and the rest of the family sat in the row behind. At one point, irritated by my unenthusiastic response, she wormed one sharp knee under mine and dug it in. She got out after an hour or so, greeted her husband soberly, and refused to give me a backward glance.

I intended, on my way to El Salvador, to cross into Honduras to view the ancient ruins of Copán. Next day, my bus was approaching the point of no return on this journey when I realised that if I left Guatemala I would have exhausted my visa. I would have to travel hundreds of miles into Honduras to get another one. So in a small town whose name I did not know, I got off the bus.

A very informative woman told me that a bus was returning in the required direction in a couple of hours, and directed me to a house where I could shelter from the sun. She talked to me like an old friend. I carried my cases through the excessive heat to the house in question and crashed through the door. Small sensation; then an old man said, 'Please be seated.' Within three minutes he had described his entire family to me. The heat makes brothers of us all. On the wall hung *seven* teachers' diplomas. He said three of his sons were teachers, so was a daughter. Another son was an architect. His wife offered me lunch, with herself and her daughter, in the kitchen. Lunch was soup and tortillas and chilled Coke. We got to the point almost at once.

'Are you married?'

'No.'

'Will you marry?'

'Yes.'

'But you will wait?'

'Yes.'

'Would you consider marrying a Guatemaltecan?'

(Nervous glance at daughter) 'Er . . . yes.'

'How old are you?'

'Thirty-nine.'

Horror. 'I am thirty-seven,' she said. 'And my oldest child is twenty-three.' Then her daughter said:

'And I am twenty and will be married on 23 May. Do you want to come to my wedding?'

'Yes.'

'And we will come to your wedding when you marry a Guatemaltecan.'

Later she said. 'How tall are you?'

'Six foot, two inches.'

'Ah. You will need a big woman then.' I looked down at her. It was a considerable drop. 'I assure you,' I said, 'small women please me much.'

'Yes,' she said. 'Better for cuddling probably.' This was better than the conversation in the average English bus queue.

Then her husband asked me if I had been told that I was identical in appearance to the priest. Sensation! And not only that: the priest he referred to was one from *Los Estados Unidos*. He had become *inamorata* of a Guatemaltecan, and had been sent away. I resembled him closely. This announcement explained several puzzling events. I had been wondering all morning why I had been greeted several times on the bus. One old chap had been almost incoherent with pleasure at the sight of me. Fortunately nobody had asked me to hear their confession. My hostess went over the story of the priest and the Guatemaltecan again. She melted as she recounted it; it was two feathers, one in the national, one in the female cap.

After lunch I asked for a shower. After the shower I retired to a bedroom to dress. As I pulled on my trousers I noticed with the corner of my eye an insect, possibly a horse fly, on my knee. It was a small red and black spider. At last! The celebrated evil spider of Central America, and, unfortunately, on my knee. For two months I had lifted the lavatory seat before sitting on it in order to avoid this meeting and now, in the jungle, a month before the rain, two days' journey from the hospital, it was here. It must have entered my trousers while I was in the shower and left them when I inserted my leg. Civilised. I moved to flick it off with my pen. It survived one flick by stepping unhurriedly over the fast-moving pen. Before I could make a second flick it had leapt about three feet across the floor. It then leapt on to another spider and began to bite it. Some weeks later I described this spider to an entomologist in El Salvador. He said it sounded like a black widow spider, whose bite is frequently fatal.

I spent the rest of my time waiting for the bus with this family. The wife was proud of all the teachers' diplomas on the wall. 'But,' she said, 'in this country the government is not interested in teachers. Only in soldiers.' Several of her children were out of work. The bus arrived and we bade each other affectionate farewells. She gave me one tip. In Guatemala, she said, the Spanish for bus was '*bus*', not '*coche*'. In Guatemala '*coche*' meant pig. I had been asking 'what time is the next pig?' from one end of the country to the other.

PART THREE

New Spain

9

The Third Border

> By indolence and recalcitrance the Spaniard has preserved his individuality, a creature unashamedly himself, whose only notion of social obligation is what old custom dictates.
>
> V. S. Pritchett, *The Spanish Temper*

I crossed into El Salvador from Guatemala at the Anguiatú border post, on a quiet road linking the Guatemalan backwater of Esquipulas with the Salvadoran backwater of Metapán. There were once silver mines in this part of Salvador, but the metal ran out as it did in all the precious mines of Mexico and Central America. It was a Saturday afternoon, very hot. The bus dropped us on the Guatemalan side of the border, and we carried our bags through the heat towards the luxuriant blue and gold uniforms of the Salvadoran border guards.

The town I had left, Esquipulas, is one of those places famous to Central Americans and ignored by the rest of the world. It is a little town, almost a one-street town, which lives off the 'Black Christ' guarded there since it was carved in 1594. My guide book described Esquipulas as 'a tourist centre'. In fact it is a place of pilgrimage, a rather different matter, and one of the pleasantest towns I visited. I arrived in the evening and went for a walk after dark. There was a loud disturbance caused by a girl riding a large motorbike through the market, very slowly. Her drunken boy-friend climbed up behind her, pushing her forwards until she was astride the petrol tank. Then they rode off, abruptly, into the night, both wrestling with the handlebars. As they did so an older woman ran out of a nearby shop, shouting after her into the darkness, but too late, '*Me-eere*! *Me-eere*!' 'Look here!'

> Nor does the family even move about together,
> But every son would have his motor cycle,
> And daughters ride away on casual pillions . . .

or, in this case, on casual petrol tanks. The older woman laughed when she saw that I was watching her and had realised that it was too late. '*¡Miré!*' '*A sus ordones*', '*Digame*', '*¿Como non?*', '*¡Que Barbaridad!*'; I still found pleasure in the catch-phrases of Spain. Another one was 'Bvah!', the quintessential noise of a Spanish woman, satisfied.

Next morning, walking up the main street, I met a lawyer who said that he had seen two Italians in Esquipulas eight months before, otherwise no Europeans or gringos in three years. He was very anxious for conversation. He was from Guatemala City but had come to Esquipulas 'to get away from the death squads'. It was safe in this part of Guatemala. 'There are few Indians, so few *comunistas*.' That was a joke. The lawyer lived with a beautiful girl. He introduced her as his wife, and then told me, rather proudly, that they were not yet married, they were 'living-in-sin'. It seemed the sort of sin that might escape God's attention on the Guatemalan-Salvadoran border. The lawyer was lost in Esquipulas. He had discovered by going through an old deed box that he and his 'wife' had been related a hundred years before. He was proud of this, he hoped it would recommend her to his parents. He had a love of Spain and of history, and a fine collection of jazz records, and he had become a foreigner in his own country.

Earlier I had watched the pilgrims, whom the lawyer distinguished from tourists, at work in the Benedictine church. At 6.30 in the morning the monks sat on chairs scattered along the nave hearing confessions amid the bustle of family groups arriving from all over Guatemala, as well as from El Salvador and Honduras. There were Indians kneeling on the flagged floor setting up little shrines with candles and rosaries. Some knelt holding a candle in each hand, others returned from the communion rail wearing a smile. The women's costumes showed that they came from all the villages of the Highlands. I recalled that in the Highlands it had been hard to think of the Indians as anything but political people. Whose side were they on? Were they sheltering guerrillas? Would they join the Civil

Guard? How could one persuade them to talk about the army? Here, out of journalistic context, they were just people on pilgrimage, excited and happy. Some of them had babies, carried in white cloths across their backs from head-bands, but suspended horizontally so that the babies lay as though in hammocks. To soothe them the mothers, frequently teenagers, tossed their babies in the air, swinging them from the hips in semi-circles. This did not soothe the babies. The noise of children crying during mass was extraordinary but not distracting. It was not urgent, it just drifted up to the roof of the church like incense, and failed to rebound.

After mass there was the benediction, a local rite. The Indians lined up outside the church, and the monks, mostly from Louisiana, walked past them carrying large brushes and plastic buckets full of holy water. Something similar used to happen at high mass before the Church reformed its liturgy. There was a chant taken from Psalm 50, '*Asperges me*: Thou shalt sprinkle me with hyssop, Lord, and I shall be cleansed; Thou shalt wash me, and I shall be whiter than snow.' At school we used to duck to avoid being soaked. But at Esquipulas the monks had to give each pilgrim and all their belongings – which were spread out on the ground in front of them – a thorough dousing. The Indians became agitated if anything remained dry. To them the holy water was a medicine: it had to be administered in the correct dose.

The previous evening I had watched as the shrine, abandoned by the monks for the night, was enthusiastically taken over, like shrines all over the world, by the faithful. The blaze of candles around the 'Black Christ' could be seen for half a mile down the street, framed in the gloom of the nave. The family parties arrived, knelt across the west doorway, and started singing the shrine's hymn. The old women wailed it like *muezzins*, then advanced on their knees into the building. Inside some wandered around chatting, others made directly for the ramp behind the altar which led up to the silver and crystal casket around the image. This they touched and kissed and here they emptied their pockets. When they left it after a few moments of prayer, patiently observed by those to come, they walked backwards down the ramp, eyes still fixed on the *Cristo Crucificado*. Such devotion can be seen all over Latin America – a region which, according to its priests, contains a church in crisis.

It happened that the bus to the border carried a number of pilgrims, not Guatemalan Indians but Salvadorans returning after one night in Esquipulas. El Salvador has only 10 per cent pure Indian people and less than 10 per cent pure white. Its 80 per cent *mestizo* majority is by far the largest in Central America. The country's present troubles are said to be due to its recent history. It seceded from Guatemala in 1849 shortly after coffee was introduced to the region I was about to pass through. At that time the population was only a few hundred thousand. But the coffee led to prosperity and the population, that is the *mestizo* population, grew fast. Coffee, which is El Salvador's chief wealth, is also a curse. By 1930 there were one and a half million people, by 1966 three million, by 1979 nearly four and a half million. There are now one hundred and fifty-seven people to the square kilometre, which makes El Salvador the most densely populated country on the American continent. Furthermore, the land is mountainous and much of it is useless. Traditionally the land has been owned and run by fourteen families. It is not hard to see how the trouble started.

At the border I lost my pilgrims. They were waved through and on to another bus, leaving me to face Salvadoran immigration for the second time in twelve months. On my first journey I had entered El Salvador not by a back door but from Honduras by the Pan American Highway. I did not know it but the southern customs post which I had used before had been destroyed on the previous day. The few soldiers on duty had fled into Honduras when the guerrillas attacked. Eight border guards had stayed at their posts and all had been killed. The buildings and the bridge had been blown up. All traffic along the Pan American Highway had ceased; it had been one of the guerrillas' most spectacular coups for many months. The Honduran army had opened up with artillery from their side of the river. For members of the immigration service it must have been their worst experience for many years. Quite unaware of any of this, I approached a burly woman who started to search my baggage.

If you ask experienced observers of Salvador how *not* to travel through the country, they will tell you not to travel by bus. For some reason this advice never reached me until I had crossed the country twice by bus. One was told that the main danger on these buses came not from the guerrillas but from the army. I was eventually issued with a *laissez passer* by the Ministry of Defence. It was a fine piece of typing addressed to *Señores Comandantes y Jefes de Cuerpos Militares*. It identified me as a correspondent for the *Spectator*, London, and said that as long as I did not breach military security I should be assisted in my journalistic labours. It was signed not 'yours sincerely' but 'God, Unity, Liberty', and stamped with the military motto 'TODO POR LA PATRIA, JUNTOS, PUEBLO Y FUERZA ARMADA'. I eventually showed it to the foreign correspondents based in El Salvador and suggested that this would see me safely off the bus. They laughed quite a lot.

The Ministry of Defence nearly did not give me the *laissez passer* because my press card was 'out of order'. It was out of date by one year. I thought of the National Union of Journalists, their office in the Gray's Inn Road, London, called Acorn House, their fidgety demands for my subscription, their confident proclamation of the recognition of the Association of Chief Police Officers of England and Wales. I discussed the problem with Captain P. A. Luis Mario Aguilar Alfaro. I pointed out that my subscription arrears were usually only cleared in June, two months away. He replied that my credentials were out of order. Then he was distracted by the arrival of an assistant press officer who wanted to show off her new khaki uniform, so I got my *laissez passer*. It carried one of those passport photos, several years out of date, which always look a little ominous.

'How do you intend to leave our country?' The customs woman was not very friendly.

'By San Miguel.'

'You can't. That road is closed.'

'But that is the Pan American Highway.'

She explained the events of the previous day. She began to go through my books and papers. *Anna Karenina* passed, despite a reported prejudice against Russian authors. She opened Donne. '*Poemas*,' she said.

'Yes,' I said, 'about love.'

She did not respond. 'You are here simply as a tourist?'

'Yes.'

She looked through the piles of books, notebooks, newspapers, photocopies, the usual working junk of a journalist. *Viva Mexico!* by Charles Macomb Flandrau, *The Catechism of Christian Doctrine*, *Scarlet and Black*, *The Country Between Us* by Carolyn Forché, *Il Principito* by Saint-Exupéry, *Guatemalan Indian Costumes*.

'Your profession?'

'Barrister.'

'You understand our situation?'

She began to flick through a notebook, *libreta espiral*, marked No. 8 on the cover. 'Heads too decomposed to know the sex. Many died. Sixty cadavers one morning.' This was only page two.

'You know our condition?'

'Yes.' It was not clear whether she repeated the question because she was concerned about my lack of information or because she was emphasising her suspicions. But she remained courteous. She was bound, as so many people are in Latin America, by the Hispanic tradition of courtesy, by social obligation.

'Enjoy yourself.'

I was free to go. As I climbed up the slope, carrying my books, I looked back to the desk beneath the high roof. The woods and slopes pressed down around the customs post. She was still standing there, staring after me. There was no one else to attend to. The *abogado* from England would be remembered for a while. I was reminded looking at her as she stood alone of how lightly Salvadorans accept danger.

From Anguiatú I drove to Metapán in the back of an open pick-up. By now it was late afternoon. Long shadows lay on the hills, chilling the collected heat that rose from the tarmac. There was no sign of the teeming population. The hills looked quite empty. In the truck there was a woman dressed in red with her husband and a small girl, and another woman, a stray pilgrim from Esquipulas. After a while the empty hills began to give the impression that they were looking on; one was being watched. This impression was supplied simply by the knowledge that I was in El Salvador, that this was not Mexico or Panama.

Uniformed men with guns stopped the pick-up and demanded to see papers. Their shoulder flashes said Border Police. As we drove on they started to insult each other roughly. One snatched a cigarette from the other's mouth. The open hostility was unusual. I wondered what was making them so irritable.

The pick-up stopped again to let a country woman clamber up. She was brown-skinned and blue-eyed. She had a kind face, although I did not notice it for a while for fear of looking at her too closely. Beneath the face she had two throats. The original throat was pushed to one side. Beside it a lump had formed which had grown in time parallel to her original throat and which, from her chin to her shoulder, was just as thick. It must have been the world's largest goitre. We all avoided her gaze. She did not mind. Her expression remained kind. She was accustomed to being ignored by strangers. She said nothing. Perhaps she could not speak.

The stray pilgrim, a heavy elderly woman, was perched on the wheel hub. There were no seats in the pick-up. Twice she refused my offer of a seat on my case. We talked about her pilgrimage, about Santa Ana, about my journey. Nobody mentioned problems. Away from the hills, the wind rushing over the edge of the truck grew hot again. The woman in red crouching opposite me allowed her foot to touch mine. She had gold teeth and thick black hair. She would have been beautiful but for her jaw which was large and slack. Her husband leaned forward and noticed her foot and suddenly stopped smiling at me. Our feet separated. Then her daughter fell over and we all laughed. There was an innocence and happiness in her face when she saw that I admired her child – which was quite different from the calculating friendliness there before. It made her look five years younger.

In the boredom of riding day after day on crowded, uncomfortable buses, watching the behaviour of the women and children of Central America became more and more of a pleasure. The children were frequently polite, obedient and curious, at first alarmed by the sight of a gringo, later trusting. I remember two of them on an evening ride in Guatemala playing some version of 'I-Spy' for an hour. The girl – quick-witted, younger, the dominant partner – evaded the sharp nudges of her larger brother which were directed at her whenever she broke the rules. She broke the rules at every opportunity and always to her own advantage, and then she fiddled the score. But – she was quick-witted after all – she fiddled the score to *his* advantage. Again and again, at some pause in the journey, there would be such children, frequently looked after by a thin woman in a thin dress whose graceful movements were a constant solace in solitude. I grew to love the cheap colours and materials which these women wore so well, their large eyes and modesty and nervous strength, their endless pride and care of their appearance however tired they might be, and their remarkable lack of self-consciousness. While quite aware of their easy power to attract they also seemed aware of its unimportance. They played the game very well, to win, and then got on with life. Life, after some years, altered their appearance. Equally lovable were the slatternly, fat women, their bulging rolls of tummy barely contained by the same cheap materials that clung so sparely to the thin women, their infants constantly at breast, the confidence the mothers had that they could impose the necessary area of privacy with a single glance. The thin women were usually aunts or mothers of one child. The fat women were the same women three children later.

At Metapán the pick-up stopped at a bus station. I crossed the road and people called out in English, amused to see a gringo in this part of the world. 'Not many gringos in town,' they said mockingly. The newspaper seller, an intelligent-looking European, unshaven and unkempt, made a joke of selling me a Spanish paper. The news that a gringo had arrived from Anguiatú spread up and down the street. Things must be looking up. 'The situation' was improving. The bus from Metapán to Santa Ana was an express and only stopped when ordered to do so by the soldiers dug in at every road bridge.

I spent that night at Santa Ana's best hotel. The war which has wrecked the economy of El Salvador has done so more obviously in this once pretty town than in other parts of the country. Paul Theroux visited it in 1978 and described Santa Ana as 'a perfect place . . . perfect in its slumber, its coffee-scented heat, its jungly plaza, and in the dusty elegance of its old buildings.' Five years had changed all that. The hotel was run by a family of Spanish refugees from General Franco. They were from Bilbao but had not seen their home since 1938. They had locked their hotel up like a fortress, and it remained locked up like that all day. I rang the bell in the steel door, and eventually a very, very old man in a greyish-white starched jacket opened it a crack.

'Do you have a room?'

'*Securo.*'

I dined alone in a dining room that would have seated seventy-five. The building had been comfortably planned with stone floors and vaulting and a spacious arcade to cool the rooms. But the money had long since run out. There was little money in Santa Ana. The dust and the insects were breaking through every chip in the plaster.

The Basques accustomed themselves eventually to the unexpected presence of a visitor in their hotel. The mother spoke of Franco: 'You will never know how many bottles of champagne we drank in this room the night he died.'

Their daughter admired England. Why? 'Because it stood alone in the war against Hitler for one year. And because it is always raining there. The same weather as Bilbao.' She had never left Salvador but she wore a T-shirt with *Euzkadi*, the Basque name for the country of the Basques, printed on it. She read a lot about Europe. They asked me what I was doing and I said I was a tourist. I could see the daughter did not believe me.

Her mother talked of Barcelona when *los rojos* defended it. Their friends now appeared to be of the Right – businessmen, officials. They had a hotel. They were against the *subversivos*. The mother said, 'When we came here we never dreamed that one day Spain would be the safe country.' She could not go back. 'My life is here now.' She did not say it but she could hardly have dreamed when she left Spain that *los rojos* would become as much of a threat to her as Franco had been.

They told me it was safe to go out at night. I had heard of a casino in Santa Ana and I thought that I might spend a few *colones*. There was very little lighting in the streets around the Plaza Mayor. Eventually I found a bar which had not closed and sat down to write my notebook. I was vaguely aware of several men at another table, watching me. The beer, added to the wine at dinner, made me feel rather sleepy. I started to wander back across the plaza in what I regarded as the probable direction of the hotel.

'*Venga*! *Venga*!' Outside the heavily-defended police station on one side of the plaza, which was now quite deserted, the three men from the bar were sitting in the back of a truck. One of them snapped his fingers impatiently. They were dressed as civilians. They were quite confident that I would obey them. Somewhere in the darkness beyond the edge of the plaza there was a single shot. 'Papers,' they said. 'Who are you?' Something seemed to have happened to the Hispanic tradition of courtesy. I remembered that I carried no papers.

'You're not a member of the press, are you?' said one.

'The *international* press?' said another. They asked again for my papers. I tried to look helpful. There was a small plastic wallet in my pocket. I pulled it out. It contained the record slip for my travellers' cheques. At least it was typed. The light outside the police station was not very good. I handed the wallet over and said it was my English identity card. One of them began to study it carefully.

'It is dangerous out here at night,' said another. 'There is a curfew. Why are you out? Where are you staying?'

I tried without success to remember the name of the hotel.

'Where is it?'

I pointed in what I hoped was the right direction.

The first man brandished the wallet at me. 'If this is your identity card, where is your name?' I peered at the record slip. Ah yes, my name. He read it out carefully. 'Thomas . . . Cook. Very well, *Señor* Cook must return at once to his hotel.' *Señor* Cook was behaving very foolishly. I agreed and set off in the wrong direction. They called me back. They had to redirect me. My behaviour could hardly have been more conspicuous.

There were more shots as I left the plaza. A file of police started to walk past me. They kept close to the wall and checked the bolts of their rifles. They were stalking along the street as though it were a jungle. Is this what Paul Theroux had meant? Their behaviour seemed to me rather exaggerated. Then there was a blaze of light ahead. An armoured car had come round a corner and was now lighting up the wall of a house. The police stopped moving. Seeing a lighted doorway to the right I decided to take refuge, passed through and found myself happily in 'the casino'. A waiter came forward to welcome me, everything was reassuringly normal at last. At the end of a long corridor I could see palm trees, a bar, men dressed in well-cut suits sitting on stools, more waiters. There was music playing somewhere.

Then it all started to go wrong. The welcoming waiter, another very old man, was not so welcoming after all.

'What do you want?' he said.

'A drink.'

'But not here, *señor*. This a club.'

'This *is* the casino?'

'Yes, señor, the Casino, a private club.' He looked quite distressed. I should not have been allowed to pass the door. 'Please, *señor*, you must leave.' Outside the firing had started again.

'Of course,' I said. Who did he think I was? A private club, just like in London. Rules, waiters, what old custom dictates. One never entered a private club uninvited. I was concerned to reassure the waiter; no one had noticed me come in. He looked so grateful as I stepped back into the darkness and disturbance outside.

When I got back to the hotel the Basques also looked relieved. They had heard the firing. 'Most unusual,' they said, as they locked us all in yet again. I slept badly that night. It was terribly hot but I did not want to open the window. And so the day which had started amid the candles and hymns of the Indian shrines ended in a sealed bedroom with the noise of army lorries changing gear, occasional shouts and, when there was no other sound, the sound of running feet.

I read later that four soldiers had been killed in *un ataque terrorista* that night. Three decapitated bodies had been recovered and subsequently recognised. Three other corpses had been taken to the Santa Ana mortuary and named.

10

Inside the Zoo

Liberals! The words one knows so well have a nightmarish meaning in this country. Liberty, democracy, patriotism, government – all of them have a flavour of folly and murder.

Conrad, *Nostromo*

Next morning was a Sunday, and I needed money; I wanted to take the bus to San Salvador. Cashing fifty U.S. dollars is not usually a problem in Latin America, but Santa Ana was so impoverished that no one I asked could provide enough *colones*. Eventually I found a taxi-driver with a confidential manner and putrefied breath. He said that he could help but that he was too frightened of the police to change money in the plaza. In truth he had no more money than anyone else. Instead he drove me very slowly through the Sabbath calm of the town. Occasionally he turned to face me with a confident smile and an explanation of his plans, suffocating me each time with the odour of gum gangrene. He assured me that he knew a gentleman, a *fincero*, a coffee rancher, who would certainly have the small sum involved about his person. We went to the houses of several *finceros*, each of whom recognised the taxi-driver but regarded me with deep suspicion. They all denied that they had any money in the house.

At the last call, the house of a doctor not a *fincero*, we were left standing in the street for about fifteen minutes, our illegal mission, as it seemed to me, all too apparent. Then the doctor, deadpan, polite, unfriendly, changed my money at a handsome black market rate and I was free to go. It had been an interesting view of the blank face of the Salvadoran ruling class. Such men, it was said, ran the country, manipulated the U.S. embassy, raked in their commissions, authorised the death squads, just as they had always done. They were quiet, watchful, correct and – viewed from the position of supplicant at the door – rather unreassuring. The doctor had been the rudest of them.

The express bus to San Salvador took itself very seriously. It made a very different journey to the bus ride to San Salvador I had taken the previous year. Then I had been travelling the other way, south to north, and had started out from Honduras. Before I left I went to see a senior diplomat in Tegucigalpa, a man widely believed to be a spy. He received me sitting behind his desk. The thick net curtains in his office were arranged so that they concealed his side of the room. His visitors, on the contrary, sat before clear windows offering an easy target for the snipers he evidently feared. I had asked him about El Salvador and he had warned me against going there at all, particularly not by bus. It was the *people* who were brutal, he said, not the institutions. The people were much more violent than the Hondurans. They were like the Guatemalans. Perhaps it was something to do with the Mayan religion. Human sacrifice had been succeeded by the brutality of the conquistadors, then they had been roughly administered by the Spanish. The Salvadorans were very energetic, unlike the passive Hondurans. They were 'the Jews of Central America', a driving force and successful at business. The problems of El Salvador, he told me, were problems of food not problems of ideology. It was not the Cubans causing the problem, it was the greed of the Salvadoran rich. The country was run by an oligarchy. He also said that the guerrillas tended to exaggerate the abuses of the right in order to encourage Congress to cut off U.S. aid. This would enable them to win any elections that might eventually attract their participation. The Catholic Church in El Salvador had been used and knew it.

Excited by this brutal analysis I had gone straight down to the hotel where the only bus to El Salvador could be taken. 'Transportes El Salvador', read the sign inside the hotel. 'Safety, comfort, responsibility'. This was the correct slogan to attract the Hondurans but since it was a Salvadoran bus, 'Speed, swerves and the possibility of seeing your bus blown up' might have been more accurate. I remember as our bus departed that morning, rather regretting that I had not made a will. Stories of the dangers of this road had spooked me. The bus was white and marked 'Turismo'. It seemed needlessly conspicuous. I looked at the other passengers and felt calmer. They seemed most unlikely to have made wills either.

After only one hour we stopped at the Comedor El Ocotal for the driver's breakfast. It had a fine garden, unusual in Central America. There was an irrigation system and notably tall trees. Some of the plants were even marked 'Do not touch.' In cages suspended from the trees were parakeets and parrots and budgerigars and a squirrel. Below them were tame monkeys and two savage alsatians tied on long ropes. The cooking was done on a vast, circular, whitewashed, stone oven which was fed constantly from a wood-shed by two men.

In the early afternoon we cleared the Salvadoran customs. The official who stamped us in wanted a bribe which I alone refused to pay. For some reason my unstamped passport was overlooked and I looked on my escape as a small triumph until it occurred to me that without an entry stamp everyone who examined my passport would assume that I had entered the country illegally, like a guerrilla.

Fifteen minutes into El Salvador we passed a group of men standing by the side of the road beneath a tall tree. They were in civilian clothes, but all of them were armed. Some carried machine-guns, one had a much thicker barrel over his shoulder. The tallest of them wore a cowboy hat. On seeing them our driver braked hard, but they did not stop the bus. Instead they continued to look past us down the road we had come from. They were waiting for something else. The man next to me looked worried when he saw them and just nodded wearily in answer to my question, 'Guerrillas?' As we crossed the bridge I looked down into the river where a party of women was bathing. They were not stripped, as is usual among the peasants of El Salvador, but were washing themselves with their clothes on. One girl stood with her legs apart, the sun behind her, her clothes soaked, lazily washing out her hair, looking up at the bus. There was no village near by. The men on the road had merely been guarding these women as they washed.

Our driver's technique had been to go flat out when the road allowed it. Over the radio came the commentary from a football match in the World Cup. Hungary were on the way to beating El Salvador 10 – 1. That morning the surrender of the

Argentine forces on 'Las Malvinas' had been reported. El Salvador had once started a war over a football match. It did not seem a very good day to be an Englishman travelling alone on a Salvadoran bus without an entry stamp in his passport.

We saw no more guerrillas and nothing seemed to worry our driver except being stopped by the army. I noticed how his face fell the first time this happened. A platoon of soldiers looking for arms told us all to get out and the seven men on board were made to line up against the bus, hands pushed against the windows, while a surly youth in khaki searched us. Then our identity cards were checked. Then the soldiers started going through our wallets and pockets. They were looking not only for arms – there was a fierce battle taking place about ten miles to the north of this road – but also for any evidence of left-wing political sympathies. When we saw the guerrillas I had taken the only possession I would have grieved for and put it in my sock. I had no wish to contribute my ring to 'the People's Tax'. When the soldier came to turn out my pockets he was told I was a foreigner. This stopped him, which was fortunate as I had in my wallet several propaganda postcards, purchased in Nicaragua, issued by the *Frente Farabundo Marti Para La Liberación Nacional*, the F.M.L.N., the chief Salvadoran guerrilla organisation.

We took lunch in San Miguel, a town which contains a large army barracks. It was difficult to work out the political sympathies of my fellow passengers. If anything they seemed apolitical, although that would hardly have seemed possible in El Salvador. They were clearly nervous of the soldiers on the road but quite friendly to the soldiers in San Miguel. They had not looked overjoyed to see the guerrillas.

After lunch I did learn something about the conventions if not the opinions of El Salvador. Our bus would not start. We had to bump start it backwards up a hill. Seven male passengers pushed this rather heavy vehicle up the slope, watched by the fifteen women sitting in the bus. In some ways Central American society remains very conservative. If female guerrillas run a risk by washing in a river they expect to be guarded, and if a bus breaks down it is the male passengers who push it. The women remained in their seats looking down with interest and prepared to offer critical advice. It clearly never occurred to them to stand, attractively grouped perhaps, by the side of the road, but then it was raining. Eventually we achieved success and rejoined the ladies. I felt hot, wet and irritable. The Salvadorans felt wet, hot and immensely strong. Although the driver had not been pushing, he too was lifted by the masculine triumph. He drove even faster. The faster he went the less worried he looked. After any famous piece of overtaking he glanced back at his passengers as though expecting applause.

We were stopped by the army again towards the middle of the afternoon. By this time I had removed the incriminating postcards from my wallet and placed them in a book in my suitcase. This was just as well. The second group of soldiers were far more inquisitive than the first. When the search was over I found that one of them had checked the inside of the bus, had found my wallet in my suitcase and had emptied its contents on to my seat. He had not, fortunately, gone through my books.

As we approached San Salvador the road became quite clustered with the signs of battle. There were burnt-out buses, petrol tankers and bulldozers every few miles. The Pan American Highway is the only reliable link between the various countries of the Isthmus from Panama to the United States. And just as fast as the government tried to upgrade the Highway, the guerrillas disrupted its efforts. It was an illustration of the revolutionary's vested interest in destruction, of how it suits him to impoverish the poor. The men who owned the buses which were left burning on the road frequently owned little else. The passengers who were induced in this way to fear a journey to their own capital city frequently had to save up for the bus fare. One could see how, if one was caught between these weighty historical disagreements, one might have settled for the quiet life. 'How bad my country is,' said a poor man who made it his concern to stand near me during the army searches, and who may have saved my life by dissuading the soldier from going through my pockets. 'I am sorry.' He was embarrassed that I was inconvenienced while ten miles away his fellow countrymen were engaged in a pitched battle. 'These soldiers catch me every week,' said another, 'but they never catch a guerrilla.' It had clearly never occurred to any of them to report the presence of guerrillas to the nearest troops. In so far as possible they just wanted to make a normal life for themselves and that meant keeping out of trouble. Even on the most bitterly disputed stretches of the road one could see where other Salvadorans had taken the same decision. Farmers would be quietly rebuilding a burnt-out house. A man lay in a woven Indian hammock, in the shade of his porch, sleeping off his lunch. And as we drove past the wreckage of warfare, and negotiated the dangerous road-blocks, and nervously surveyed the company of guerrillas, my fellow passengers remained phlegmatic. The strongest emotion they displayed, all through that hot afternoon, was derision and disgust at the performance of their football team. They cheered every Hungarian goal. When we reached San Salvador and I took a taxi to the hotel, the driver, seeing which bus I had arrived on, merely said, 'Any problems on the road?' 'None,' I said, 'and how about the city?' 'Peaceful,' he replied. The previous week the guerrillas had fought their way right into the centre of San Salvador, hijacked forty-three buses and blown them all up.

On this second bus journey to San Salvador nothing unusual happened at all. We drove into the city past the heavily-defended military headquarters which, though close to the centre, frequently comes under attack. At the bus station I asked the taxi-driver for the Hotel Camino Real. '*¿Como non?*' he replied, and 'why not?' seemed one of the most irritating responses in the Spanish language.

The Hotel Camino Real is the centre for the international press in El Salvador. My bedroom window provided a fine view of what was apparently a peaceful and prosperous district of United States suburbia. In front of the hotel there was a four-lane highway. To the right there was a revolving 'Motel' sign and hoardings for Toyota, Pepsi-Cola, Marlboro, Smirnoff, Toyota again and McDonald's. There were several modern, slab buildings, a water tower, pine trees, yellow cabs and a parking lot painted with neat white lines and arrows. The national flag, blue, white, blue, '*Dios, Union, Libertad*', flew over the parking lot. Along the pavement by the highway a jogger in a track-suit and baseball cap moved from right to left. I noticed the pear-shaped outline of a Dutch travel agent last seen twelve months before in Nicaragua, ambling into the Metrosur shopping centre. And then, quite suddenly, there was an incident.

Outside the bank, on the edge of the shopping centre, a crowd was gathering quietly to watch an argument. A man in a loose, grey shirt was attempting to 'restrain' a dark-haired man in a blue shirt with short sleeves. From the distance of my window nothing very dramatic occurred. The man in the blue shirt tried to get his arm free but the other man would not let go. After a while two white-helmeted security guards from the bank arrived. The blue-shirted man struggled briefly, then he seemed to give up and they led him away. The grey-shirted man turned to the crowd of shoppers and gesticulated. He seemed to be explaining to them what had been going on. I wondered if he was a store-detective who had caught a shoplifter. Then he pulled a long-barrelled pistol from beneath his loose shirt and glanced at it. He no longer seemed like a store-detective. The crowd broke up. He replaced the gun in his trousers and walked away. A shorter man went with him. The man with the gun was solicitous towards the shorter one as they threaded their way across the busy highway. The whole thing caused so little stir that the taxi-drivers on the rank directly opposite didn't even notice it.

Next morning I got up at 8.30 and looked out of the window again. Another sunny day, the motel sign still revolved. The traffic was light. Then along the highway came a loudspeaker van. It was followed by the Girls' High School run. This quickly degenerated into the Girls' High School walk. They were spread out over about half a mile and took fifteen minutes to pass my window. I watched them as I ate my breakfast. They were handsome girls and well-fed. They joggled along, giggling, sometimes hand-in-hand, sometimes in track-suits and pretty head-bands, sometimes in their usual uniforms. Behind them came an ambulance, a rather helpless-looking police car, and a vast, walking-pace, traffic jam. What could be more normal, more healthy, more innocent?

Beyond the girls, on the lawn outside the *Banco Financero* (*'mas servicio por su dinero'*) lay a body. It had dark hair and wore a blue shirt with short sleeves. It looked like the body of the man who had been arrested on the previous evening. A few women, smartly-dressed for work, stood on the pavement, not too close, and looked down at the body. They kept glancing back along the road and I thought they were looking for the ambulance, but it was the bus they were waiting for. They didn't want to be late for work. When the bus came, nobody stayed with the body. After about half an hour it was taken away.

I went to see W. H. J. Chippendale, the honorary British consul in El Salvador and the only representative of his government left in the country since the embassy withdrew to the safety of Honduras in 1980. I asked him about the 200 British citizens still left in El Salvador. He corrected me. 'There are twenty-three men, thirty-four women and ten children here at present, and I know where they all are, because we've had an evacuation policy for some time now.' I told him that the man from U.P.I. had said that life in San Salvador was almost normal. 'You wouldn't have thought so two nights ago,' said Mr Chippendale. 'They attacked the police station and the army barracks just round the corner from me. It was coming down like rain all night on my roof.

'Last year I had a British student through here, a backpacker. He lost his passport somewhere between here and the Guatemalan frontier. He said he'd come round to the office on Saturday morning. Doing Latin America on a shoestring, that sort. Just down the street a man stuck a gun out of his car window and shot him through the ears. Just because he was a foreigner I suppose. He was completely non-political. I got him to hospital and then on to a flight to the States the same day. What happened to him next I don't know. He was seriously ill.'

Mr Chippendale was an old man. He was seventy-five. The walls and staircase of his office were plastered with Union Jacks, and there was another one outside the office. He had retired from the Foreign Service sixteen years earlier and been attracted to El Salvador by the climate. He had a framed picture of himself and his wife and daughter standing outside Buckingham Palace on the day he received his O.B.E. The British Tourist Board's colour poster of the Queen added another incongruous touch. I wondered how he came to be in this position.

'In 1979, they kidnapped the two top men in Lloyds Bank.

The embassy thought it was getting too dangerous and closed down overnight. I used to represent Lloyds Shipping Agency then and I didn't want to move so I was redrafted. I replaced the entire embassy. Glaxo, Unilever and I.C.I. all went at the same time. Now there's just me and a chap from the bank. I suppose they thought an old work-horse like me didn't matter.' Shortly before my visit his office had been machine-gunned and the window shot out. For some reason he described this as 'a mistake'. He said that 'Her Majesty' had 'come across with some new curtains.' He seemed to be completely baffled by my presence in the country. When he heard that I had come by bus he looked rather anxious. 'You're not going to suggest to your readers that they should use the roads, are you?' He said that the situation in the country had been really bad for three years. He said he kept telling people not to come.

Later that week the National Assembly passed an Amnesty Law for guerrillas who would surrender. The motion was fiercely opposed by parties of the Right. Before the debate started there were two hours of heated argument about whether or not there should be a National Day of the Librarian. Having decided that there *should* be, there was more heated argument about the date. Eventually the National Assembly decided on May 25. Previously they had been concerned about whether or not the 'Señorita El Salvador' contest should be granted tax-exempt status. It was.

Sometimes the national days make strange conjunctions. There is, for example, the proximity of Mother's Day and the Day of the Soldier. 'Thank you Salvadoran Soldier!' said the newspaper advertisement placed by the National Pipelines Board, and there were pictures of bombers, tanks and soldiers charging barbed wire. On the next page, electric fans, watches and furniture are all advertised 'for Mama on her day'. If one restricted one's knowledge of El Salvador to its newspapers one would have a peculiar but possibly quite accurate impression of the country. It is a country with strong U.S. connections. Cheer-leaders in rah-rah skirts and pompons inaugurate the national student games. Mrs Kirkpatrick's suggestion that the military regime in Argentina should aspire to government on the model of El Salvador was reported with approval. Then small-town U.S.A. is dispersed by a single news caption: 'A bus on the road to Sensuntepeque rolled over and killed la Señora Anselma Martinez de Cornejo. The bus driver was injured.' The picture shows the bus in a ditch, lying beside it in a pool of blood is la Señora. Kneeling in the road is a younger woman, grieving; looking over her shoulder are a group of curious children. The newspapers are full of mug-shots, but one never knows until one has read the caption whether the mugs are wanted for armed robbery, or have just passed their accountancy exams, or have been taken away in the night never to be seen again.

The Hotel Camino Real did a lot of business in receptions and tea-parties. It was the smart place to hold a celebration. These events were subsequently reported in the social columns of the daily press. While I was at the hotel there was a tea-party to celebrate the 'unforgettable date' of Señorita Ana's fifteenth birthday, there were the preliminary heats in the 'Señorita El Salvador' competition, there were various parties to mark El Dia de la Madre, and there was a little celebration of the engagement of Señorita Regina. The people who came to all these parties looked virtually identical to me. One would be sitting in the bar, brooding over one's notebook, and suddenly the room would be full of small, round women looking almost as succulent and luscious as the chocolates they were presenting to each other. Most memorable were the parties organised '*con motivo de la proxima visita de la cigüeña*'. Baby-showers! All the guests looked like extras from an Hispanic *Dallas*. Here they were again, la Doña Vilma, la Señora Romero, etc., etc., with their gift-wrapped offerings, beautiful frocks, shining hair, tinkling laughter and doe-like eyes; and none of these women appeared to be aware that there was anything untoward happening in the country at all. No one spoke of 'the war'. That was somewhere else, in a distant part of the land, if any part of so small a land could be described as distant. The 'war' was in Morazán Province, that is in the extreme north-east of the country, that is about sixty-five miles away from the city. Or the war was in Chalatenango, that is on the northern border with Honduras, that is thirty miles away on the road to that border.

These partygoers, preoccupied with their pregnancies, their hair, their clothes, and all the trivia of peacetime, were prosperous people whose interests were well-represented by the right-wing government and by the North American connection. Were they irresponsible or brave? It was a propaganda point, the Dunkirk spirit or bourgeois selfishness. These beautiful, elegant creatures, the daughters of the new middle class, were the people who had stayed on to make money in the state of siege, and who aspired to the old oligarchy.

One day I went to the military academy for a passing-out parade. It was a blazing hot day and there was an enthusiastic gathering to watch the annual parade of graduates from this Sandhurst of Central America. The baby-shower crowd were out in force. Before the march-past an army chaplain asked God to protect the brave young men before him, ready to die for the country. Between the chaplain and the official guests stood the raggle-taggle army of the international press, hogging the best positions, irreverent and inattentive during the invocation, unaware that the Almighty was being called down on to this particular parade-ground. I looked round at the official guests: not a reassuring sight. There in full uniform were the assembled grey-jowled ranks of the military-politicos who ran the economy and the arms rackets and who manned the death squads of El Salvador. The national anthem started up but the press corps chatted on. The Salvadoran national anthem is an ordeal. It goes on and on, dying out and then starting up again and again, requiring everyone to sing a succession of sub-operatic choruses. The baby-shower, in their immaculate silks, laid plump hands on plump breasts in the American civilian salute. Their painted, rosebud lips opened and closed in soundless obedience to the lyrics, while the cadets bellowed out the song from across the playing fields through the heat. And the press chattered on. The baby-shower looked embarrassed; they knew it was a small country, they knew it was a bad tune. But they were embarrassed at the discourtesy of their 'guests', they felt that they still had to regard this group of foreigners in that light. Then at last the anthem ended, the march-past began and honour was avenged as the baby-shower broke ranks, overran the press corps' position and, with squeaks of pleasure, charged past the heavily-armed troops at the edge of the parade to blow kisses and throw roses at their favourites.

I asked a North American who had grown up in El Salvador about the mindless innocence of these women. He said it was just as it seemed. The women and children were kept in the dark. He had gone back to his old parish church and talked to some of them. He had asked the children about the dangers of their life. They had been surprised. For a few months, when the guerrilla attacks in the city centre were at their worst, they had not gone out at night. They were always picked up from school. They were so well-protected from the events around them that they were not scared. But my friend also noticed during his visit that his old parish church was now half-empty. It served a wealthy district. He was told that one day one of the young priests working there had been caught with guerrilla literature. The wealthy parishioners no longer went there because they no longer felt it was their church.

The position of the extreme right in El Salvador is not as simple as at first appears. They are not, for instance, in straightforward alliance with Washington against a communist guerrilla movement. Indeed, as rightists, they are fierce nationalists and as nationalists they are passionately anti-gringo. Roberto D'Aubuisson, the leader of the right-wing ARENA, made a succession of violently anti-gringo speeches in the last election campaign and was even accused by the U.S. ambassador of trying to murder him. D'Aubuisson, or 'Blowtorch Bob' (named after his favourite instrument of torture), is an eccentric. He was once told by a gauche French woman that in France he was regarded as a psychopathic killer. He replied, 'Killer, yes. Psychopathic, no. I always retain my lucidity.' But eccentric or not his anti-gringoism is genuine. It is one of the basic political instincts of Latin America. This makes the task of the United States Foreign Service even more complicated.

In El Salvador the man responsible for turning the military cadets into real infantry officers, the 'western observer' of newspaper dispatches, is the commander of the U.S. military mission to El Salvador. He was a muscular, noisy colonel who conducted a weekly briefing for the foreign press corps on an informal basis. This was held in the heavily-secured basement of the U.S. embassy. It was a comfortably furnished room. The deep carpet and deep chairs distracted one from the bars on the windows and the anti-blast wall which blocked out most of the natural light. When I attended the Colonel's conference there were twenty-three journalists present, including six women. There is no shortage of female reporters in El Salvador and most of them seemed to understand the Colonel's strange, military vocabulary more readily than I.

The Colonel lit a cigar, adjusted his horn-rimmed spectacles, leaned back, crossed his legs and exposed the elegant high suede boots which he wore beneath his rather tight pants. 'The Hondurans killed about 40 g's last week,' he said. G's? Ah yes, wake up, 'guerrillas', '*guerrilleros*'; in this room simply 'g's'. 'How did the g's die?' It was one of my female North American colleagues who asked. 'Same way g's usually die,' replied the Colonel. 'G's die trying to defend a fixed position. That's how Che Guevara died.'

This was an interesting example. Before the Colonel arrived I had been told by two of my female North American colleagues that he had been *personally responsible* for the death of Guevara – who, by romantic legend, went down, guns blazing, in a Bolivian rain forest. There is absolutely no evidence for the truth of this rumour but I thought my female colleagues seemed a little flushed and breathless as they repeated it. Yum-yum. The Colonel continued his seductive list.

'There was a night ambush in San Vicente. Small army units killed 15 g's in a road clearance Sunday. The new airborne company we trained three months ago had its first kills. Since the unit was freshly graduated this was a good opportunity for them to get blooded. They did a good job.'

The Colonel's idea of a press briefing was to show the Salvadoran army in a good light. Since the army frequently preferred to exercise its skill against unarmed civilians rather than heavily armed g's, the Colonel's task was not easy. It was made no easier by his audience, predominantly North American, who adopted an admirably direct method of questioning.

The previous week the g's had attacked and destroyed the frontier post, blowing up the bridge which carried the Pan American Highway. Had the Colonel heard that many of the soldiers supposed to be guarding the bridge were absent at the time attending a celebration for 'the Day of the Soldier'? Yes, the Colonel had heard that rumour. Was it true? He did not know. Why were two large American warships anchored off the Salvadoran port of La Libertad? 'They were landing a female naval lieutenant who had developed an acute appendix.' This explanation caused some mirth. Were they also engaged in a surveillance mission on the Nicaraguan coast? The Colonel had no comment.

The Colonel's task was made even more difficult because he was under fire on two fronts. Most of his audience represented North American liberal opinion. They were concerned to show that the army was losing the war and that it was time to negotiate with the guerrillas. But there was also present Señor Mario Rosenthal, editor of the English-language weekly *El Salvador News Gazette*. Sr Rosenthal is a man of right-wing opinions extreme even by the standards of El Salvador. He speaks English with the speed, volume and accent of the Bronx. He was concerned to show that the army was losing the war *and that it was time for some more American military aid*. 'The American military mission to El Salvador is too small,' said Rosenthal. 'I'm working under a fifty-five-man lid,' said the Colonel. 'So why were you down to thirty-seven last month?' growled Rosenthal. '*If* I was down to thirty-seven it was because I was out of bread,' growled the Colonel.

Rosenthal beamed in triumph, then looked around the room, searching for approval. He received none. Privately the Colonel and Rosenthal might have agreed that the g's would never be defeated until the U.S. sent in the 82nd Airborne, who would clean the place up in three months. But not even President Reagan was proposing this step. Until he did so the Colonel had to spend his time pretending to be enthusiastic about an army that would not fight. And Sr Rosenthal, for reasons of national pride, had to pretend that with just a few more advisers or planes or guns the Salvadoran army would be able to solve the problems of El Salvador.

There was another man present, a European who acted as transport manager for one of the television news companies. I was surprised to see him there since he was not a journalist. Throughout the press conference he stared nervously at the muscular, hairy colonel. He looked quite frightened when a reporter contradicted the colonel or pressed him on a point he wanted to evade. I wondered why he had come to this conference held in this heavily fortified room, and why he looked so nervous. I wondered if he was 'an idealist'. Later I had a meal with him and decided he probably was an idealist. I thought of saying 'I know your secret', just to see his reaction; then I thought better of it. His side weren't exactly sweetie-pies either.

Three weeks later the Colonel's second-in-command, Lieutenant-Commander Albert Shaufelberger, was shot dead as he sat in his car, waiting outside the Catholic university for a friend. He should have been safe in the car because it was bullet-proof, but for some reason the air conditioner was not working that day, so he had wound down the window. Four weeks after that one of the reporters at that meeting, Dial Torgersen of the *Los Angeles Times*, was also killed. He was looking for a story on the border between Honduras and Nicaragua when his car drove over a mine, probably laid by one of the Nicaraguan rebels trained by a colleague of Shaufelberger's. A few months after that another of the reporters present, Susan Morgan of the *Observer*, was seriously injured in a bomb explosion during a press conference held by the leader of those Nicaraguan rebels who were not backed by the C.I.A. It was to be some months before it was discovered that the Colonel's mission had unwittingly been training Salvadoran guerrillas for the previous three years.

I went to see Maria Julia Hernandes who works for the Archbishop's Commission for Justice and Peace, a bureau that records all the atrocities committed by both the death squads and the guerrillas, and tries to find those who have disappeared. It is one of the leading civil rights organisations in the country. In her waiting room all the chairs were occupied by women. They looked exhausted, dull, worried or griefstricken. This was the room to which women came from all over El Salvador after their men had disappeared. One nursing mother sat slumped asleep, her baby on her knee, its sleeping face pressed to the teat. Another woman, on the verge of tears, had deep lines across her face. Several had carried supplies of food, a bag of grain or rice, with them. Some seemed poorer, more tired or hungry. They had been waiting a long time and would continue to wait until a corpse was found and they were released from hope. Others became desperate or angry every time a different name was called. They had the dreadful concentration of people who know that they must be patient and calm if they are not to damage their own cause.

The commission is in a house owned by the archbishop. It is unguarded, nobody there carries guns, but it is one of the few public expressions of opposition to the death squads that roam everywhere in El Salvador. The figures for weekly political murders, the most recent at the time of my visit was 253, are compiled here, supplied to the United States embassy and spread around the world. Maria Julia Hernandes works in a small office on a floor above the waiting room. When she produces a weekly total of victims it is based on as many details as possible: a name, age, address, profession, date and place of arrest or capture, name of captors (if known), manner of arrest, legal remedy sought, size of family, place of confinement.

So, under the heading of Denuncias de Capturas is 'Case No. 54, José Daniel Perez Hernandez, aged nineteen, of San Salvador, single, day-labourer taken from his house on 10 March 1983 by uniformed men, violently, habeas corpus sought, two brothers, prison unknown'. Señor Perez Hernandez was probably dead. Certainly dead was Case No. 8, under the heading 'Victims of Political Violence': name unknown, age about thirty, occupation unknown, died on 1 March 1983 of bullet wounds, two fillings in upper teeth, blue trousers, weight 165 lbs, 1 metre 60cm in height, thin moustache, swarthy, found in San Luis, responsible party – unidentified paramilitary group'.

Mrs Hernandes spent her time compiling these lists and interviewing the women in the waiting room. 'People come into this room to cry,' she said. 'Every day.' Then she showed me one of the ways she could help them: photographs of the unknown victims. Bodies, half-stripped, lying in a ditch, needing to be identified. Then she showed me photographs of the decapitated bodies found in San Salvador during the previous week. She showed all her visitors such pictures.

She was a brisk, comfortable-looking woman, aged about forty-five, the sort of person one would expect to find doing parish voluntary work, warm-hearted, once light-hearted, now become shrill-voiced in argument, no longer apparently living 'where motley was worn', yet she too was dressed for a baby-shower at the Camino Real. I asked her two questions. Was she not frightened of a communist government? 'The United States is maintaining the government we have here. Rather than continue with this situation I would prefer to experience something else.' Who organised the death squads? 'Our government needs the death squads. It needs to put fear into people.' Since 1980 at least three civil rights workers occupying positions similar to that of Maria Julia Hernandes have been murdered or abducted. They were called Marianella Garcia Villas, Maria Magdalena Henriques and America Fernando Perdomo.

I heard there was an Englishman working at the zoo so I took a taxi in that direction. On the way I stopped for a coffee. The waiter's conversational approach was pointed.

'Are you extraneous,' he said, 'or are you of this place?'

'I am extraneous.'

'I thought so. Your comportment is *recto* and how the strengths of your character shine from your face.'

'Thank you.'

'Are you, by chance, Swiss? We, the waiters, have been discussing this and it is our conclusion.'

'No. I am English.'

'English! Son of a whore! I would never have taken you for English from England.'

'Why not?'

'You are too courteous. Here, in El Salvador, it is our experience that those from England are *brusco*.' We simpered at each other as courteously as we could, and I prepared to pay a tip such as only an extraneous of my comportment could afford.

When I got to the zoo it was closed. Needless to say Philippe and Manuela were outside. I had not seen them since a chance encounter at the main post office in Guatemala City where they had been trying to post letters without paying for the stamps. If you wanted to know which day a zoo was closed the simplest method would have been to ask Philippe which day he would like to visit it. On this day it was only open for educational visits from school parties, but I showed my letter from the Ministry of Defence (*'Señores Comandantes y Jefes de Cuerpos Militares Presente* . . . ') and asked to be taken to the Englishman. I tried to inject a little *brusco* into my manner, and it worked.

My first impression of visiting a zoo which was closed was that an alarming number of animals seemed to be allowed to wander free of their cages. A cage full of magnificent black panthers was still secured. Then I realised that the wandering animals were ducks. A guide took me along the walks, deserted except for a small party of schoolgirls, to the snake house. He took me round to the back of the building then shook me by the hand and left. He said that the keeper of snakes was somewhere in there. I found myself looking down a corridor which was lined with doors to the back of the snake cages. At the far end of the corridor a slight figure could be seen with head and one arm thrust into an open enclosure. This was the Curator of Reptiles. He was too far away to hear me so I started to walk down the corridor, down the line of plywood doors, several of which were open. I decided not to look inside. 'Oh,' he said eventually. 'You're English? How did you find me? What do you want to talk about? My work? Life? Atomic war?'

The Curator of Reptiles was a slim, bald, bespectacled, and absent-minded man. He started to open several more of the cages. As far as I could judge I was now standing in a snake house, with about six poisonous snakes between me and the door, embarked on one of the least comfortable conversations I could remember. With all the doors open it was possible for the Curator and I to look through the snake boxes, through the glass panel at the front and so to the pathway from which the public viewed the collection. The party of schoolgirls was now assembled on the path. They seemed surprised to see, behind the snakes, two gringos in earnest conversation.

The Curator started to discuss the snakes. There were a rattlesnake, a cottonmouth, a hooded viper, a boa constrictor, a coral snake and a nocturnal snake that seemed annoyed to have been woken up. The Curator was unusually deft. He demonstrated the speed of the nocturnal snake's movements. 'Oh, you *are* a silly. What a silly,' he said as the snake struck again and again to within a few inches of his hand and face. 'Stop it at once,' he said. 'You really are very silly.' He didn't flinch at all. I noticed one schoolgirl's surprise change to alarm. We moved on to the rattlesnake, which seemed enormous. It lay close to the open door and was making a most disagreeable noise. It was rattling. Just as we reached its cage something whipped out, brushed against the curator's shirt and fell to the ground. 'Gracious,' he said. 'What's that? Oh it's a little *gecho*.' The lizard recovered itself and shot under the cage. The next moment there were screams of hysteria from the schoolgirls. It had run straight under their feet. They were convinced that a small rattlesnake was upon them. '*Niñas*! *Niñas*!' piped my companion. 'It won't kill you.' This had little effect on the girls, who were forming the opinion that two maniacs were at large among the snakes.

When we came to the boa constrictor the Curator took it out and coiled it round his head and shoulders. He pointed out a scab on its mouth that dated back to when it had shed its skin. There was dried blood round the wound. 'It could have been the rats,' he said, 'but I think it's the scab. I've put Listerine on it.' He was particularly proud of another snake he had found in El Salvador which he had identified as an obscure cousin of the cottonmouth. He said that it was very rare and that the London Zoo had wanted him to send it to them, a proposal which he had rejected. 'I couldn't really do that,' he explained. He picked it up and asked me if I wanted to handle it. I remembered that in the Florida swamps the cottonmouth is more feared than the alligators, and declined. 'No? Not many people accept my offer,' he said. He had a precise, humorous manner and used a wonderfully dated English, but as he proudly showed off his collection I began to wonder to what extent his evident isolation had begun to affect his judgment. Could the schoolgirls be right?

The Curator had lived in El Salvador since 1944. At first he was a teacher. For the last twelve years he had been curator of reptiles and insects at the zoo, mainly on the grounds that he knew more about snakes and spiders than anyone else in El Salvador. He was paid £37 a week, which he described as 'ridiculous'. We left the snake house eventually, and only after he had chanced to notice an unlocked cage, and I was surprised at the strength of the relief I felt as we passed out and I could regain the pathway. Then, on our way to the exit, and to the safety of San Salvador's streets, we passed the alligator pool and I heard myself, with a sinking feeling, making some smart remark about the length of a half-submerged snout.

'Would you like to have a look?' He had seized on my mistake with glee. My God, he was fiddling with the gateway to the enclosure. What did the old fool think they put these cages up for? Fortunately the gate was jammed. Unfortunately he was able to release it.

The enclosure which we now entered contained two large pools divided by a narrow path, along which the Curator led the way. To the left an enormous alligator, heavily camouflaged in green slime, was watching our progress from about four feet away. 'There's another one over here.' The Curator had taken a twig and was bending down towards the water intending to tickle a snout. There was a swirl, a gulp (a roar, or did I imagine that?) and suddenly a vast yellow softness, ringed by teeth, was gaping beside his hand. 'Looks quite hungry . . . ', he tittered.

At the end of the path there was another pool on the banks of which ten small caymans were sunning themselves and looking on. Turtles circled, numerous little black snouts poked out from the water. The Curator told me that they had recently introduced a newcomer to the enclosure but it had been pretty well ripped in two by the older inhabitants. He said that the largest alligators were from Honduras and that one of them had walked out one day, just pushed his way through the wire and set off down the path. Several keepers lassooed him and after a terrific struggle had succeeded in getting him back.

However the pride of his collection was the original black snout. It was a most unusual sub-species. 'Ah yes, there he is . . . ' I looked round. The alligator in whose enclosure we were conversing had moved round the island without a ripple and was now stationed just below the surface about a yard from the path, cutting us off from the gate. 'He's come to have a look. But he's just curious. He can't be hungry because he's just been fed,' said the Curator. 'At least he should have been. Although sometimes when we are closed the staff get a bit slack. Still I don't suppose he's looking for food.' The eyes of the alligator did not blink. I decided to avoid eye contact and set out for the gate. Half a pace past the submerged snout there was another swirl and then a snap and a splash. From behind me I could hear the Curator giggling with delight. 'He was after your leg! Reared out and had a go at it.'

Back on the path, among the schoolgirls, who had decided by now that we were the best show in the Zoo, the Curator asked me if I wanted to meet the elephant. No. 'Pity. Sweet little Indian elephant. Very fond of me.' I discovered subsequently that the elephant had recently killed a part-time keeper. The Curator blamed this entirely on the keeper. The elephant had the habit of removing the keeper's broom when its enclosure was swept. The part-timer had 'mishandled' the situation because the elephant had picked him up with its trunk, smashed him down and knelt on his chest. That had been at 8.30 in the morning. He had been dead by lunch-time. When he was carried away he was bleeding from the nose, mouth, eyes and ears. The press had been very good about it, the Curator said; there had not been much publicity. I thought what a relief that must have been to the animals. I presumed they could read. They were clearly in charge of the asylum.

On the path outside the alligator pool the Curator found a stinking duck which had apparently been taken for dissection and then just left around. He tossed it over the wire into the pool. Two of the brutes went for it at once and there was a flurry of feathers and wonderful tugging and splashing before the duck disappeared beneath the surface. This incident led the Curator to some reflections on the staff. The previous director had been 'frightfully nice. But he used to steal all the time.' And getting the present staff to feed the animals was a terrific problem. The curator thanked God for the abundant supply of Salvadoran rats. 'The maternity hospital is the best source,' he said. 'Do they have a better rat-catcher than the other hospitals?' I asked. He giggled again. 'No. It's because they still use rats for pregnancy tests. God forbid they should ever go over to modern methods. That is the *last* thing I would suggest.' His work now, apart from caring for the animals, was in lecturing to the schoolchildren about conservation. But he had few illusions. He was discouraged by the certainty that his audience would still go away and kill the first snake they saw. He had the disadvantage of working in an unacademic country. A European archaeologist told me that he had once been lamenting the complete absence of Mayan sites in El Salvador to an official of the national archive. 'Oh, but we do have Mayan sites,' replied the official. 'It is just that we have not yet discovered them.'

Later I went to the Curator's house for tea. He interested me. He had a square jaw, a scrawny neck, and prominent flickering eyes, that seemed to be without lids. He was bald and darting in his movements. He resembled one of his reptiles, possibly a lizard. When he wore a tie it emphasised his thin neck and he looked more than ever like a lizard; a lizard in a necktie. I had trouble finding his house. When I arrived he was peering out eagerly from behind a wired windowframe. He was no longer a lizard. He had changed into a tortoise in a cage.

Some people get washed out of the mainstream of life. The world flows on. They remain in a time of their own. I asked the Curator about England. He had been there recently, for the first time since 1939. He mentioned the trains. They had doors which opened automatically as you approached. They were silent. They went like a bullet. It sounded like something out of Jules Verne. I had to remind myself that he was describing British Rail. He had been upset by the state of London Zoo. 'No stick insects. And nothing like as many spiders as there were before the war.' He did not want to return to England. 'They wouldn't have me at the London Zoo or at the Natural History Museum. I'm an old man. Before, when I lived with my parents, we had a lovely house in Kensington. My father had a business; he imported champagne. Now it would be very different. I have no friends or family in England. I can't drive a car. I'd need a house within walking distance of a zoo and a church.'

His English was so correct that I wondered how well it would be understood in England. Talking of a snakebite he said, 'So I submitted the blister to the doctor.' Describing the leaders of the British Labour Party he said, 'the scamps'. That was a serious criticism. Fidel Castro was worse; he was 'the dirty scoundrel'.

I asked him what he would do if the communists came to rule San Salvador. He said he would have to leave. 'No civilised man could live with them.' He was very frightened of an upheaval in his life, but spoke of it as almost inevitable. He said that when he went he would take all his snakes with him. He had the boxes ready. I thought of the W. H. J. Chippendale evacuation plan and wondered if the consul knew about the Curator's boxes.

The traditional death of snakekeepers is by snakebite. There had been the case of Constantine Ionides in Kenya. And the Curator told me of another great authority called Dr Morton. This man had been bitten in Germany in the 1960s and taken at once to a good hospital. He had died there, despite the most skilful treatment, after three weeks. He had been killed by the collapse of numerous internal organs. Snake venom destroys the blood vessels and the blood cells and the vital organs, said the Curator. But even in the act of dying Dr Morton had added to the sum of knowledge: he had been bitten by a back-fanged snake not previously considered very dangerous. The Curator had some stratagems for avoiding snakebite. He thought that the creatures recognised him and that his familiar movements did not alarm them. He always noted how much of the snake's body immediately behind the head was uncoiled. If he approached them closely he kept his hands below their line of vision.

Nevertheless he had been bitten three times. When he first came to El Salvador he had decided to return a family of coral snakes to the jungle. The coral snake is the most venomous snake in America. He had fallen asleep on the train. The snakes had escaped and he had been woken by the general alarm. One of the baby coral snakes had bitten him on the hand. Nothing had happened except that his thumb and hand had swollen up for twenty-four hours. It was possible that this slight bite had helped to inoculate him. Later he had been bitten in the zoo by 'a viper'. It had been an unfortunate accident. His arm had swollen up like a balloon for three weeks. 'It felt as though it was filled with dirt,' he said. It was on that occasion that he had 'submitted the blister to a doctor'. But the doctor had been unable to help him. As far as the Curator knew, *there was no anti-snake serum anywhere in El Salvador*. The doctor had told him to go home and await events. After three weeks the swelling subsided. On the third occasion a puff adder had been lying in a straight line facing away from him. It is thought that a snake cannot strike unless part of its body is coiled. In the nature of an experiment the Curator had touched the puff adder's tail. This had been 'very silly'. Immediately the snake had turned and bitten his hand. His arm swelled enormously. The Curator knew that when the swelling reached his heart he would die. But the swelling reached the shoulder and stopped. Then his body turned the colour of chocolate from neck to waist. It was '*very* uncomfortable'.

After tea he asked me if I would like to see his garden. He had planted it all himself and it was full of rare shrubs, trees and cacti, some of them, needless to say, highly poisonous. We had to pass through several locked doors to reach the garden. The Curator was nervous of intruders. Outside the french windows there was a pool full of turtles and beside that a tree in which a wild basilisk lived. The Curator had tamed this creature so that every morning it would descend and he would feed it on cockroaches with a pair of pincers. There was no clear reason why he should have ended up this way. As a boy in England he had loved collecting butterflies. That had apparently been the only sign. Otherwise he had done it all by himself. He was made for solitude and the company of reptiles. We walked towards the bottom of the garden. On the way we passed a rickety shed. Without my saying a word he asked me if I would like to see his private collection. He said it was quite safe, but I noticed that the intelligent-looking mongrel he kept had no intention of going in. Inside the shed there was a hooded cobra, a rattlesnake, a boa constrictor, a short-tailed python and a yellow beard, *barbaramarilla*, last known and feared outside Oaxaca. There were also several other snakes whose names I have forgotten. The Curator said that he had made the shed and the cages himself. He had not, unfortunately, been able to make them as *strong* as those in the zoo but he thought they were 'pretty safe'. It was too narrow to turn in the shed without brushing against the cages. The rattlesnake rattled away incessantly throughout my visit. The fragile glass enclosing it was smeared with streaks of venom. The python was not in a cage but on the floor. The Curator thought it had broken its back. It had not eaten for months. There was something else in a paper bag by the door. I didn't enquire. The crowded little hut stank, of snakes.

After the hut we continued to the bottom of the garden. On the way we passed another cactus, the maguey, the type from which *mescal* is drawn. The garden ran down to the edge of a cliff which plunged into the *barranca*. This was the ravine that served as an underground highway for the guerrillas when they launched an attack on the army barracks or on the centre of the city. On the other side of the ravine there was the usual settlement of shanties and crumbling huts, the houses of the poorest people in San Salvador, the dispossessed peasants of the overcrowded countryside. It was these people whom the guerrillas counted on for shelter. A woman was hanging out her washing there. She looked across to the tall trees and shrubs in the gardens of the villas on our side of the ravine. In the Curator's garden she could see the little alligator he kept in a pool on the lip of the cliff. His servant came down every day and fed it on rats or chicken or any other meat that was going cheap. The alligator looked like an effective watch-dog but the Curator said that one of the terrorists had once climbed up from the ravine into his garden. He had been alone at the time. The man said he was a *comandante*, that there was a price on his head because he had killed so many people, that he was very hungry, and why was there an alligator at the bottom of the garden? The Curator said that he had managed to lock himself into the house and the terrorist had disappeared. Inside the house he had various rarities, mostly pickled, but the contents of his bottles included a grey and oily scorpion about the size of a box of matches which he fed attentively. And there was a bird-eating spider. As I now remember, the spider's hairy body was the size of a fist, but at the time I noted it, too, as the size of a box of matches. I thought, looking at those two jars, standing on a bare wooden table in a cold, white room without other furniture, lit by one naked light bulb, that I would not have wanted to be locked in with them. I would have preferred the company of the *comandante*.

When I left him it was raining heavily. The Curator had wanted to continue talking about communists, and the poisoning of the oceans and the state of the London Zoo and his collection of mediaeval ivories. But it was dark and I was thinking of the difficulties of finding a taxi. The pavements in that district were deeply potholed. There was no moon and no street lighting. I walked through the rain towards where the main road should have been; occasionally a car would drive past, very slowly, two thin beams of light bouncing wildly over the bumps and quickly lost in the sheeting rain. Eventually I found a highway. The passing lorries drenched me in sprays of filthy water but I felt grateful for their company. A taxi took me back to the hotel. At every red light the driver indulged the usual habit, the commonest sign of fear in San Salvador. Waiting for the lights to change he would turn his head as casually as he could and check who was in the car that had drawn up beside him. And the people in that car would invariably be staring back.

The Camino Real gave journalists a discount and lodged them all on the sixth floor. This made it easier for the police to tap their telephones. Nobody objected to this arrangement, or to the fact that the barmen who spoke such easy English were police informers. The sophisticated view was that at least it was better than the El Salvador Sheraton where, on one celebrated occasion, the waiters had dragged one of the guests out to his death. John Sullivan had also been staying at the Sheraton. He was a young freelance journalist from New Jersey on his first foreign assignment. Immediately after arriving in El Salvador he booked into the Sheraton, made one telephone call from his room and then left for a rendezvous in a nearby bar. He was never seen again, but an investigation suggested that he was taken away from the bar by several unidentified men. Some time later a body was found in a shallow grave outside the city. An anonymous tip-off said that it was John Sullivan's although identification was impossible because the head had apparently been blown off with dynamite. To strap dynamite to the head of a member of 'the international press' is the sort of symbolic murder which would tickle the fancy of members of the Salvadoran Right. Their hatred of 'the international press' is an institutionalised hatred, vividly underlined by the notice displayed on the wall of the Ministry of Defence press office: 'Like a voice crying in the wilderness, we beg members of the foreign press to earn their wages honestly, and suggest that if they must lie they do so about their own countries, *but not about El Salvador*'. The right-wing in El Salvador does not lack insolence. When asked to explain why the killers of Archbishop Romero had never been caught, they said that a description had been circulated to Interpol, but there was no response because El Salvador's subscription to Interpol was in arrears.

There was a man in the bar of the Camino Real one night, a

prosperous Salvadoran, dressed in a sports shirt which he wore outside his trousers. He was a most unpleasant man. I had noticed him earlier in the day, sitting by himself in the dining room and openly staring at the foreign journalists. He had been in the hotel bar all day and was now extremely drunk. He was built like a slab of concrete, fat, and as broad as he was tall. He had a very long upper lip. It made his mouth look like that of a fish. He had a younger man with him who said nothing at all. The barman watched him with a nervous smile.

Failing to notice this man when I entered the bar I found myself sitting on the bar stool next to his. He used my arrival as an excuse to offer a drink to the members of 'the international press'. I declined politely. He took my arm in his hand. Why did I not wish to drink with him? Was there some reason why I did not wish to accept a drink? He had an uncomfortably strong grip. I decided that if this man ever released my arm I was going to go to bed. When I reached the lift I found that every single other journalist in the bar had joined me.

Guests at the Camino Real got into some other funny habits as well. No one, even in broad daylight, sat in his room with the door unlocked. And if three or four were gathered together in one bedroom for a drink, they would lock the door then too.

One evening members of the international press returned from a lobster dinner to find that the hotel car park was in a state of mild commotion. An N.B.C. crew had set up its floodlights and was filming a battered green sedan. A young man was lying beside the car; he was dead. An anonymous telephone call had alerted Cecila of N.B.C. to this convenient opportunity.

The young man, with long, dark hair and a moustache, was lying gracefully on the tarmac dressed in an olive green uniform which appeared to have been recently laundered and pressed. The letters F.M.L.N. were stencilled above the breast pocket. Someone had cut some branches from a tree and placed these, with a No Parking sign, beside him. A policeman in plain clothes stood at the back of the crowd, showing little desire to assert himself. The explanation for this body was to be found in a pile of leaflets stacked beside it. Issued by a previously unknown organisation called 'The Secret Anti-Communist

Army', the leaflet stated that the body had been left 'to draw the attention of the international press to the way in which the amnesty laws, and other Salvadoran laws, tended to favour the communist-criminals of the F.M.L.N. We have accordingly apprehended one of the terrorists who had blown up the Esso station at Apopa. There was no difficulty in establishing the guilt of this man, he carried the proof in his hands, and he was accordingly condemned to death . . . The blood of our soldiers will always be avenged!'

A young man from Detroit, bending over the body, announced that he could see no sign of blood but that there were strangulation marks around the neck. How did he know about strangulation marks? I assumed it was a tribute to a childhood spent watching gringo television. Behind him, ten or fifteen members of the international press had gathered to film and photograph and argue. They paid little attention to the Salvadoran policeman, who was trying to keep the scene undisturbed, until the policeman told them that the body or the car, or the pile of leaflets might be boobytrapped. This had a remarkable effect on everyone's curiosity.

I fell into conversation with a young Salvadoran who was standing beside me on the outer edge of the circle, apparently in a state of shock. He said that he had come to the hotel to pick up his mother, who was attending a baby-shower. 'This makes me want to get the press,' he said. I pointed out that everybody else there was *from* the press. 'It makes me want to get them,' he repeated. He meant 'kill them'. 'Why do they always publicise this?' he asked. He told me that he worked for an Arena firm, that is a business that backed the right-wing party in El Salvador. 'Nobody in my firm gets killed. We all lead a normal life. Yet everyone in the United States thinks this is such a bad country. It is the press who do this. Remember William Randolph Hearst.' It was baffling enough before he asked me to remember Mr Hearst. Here we were standing in the car park of the hotel where his mother was attending a baby-shower. Beside us lay the body of a young man of about his age who had been strangled. The deed had apparently been done by a group of men who would certainly have voted for Arena. And he wanted me to know that if you were under the protection of Arena this sort of thing did not turn up in your car park. His solution was to kill the press.

I looked around me. The ring of reporters standing by the body seemed to have lost all interest in it. The television lights still blazed down, picking out the details of the corpse's clothing, but the press were not looking at the corpse; they were all talking to each other. Men, women, American, European, stood around the dead man like guests at a cocktail party going over the possible explanations for this peculiar incident. They were making the usual 'rhubarb, rhubarb' cocktail-party noises. It was an almost incredible sight and did nothing to soothe the feelings of the young Salvadoran who was becoming incoherent with rage. I suggested to him that we might go back to the hotel and that his mother was probably waiting for him. On the way there we passed some of the departing guests from his mother's party. True to form this elegant group stood chatting happily thirty yards from the floodlit corpse and quite oblivious of it. I thought of how peaceful the body of the young man had looked, of how surprised he would have been if he had known this was going to happen to him. I wondered how often he had driven past this hotel, of how little he could have expected this brutal and slightly ridiculous turn of events. I wondered who he was, and whether he was indeed a terrorist or just some nondescript victim who had come conveniently to hand. He could have been anyone. He could have been killed by either side to make some obscure point of black propaganda. He looked peaceful enough, but he also looked abandoned. Looking at him with his clean hair and clean clothes I had understood for the first time the meaning of the Seventh Corporal Work of Mercy, to bury the dead.

In the hotel lobby I met a reporter from I.T.N. who was eager to enlist the incident as support in an argument we had been having earlier about the relative merits of life in Nicaragua and El Salvador. This reaction interested me. I asked him if, looking at the body, he had not felt that it should be buried, or that someone should pray for the man, or send for a priest. He guffawed happily in response, and assured me that he felt no such thing. Perhaps most of all, I remember from that incident the dignity of the few Salvadorans there, the detective, the angry young man, the taxi-drivers and others. They stood back out of respect for death, though they were so familiar with it, and though the corpse was that of a hostile stranger. Nor did they say, 'Rhubarb, rhubarb.'

One of the more convivial visitors to the bar of the Camino Real was a French diplomat called Pierre. I teased him about the idleness of his job and he replied that, on the contrary, France and El Salvador did some very good trade. There were very few cows left in El Salvador, but a considerable need for milk. France made up the deficit in the form of huge amounts of milk powder. The powder was supplied to the Ministry of Agriculture and then distributed round the country by the regional military commanders, chiefly to refugee camps. He had noticed that the colonels who handled this trade made a 100 per cent profit on the deal. They were in a strong commercial position since they enjoyed a monopoly of milk supply to a captive market, the refugee population, whose size they were well-placed to increase.

Pierre said that these colonels were characteristic members of El Salvador's new prosperous class. It had always been said that the country was run by fourteen families, the original 'oligarchy', but most of those people had left the country by now. (I had looked up the names of the fourteen families in the San Salvador telephone directory, but had only found four of them.) The rest had taken their profits from 150 years of coffee planting and gone to live in Miami where life was more comfortable. The fourteen families had been replaced, at the latest count, by 244 families, the new oligarchy who were making a fortune out of the economic crisis. U.S. aid was running at $400 million a year and Pierre estimated that half of that was being pocketed. This was a very lucrative civil war to be involved in. Profits were available for everyone, from senior soldiers who took commission on helicopters to infantrymen who sold their guns and ammunition to the guerrillas. He was not at all surprised by the elegance of the baby-shower crowd. He foresaw no early solution to the national crisis. Meanwhile he recommended the beach.

The road to La Libertad was excellent; broad and newly-surfaced it swept down between woods and hills to the tatty, humid little

Pacific port named for liberty. I went there with Bill from the *Los Angeles Times*. Bill said that one could eat very well on the beach in La Libertad. There were open-air lobster restaurants, cold beer, and surf. Bill described food very well. Once I went with him to 'the best Chinese restaurant in San Salvador'. Bill insisted on discussing the menu with the proprietor, in Mandarin. This took some time. He then described in detail the succulent meal he had ordered. We then ate a reasonably good dinner of a somewhat different description. I asked him why the dishes appeared to be so different from the ones he had described. Bill explained to me that the proprietor had lived for so long in El Salvador that he no longer spoke very good Mandarin.

La Libertad was a surprise. It was hot and humid, but sitting by the sea wall under a palm roof, it was possible to catch a little breeze as the waiter brought the uncooked food around instead of a menu. There were lobsters, shrimps, oily black crayfish, fresh white fish and trays full of crabs in dressed psychedelic colours. Noisy, family parties sat around, sipping their well-chilled beer. A swollen, wrinkled old lady in a purple mini-skirt ordered a handsome group of grandchildren on and off the beach. These people seemed to have very little on their minds. Several groups of musicians wandered around touting for custom, and, at the next table, a little boy was stood on a chair to sing *mariachi* songs in a piping voice to the accompaniment of a full Mexican band. The band were amused but did not stint their efforts, and the infant's mother encouraged him by loyally fixing on him a soulful gaze. On the black, volcanic sand below the wall a fair-haired girl with olive skin and pale green eyes, dressed in a bikini, was permitting a group of younger boys to bury her in mud. Above her a line of plumper girls sat on the edge of the terrace, painting their faces in vivid colours with the aid of tiny mirrors, the final result clashing horribly with the astonishing shades of their swimming costumes. They kept a pet squirrel on a lead, fed it on scraps and leant over the balustrade to appraise, with expert innocence, the exact degree of surrender offered by the mud-covered girl below. Long, high Pacific rollers crashed on to the beach a few yards away. The occasional swimmer ventured out, ducking beneath the waves as they broke, to avoid swallowing the thick, yellow foam.

Somebody said that the beach was noted for its sharks and undertow, but La Libertad was too peaceful to make it likely. Here on a Sunday afternoon one could almost believe oneself in a country like one's own.

11

Detour through a Backwater

One of the greatest things the entire Central American area has 'going for it' is the people. They are smiling, genuinely friendly and a kindly people. The do not resent the presence of foreigners in their country.

From *A Guide for North Americans to Retirement in Central America*

My chosen way out of El Salvador was by the northern road to Honduras. I had met a diplomat in Guatemala who had said that he imagined I would avoid this road as it was contested. There was a sneer in his voice which I resented; all right for him, I thought, sitting in the safety of his embassy compound.

There was still supposed to be a bus running to the northern border, though the road came under guerrilla control not far outside San Salvador. Bill, not for the first time, tried to talk me out of going by bus. We went down the list of people known to have been killed on the bus. There was a human rights official from an organisation based in Mexico. She was compiling a report on army atrocities. She had become an army atrocity herself. Three Christian Democratic mayors had been taken off a bus and shot. A reporter from *Time* – carrying a letter addressed to '*Señores Comandantes y Jefes de Cuerpos Militares*' – had been seriously wounded by soldiers while making a bus journey. A social worker had been taken off the bus one week before the Pope's visit and shot by the army. Michael Klein, a holiday-maker from the United States, had taken the bus to San Miguel, the same bus I had travelled on the previous year. Soldiers searching the bus at a routine check-point had taken him away and shot him, after a cursory examination, on the grounds that he was Chinese and therefore communist. On this occasion a more thorough investigation than usual was mounted by the United States embassy. Eventually some relatively responsible person said that it was not because he was Chinese but because he had been confused with a guerrilla of similar name. He had been shot 'while trying to escape'. But the bullet wound in his back was inflicted at point-blank range. For the murder of Michael Klein one Salvadoran soldier was eventually arrested.

It seemed to me that the chief danger of travelling by bus was of being shot casually by the army instead of, as in San Salvador, being shot by the death squad, casually. Because the murderers were supposedly identifiable these deaths on the road became better known. Still, for Bill the bus was an avoidable risk. He tried to dissuade me from travelling on it because he thought it was dangerous; but subconsciously, he may have had a further reason. Bill was a highly professional journalist. Journalists hate other journalists doing something they haven't done. It means they may have to do it themselves eventually. Bill had a nine-month posting to El Salvador and he was calculating the odds sensibly.

In the end I didn't take the bus anyway. A car hired by Bengt, a Swedish journalist, was being driven up to La Palma, a town close to the border, and Bengt offered me a lift. We were accompanied by Lucia, a freelance from Italy. Lucia looked fun. She spoke excellent English and said what she thought.

'I am very left-wing,' she told me. 'In the Italian election I voted for the communists. I work for *Manifesto*, which is a left-wing weekly. I cannot work for many Italian papers because I am so left-wing. Also I have tax problems if I earn too much. My accountant has warned me.'

We set off for the border, driven by Carlos, a taciturn but experienced guide for the international press. As we left town Carlos asked if we wanted to stop at the garbage dump to see that morning's collection of corpses. He said that there were three of them, all headless. The previous day there had been eight. Bengt and I agreed that we could do without this detour – to the surprise, and then indignation, of Carlos who could not understand why an official party of three foreign journalists should refuse to inspect the latest corpses. Instead we sped along the road north, relying on Lucia for most of the conversation. Carlos thought that since we were going into the guerrilla zone it might be an idea to get them some cigarettes. Lucia said she would buy them. Then she said 'What brand do they like?' Carlos thought that quite funny. Shortly after the 'headless corpses offer' she started to lecture me about the English. 'The English', she told me, 'are the most immoral nation in the world. That is why I like them.' She considered that the English had been driven by need to reconcile morality and reality. What they called 'pragmatic' others called immoral. She said she was fascinated by the national character although she had never been to England.

She said that she came from a town near Naples and that in Italy the English were remembered for being very brutal during the liberation. They had even been hard on the partisans. They were cold and cruel. I told her that this was because there had been a belief in Italy that all the Moroccan soldiers were English. All the atrocities carried out by this undisciplined horde had been blamed on the English. She would not buy this. 'We knew all about the Moroccans,' she said. 'The English were much worse than them.' She said that the English soldiers had stood in sharp contrast to the Americans. 'We loved the Americans. They were large, rich, generous and many were of Italian descent. We thought them a little bit stupid and very kind. But the English were very bad.' I said this was probably because the English troops involved were of the 8th Army. She must not forget that those men had been fighting the Germans and the Italians in the desert for four years before they got to Italy. Unlike the Americans, who had been fighting no one, the 8th Army had become very rough. She remained unimpressed. She said I was just trying to make excuses. The fact was that the English were very cold and very immoral. They were the most immoral people in the world. That was why she admired them.

Having established the moral deficiencies of the English, Lucia turned to Bengt and said, 'Which group of guerrillas do you like best?' This question caused Carlos to make choking noises. The idea of establishing a personal preference between the various factions pleased him greatly. Undeterred by his reaction Lucia stated that the E.R.P., the People's Revolutionary Army, were preferable because they were really Maoists, which made them 'the hardest'. Bengt and I agreed that in distinguishing the political virility of Marxist factions we were prepared to rely on the judgment of an Italian leftist.

Shortly after buying the cigarettes we reached the river bridge which marked the border of the province of Chalatenango, and the end of army control. The soldiers at this check-point were not bothering to be charming. Each of the few vehicles passing along the road was thoroughly searched and the occupants were then questioned.

'Are you from here?' said the soldier.

'*I* am from here,' said Carlos. 'These three are *periodistas*. Two of them are going to look at the frontier. One of them is crossing.'

'Which one? Everybody get out.'

Carlos, throughout this encounter, tried to keep the initiative. He drew the soldier's attention away from my notebooks towards my luggage. He then presented my passport. He told the soldier that he could ask me any questions he wished. At this stage Carlos opened up a bit of a distance between himself and me. But the soldier, who could think of no questions, had discovered that I was carrying a map. 'Let me see that,' he said. He stared at it for some time, luckily finding that it was unmarked. Later Carlos said that they were always looking for marks on a map. Because it was unmarked Carlos decided to close the interview. 'It is an Avis map,' he said. 'This is an Avis car.' Of course it was not an Avis car but Carlos was a good judge of this soldier's ability and confidence. As he folded away the map Carlos decided that we would now go. We did, and the soldier raised no objection. It was easy to see how, left to himself, such a soldier might have succeeded in causing trouble. Such a man, under the command of a drunken corporal, might well have been the person who decided that Michael Klein was a Chinaman. He would probably have been basing his judgment about Chinamen on information provided by a strip-cartoon book like *Denuncia*.

After the river, the road continued into guerrilla country, at first an empty, fertile plain. This was clearly an area which a determined military force could have occupied. Then we began to climb into the hills. There were frequent deep ravines and overhanging cliffs on all sides. This was an area for ambushes and it became obvious why the army had withdrawn across the river. Lucia, by now, was expounding her theory of travel writing. She told me that very few Italians ever travelled in the way in which I was travelling. She explained to me that this sort of travel had in fact been invented by the English in order to find for themselves a pleasant mode of voluntary exile. They did this because they did not like England. They were made uneasy by its immorality. She quite understood their point of view. Such journeys as the English made in this way were amusing, but they were frivolous. My task as a traveller could not be compared in seriousness with hers as a reporter. I agreed.

Just then we passed, by the side of the road, an elderly gringo in the habit of a Franciscan friar. So isolated did this old priest seem that Bengt suggested we should stop and talk to him. I was in favour of this idea but we were both overruled by Lucia who, glancing out of the window at the brown habit, blue T-shirt and grey hair of this stooped and frail figure said, 'No. I know *that* already.' She said that he was Italian and that she did not want to talk to him, particularly. We would continue. I asked her why she was against a roadside interview.

'Such men,' she said, 'when I see them, they are so *dirty*, on the clothes, the feet, the hands – it is *disgusting*.' We drove on.

Somewhere in the hills we came across the first sign of life, a banner strung across the road. There was no one around. The last army post was at least fifteen miles behind us. High on the hill above the banner stood a house, but there was no movement around it. The banner referred to the death of 'Comrade Ana Maria', still said to have been ice-picked to death by agents of the C.I.A. It was an E.P.L. banner. Who were the E.P.L.? I had heard of the F.P.L. and the E.R.P. There were also the F.A.R.N., the F.D.R., the F.M.L.N., the M.L.P., the M.N.R., the P.R.S., the L.P.-28, the B.P.R., the V.P., the M.R.C., the C.R.M., the P.R.T.C., the F.S.R., the F.U.E.R.S.A., the F.A.P.U., *and* the D.R.U. Not to mention the Communist Party of Salvador (P.C.S.) and at least eighteen other *un*armed opposition parties. But who were the E.P.L.? Whoever they were they had received the same version of history on this empty, mountain road as had been chanted by the students on the Alameda in Mexico City two months earlier.

We reached La Palma by midday. For the last three or four years the hills around it had been controlled by the guerrillas. This little town of 12,000 inhabitants had fallen six months earlier. Its loss was quite a serious blow to the government; by taking the town the guerrillas were able to close the international road to the north whenever they wished. There was little immediate evidence of the battle that had taken place. A crude wooden sign at the entrance to the town still said 'Welcome', as it had when La Palma was known only for its local crafts. Lucia said that she had once entered a town swarming with uniformed men whom she had questioned about 'the situation' and 'recent events'. Only when she saw one of the 'soldiers' painting a wall with the words 'Victory to the Revolution' did she realise that she had crossed the front line. In La Palma there were no uniformed men to be seen at all.

The people of the town were quiet and watchful rather than welcoming. I found out later that the guerrillas were indeed in the town, the approach of our car, prominently marked with the letters 'T.V.', had been noted, but they chose to remain unseen. The town was in truth rather over-governed by the standards of Central America. Since January all hard liquor had been banned. The E.P.L. thought that the people of La Palma were too drunk. Now they were only allowed to drink beer, and such illicit moonshine as they could improvise. Perhaps it was this sobriety which accounted for their rather thoughtful manner. In the middle of the plaza was an enormous tree ('*la palma*') beneath which a single table had been set up for the sale of fruit and vegetables. But no one was buying. The tree looked about one hundred feet in circumference. I went to the Franciscan mission church at the side of the square. Painted on the wall behind the altar was a giant St Francis in communion with a small crucified Christ. 'Peace and Love', said the poster commemorating the 8th centenary of the birth of the saint; the floor and the benches gleamed with polish and self-confidence, the whole place was spotless.

I began to take photographs of the children outside. Bengt had wandered off somewhere and Lucia started to talk, once again with great urgency. 'It is difficult for a woman alone in this country. The men of El Salvador are pigs.' We walked over to where a young mother was chopping melons into slices and setting them out enticingly on a bright, clean cloth. The mother smiled when I asked permission for her photograph. 'Their attitude to a woman alone . . .' Lucia was still whispering urgently, 'is *disgusting*.' The children of the stallholder now came forward to inspect us. Lucia, with her short black hair, olive trousers and brown shirt, could have passed for a *guerrillera*. 'They are all the same, the men.' Her tirade was reaching a climax. 'And if you go out with another one . . . *they don't even get angry*! They are pigs!'

Just then my attention was distracted from this insult, apparently about the worst one could offer to an Italian woman, by the abrupt arrival of one of the pigs of El Salvador on a bolting mule. One hand clutching his straw hat, the other tugging a rein, he was shaken across the plaza like a sack of corn and carried out of town with a great clatter of hooves, still just in place and pursued by several excited small boys. Expecting to see where he had fallen off, Lucia and I walked down the street and came to what had formerly been the government police station. It was made recognisable by the heavy-calibre holes pitting its walls. Here, in January, the army had put up some resistance. The only other house that was damaged carried the sign of Dr J. Antonio Lopez Barra, Advocate and Notary. Opposite a slogan recorded the change in municipal ownership. Beneath the hammer and sickle it read, 'Long live the politico-military campaign of the revolutionary heroes of January of the F.M.L.N. and the F.P.L.!' F.P.L.? What happened to the E.P.L.? The F.P.L. were the Farabundo Martí Popular Forces of Liberation, and the F.M.L.N. were the Farabundo Martí Front for National Liberation. Another slogan, round the bandstand in the plaza, said, 'Viva El E.P.L.-F.M.L.N.-F.D.R.!' The F.D.R. were the Democratic Revolutionary Front. So the E.P.L.-F.M.L.N.-F.D.R. was a front formed by the E.P.L. (whoever they were) and the Farabundo Martí Front for National Liberation and the Democratic Revolutionary Front. All these 'Fronts' showed that Salvadoran guerrilla organisations did not just split up, they also amalgamated. But who were the E.P.L.? Were they the F.P.L. misspelt? Lucia was unable to reach a definite conclusion on this point. Whoever they were, she was not terribly impressed with them. Their slogans were painted in yellow. There should have been red paint somewhere in La Palma.

Beyond the town the road fell steeply to the border. Here,

extraordinarily, there was a government customs post. The men who guarded it had been cut off with the fall of La Palma but they continued to do their job on sufferance of the guerrillas. They were supplied by helicopters. It would have been a simple matter for the E.P.L.-F.M.L.N.-F.D.R.-F.P.L. to have destroyed this post and so closed the northern frontier. But there was no river gorge here, and if the guerrillas had stayed on the border they would have been attacked by the Honduran army. They seemed content instead to threaten the interruption they could impose at any time. As it was, the bus service ran only with their agreement.

I said goodbye to Lucia and Bengt at the customs post. Lucia lamented the briefness of our meeting as we drove down the hill; but 'that was the life of a foreign reporter', the work came first even if she did not always like it. And I had to continue my journey. I needed, as an Englishman, to travel in order to find my place of exile. I needed to leave what was familiar in order to find what I could recognise.

I was sorry to shake her warm hand, and to look back at her and Bengt and Carlos, waving goodbye to me as I carried my suitcases across the line, my last sight of El Salvador.

My original plans did not take me to Honduras at all, a country which I had visited briefly the previous year and which had then seemed to be out of the battle. Now – forced to deviate from the direct road to Nicaragua by the destruction of the eastern customs post – I wanted to pass through Honduras as quickly as possible. This intention was frustrated as soon as I reached the border town of Nueva Octopeque. The bus to San Pedro had gone. I engaged a taxi-driver to pursue it, and as we chased up the mountain my spirits rose. The driver turned his radio to some crazy music, the air cooled as we climbed, and I felt a sense of exhilaration about leaving El Salvador. The Hondurans, anyway, made a cheerful contrast at first acquaintance with the Salvadorans. They are calmer, less defensive, happier to see a strange face. I remembered how the soldier at the last Salvadoran check-point had asked to see my *armas*. I had replied with some indignation that I carried none. But it had not been a threatening question. To him it had been incomprehensible that anyone should cross Chalatenango without carrying a gun. I was glad to have left the state of war.

We raced after the bus, occasionally catching a glimpse of it higher up the mountain – quite close as the crow flew, but separated from us by many hidden curves. When we caught it, in the blustery wind by the side of the road, I handed over a large sum of money to my taxi-driver. He was flushed with the success of the pursuit and in no mood to bargain. It turned out to be a second-class bus which was already overcrowded. I had to stand near the front in the usual hunched position but after a while forced my way to the back and was able to make a seat out of my bag. Here, wedged between the last two seats, I gazed out of the back window which bore the portrait of another gringo Christ and the words – 'Señor, into your hands I commend my passengers.'

There was very little traffic on the road; even with the Pan American Highway cut, this route between Honduras and El Salvador was not much used. But it was a slow journey none the less. Over an hour was lost at three army check-points, at each of which the soldiers insisted on going through every single item of luggage on the bus. Compared with those carried out in Guatemala and El Salvador, the searches were inefficient and poorly supervised. It was a further sign of peaceful times.

Darkness fell while the third and most chaotic search was being carried out and I finally accepted that I would not after all be taking a connecting bus to Tegucigalpa that evening, that I would not be going to Nicaragua on the following day and that my hopes of starting the last leg of my journey were over. At that point I had been travelling alone for nearly three months and was beginning to get heartily sick of my own company. One makes wild plans at such times, contrary to Lucia's theories, to escape back to something familiar or to the bright new prospect which stands waiting at the end of every long journey. To be checked in these dreams by the fumbling inefficiency of the Honduran soldiers was exasperating.

San Pedro was announced by a cloying, rich smell, evidently a sugar refinery. In the darkness we had passed over the rigid spine of the Isthmus and were now back in the steamy climate of the Atlantic littoral. Lying back by a window in the bus, for I had got a seat at last, I could watch the night, watch the stars come out, watch the fierce glow of the bush fires which were set to clear the land – some mere dots on the hillside, others jagged crescents of flame and smoke. I could listen to the babble of the little girl in the seat behind, her sticky fingers occasionally brushing my hair. All around were the heat and ease of the Hondurans, rising through the darkness; and there was the breeze, which confirmed our racing passage, and the reflections of the headlights and the dappled shadows tearing by. I felt solitary and content.

That night in San Pedro I went to dinner at a restaurant offering Castilian food. It was owned by a man from Madrid. I asked him how long he had been in Honduras. 'Eleven years,' he said. 'A long time,' he added and looked despondent. I asked him why he had left Spain. 'I don't know,' he said.

San Pedro de Sula is a tropical Atlantic town. In Central America the people of the Atlantic coast are mainly of African descent, hired originally in the West Indies to work on the banana plantations. They speak Spanish and English, a sing-song Jamaican English which is pleasant to hear. But the community is slowly changing its English culture for a Spanish one, and on a Sunday evening these African people gather in families and make a formal *paseo* through the streets and round the parks. The people of the coast are the poorest people in Central America. There is little work apart from the docks and the banana farms, which are owned by American fruit companies and are still the scene of violent strikes, violently put down.

One Sunday, in Puerto Limón, Costa Rica, while the town slept its siesta, I had walked on to the wooden quays to watch the bananas being loaded on to a boat owned by the Del Monte fruit company. The banana trains went out on to the rotting wooden piles and shunted up and down in the glaring heat. You had to keep a sharp lookout for loose wagons. If there was a signalling procedure they kept it to themselves.

The dock foreman was lying on a crate, resting. He was a vast man with a blue-black skin and pouring with sweat. I have never seen a man look so peaceful and so hot. He declined to have his photograph taken. After resting for a few minutes he stood under a water-pipe to cool off. His day's food was a yard of raw sugar cane and three cobs of sweet corn. He said his wife was living on an abandoned banana plantation beyond the swamps; that meant she was squatting. The owners call such families who work abandoned banana farms for their own profit '*parasitos*'.

The profits to be made from the tropical fruit business are very acceptable and walking round to the stern of the Del Monte banana boat I noticed one reason why. This North American company had registered the boat in Panama, thereby taking advantage of the less stringent safety and labour regulations.

However it was not in Costa Rica but here in Honduras that the power of the largest Northern American company, the United Fruit Co., was broken by the Atlantic coast plantation workers. It was in 1954. At that time the United Fruit Co. was the parallel government of Honduras. The decisions taken in its offices were of much greater importance than any taken in the presidential palace. It would not be an exaggeration to say that the successive presidents of Honduras were the overseers for United Fruit. One of these presidents, Tiburcio Carias, had been such an energetic overseer that he had introduced the air-bombing raid on to the American continent to put down one plantation workers' revolt. But on 4 May 1954 a strike started in Honduras that has remained a complete mystery to this day. Without any warning or apparent organisation 40,000 plantation workers, acting as one, refused to go back to work until they had received a 100 per cent wage increase, free housing and medical care. Four months later, after losing $20 million, United Fruit capitulated. In the words of *The Twenty Latin Americas* by Marcel Niedergang, 'this marked the beginning of the decline of the United Fruit Co. in Central America'.

Next day in Tegucigalpa I remembered a further reason for my reluctance to return to Honduras. Tegucigalpa is the only city in Central America where I have seen the extreme form of urban poverty. Honduras is a relatively large country with a relatively small population, but there is only a small area of fertile land and although the United Fruit Co. has been induced to relax its grip on much of the best of it, there is still a drift to the cities. Most of the refugees come to Tegucigalpa.

In the main square, the Plaza Morazán, built around the

statue of General Francisco Morazán, the man who nearly united Central America, a young country woman, blind, head thrown back, stood on a street corner, sucking at a warm bottle of Coke as greedily as if she had just crossed a desert. Beside her two young men, strong but drunk and destitute, staggered together for support. They had faces like angels, in Europe they could have earned £500 a day as photographic models, but in Tegucigalpa they were without hope. I booked a hotel room, wrote my notes and later walked across the town to a restaurant. On the steps of the Cathedral old men were already asleep, rolled into the ledges beneath its carved stone embellishments.

The meal when it came was poor. The rice was tasteless, the steak was tough, the sauce too thin, the beer too warm. As I sat there in critical mood, digesting it, a small boy stole into the room. He went from table to table and he wanted food. Several people turned him away. He came to a table where the pompous head of a prosperous family was entertaining his wife and children. They sat upright in their best clothes, nibbling politely at what was put before them. It was a formal occasion and the children were living up to it. Then this stinking ragamuffin was suddenly among them, his dirty little face on a level with their clean table-cloth, his fetid hand stretched out towards the food. I waited, expecting a memorable piece of bad behaviour. Instead the father ordered away the waiters and told his children to give the little boy as much as he could carry. They cracked open bread rolls and filled them with meat and sauce. They rolled spaghetti up in tortillas, they filled his shirt with fruit, and in a moment he was trotting out of the door leaving a succulent trail of gravy and ketchup in his path. I left the restaurant shortly afterwards and found him sitting on the steps, surrounded by several older children, all of them too busy eating even to beg. Further down the street more small boys had fallen asleep. They competed for the strip of pavement which was sheltered by the window-sills which projected from the city's new office blocks.

I went to a bar where the *mariachis* sang. There was an old man there in a stained brown suit; he wore a patchy yellow moustache and a dead carnation. He carried a filthy brown trilby. Not even the holes in his sneakers could puncture his faded style. Against all the noise made by the *mariachi* bands, this old gentleman went from table to table, offering to sing to the accompaniment of his banjo. His voice had gone, and he preferred to sing 'Granada'. Most of those who agreed to listen to him soon regretted it, but so dignified was his manner and so courteous were most of his customers that it was never long before he found a new audience. For this imposition he charged even less than the bands of professional musicians. Looking at his clothes more closely I realised that they had darkened over the years. I had found the white suit and the cheap music.

The bar in this room was about fifty feet long, the room as long again. The floor was tiled and sheltered by a lean-to asbestos roof. The wall behind the table where I sat was made of bamboo canes, two inches thick. My elderly troubadour, having inflicted on me 'Granada', one of my least favourite songs, asked me to choose something else. *Mas tarde*, I said, but he launched himself into a samba tune, possibly of that name. Leaning back to distance myself as far as possible from this spectacle, I found a grubby hand flapping by my ear. It had been inserted through a hole in the bamboo. Behind the hand two eyes, supplicating, an open mouth, another hand gesturing for food, urgently. An elderly chicken leg, placed on my table by the waitress, passed from me to the nearest hand and was carried swiftly through the bamboo screen. I pressed my face to the hole. He was wearing very old jeans and a ragged vest. I thought I could just hear the crunching of a chicken bone.

Most of the men in the bar wore large, white cowboy hats. These were a Honduran fashion, not requiring the presence of horses. I had not seen men as drunk as the cowboys in this bar for some time, if ever. They weaved. Young men sitting twenty yards from the door covered sixty yards of ground on their way out. When they were sitting they looked fine. The trouble started when they stood up. Interlaced with the course they set for the street was the course set by others, even younger. The street boys did not weave. They veered. They came through the door as though they were heading for the toilets on the far side of the room. On their way they tacked from plate of crisps, to bread roll, to chicken leg to sugar bowl. Anything they could eat, they took. When they reached the far side of the room they turned and veered back by several other routes. No one objected to what they did as long as they kept moving. The waitresses kept them supplied. Though dressed in trim yellow and white tunics these women spat on the floor with the best of the customers, the long, well-aimed globs providing a regular visual distraction. As the street boys made their raids, the waitresses turned a blind eye, occasionally leaving unguarded bread or sugar on empty tables. Some of the raiders limped from the after effects of polio, some were half-witted, one was blind and had to be led by a friend. The only person likely to keep them out had retired from the struggle. He was the security man, armed with a pistol, who leant against the bar, his back to events, sipping a drink and picking his teeth with the business end of a ballpoint pen.

At one table a party of farmers, evidently wealthier than the other customers, were entertaining their wives. One of them, a man built like an ox, was so drunk he wanted to sing all the songs. Unable to manage a coherent line, he seized instead an instrument from the nearest musician, a tiny and nervous violinist. This went on for some time, the enormous farmer exposing his inability to play violin, trumpet or guitar. Every time he rose the members of the band manoeuvred to avoid him. There was no question of resisting his charms, he was too drunk and far too big. On each occasion after two bars of cacophony, his even larger brother, the only man in the room prepared to do it, would rise, return the instrument to its owner and lead him back to his seat. Throughout this operation both brothers wore expressions of bemused goodwill, as though neither was sure who was rescuing whom. As they regained the table the cloud of unknowing around the mind of the younger would part; the mildest hint of embarrassment or protest would appear and, instantly, his keeper would whisk him into a violent samba, so restoring in full measure the drunk's happiness and stupidity. Thus these two enormous men would samba around for a while in each other's arms, in smart suits, high-heeled boots and cowboy hats, before returning to their seats. How clumsy they appeared, how crude, how loud; and yet how gently did the older manage the younger, dancing him with all necessary skill and patience. To save the pleasure of the party, to save the musicians' instruments and his brother's face, he was prepared to take such pains far into the night.

So absorbed was I in this scene I failed to notice that my

writing had attracted the attention of the people at the next table. One of these men stumbled towards me and, clutching my chair for support, demanded to know whether I was German, English or a gringo. It was to settle a bet. 'Come and drink with us,' he instructed. 'We are celebrating the birth of my father's sixth grandchild, my brother's first child and my friend's godson. We are very drunk.'

This was true. They told me that if the baby had been a girl they would not be celebrating, but as it was they had been drinking the little boy's health for two days. 'And there she is, the mother, my wife,' said the father, 'over there in the hospital. She cannot get drunk like us.' They asked me what I was doing in Honduras. I was a writer. And what did I write about? I wrote about Everything. And what would I write about Honduras? My story began to sound less and less probable. I said I would write that in Honduras everyone was extremely drunk. So, I had come thousands of miles from England to write that in Honduras everyone was extremely drunk? Had anyone ever heard a less likely story?

'This *hijo de puta*,' said the grandfather, 'is an *espía*. Look at his shirt.' He pulled at my shirt. 'Obviously only an *espía* would wear such a shirt! Aah! *Espía, hijo de puta*!' The situation was saved when a waitress handed me the notebook which I had left at my own table. The drunken party were then forced to agree that no *espía* would leave a notebook unguarded. For that level of stupidity you would need a man who had come all the way from England to write that in Honduras everyone was extremely drunk.

I walked back to my hotel across the Plaza Morazán. People were still strolling through the warm night, couples, families, old parties, taking the air. It was a peaceful place to pass through before one went to sleep. Somewhere in the plaza a child was crying, and gradually as I crossed the square, the noise grew into a disturbance. It bawled on, making life miserable for all who could hear. Then I saw the child in question. He was about five years old. He was walking backwards down the centre of the square, gazing up at his mother who followed behind. Round his neck was a loop of string, the end of which his mother held tightly. His mother was blind. She carried a heavy wooden box under one arm and there was an even smaller child, a girl, clinging to her skirts and walking silently behind her. In the mother's other hand she also carried a thick staff. On and on bawled the boy. His face, as he retreated, was raised to his mother's, and the string was taut. As he walked backwards he led her forward, slowly. He was on strike. His mother was trying to soothe him, she was talking to him quietly and smiling, always keeping a firm hold on the string. Her smile was ghastly. Her grey and black hair hung down to her shoulders, like coils of wire. Her face had once been beautiful, but her eyes now seemed sewn together, her mouth was crooked, the whole expression was lopsided, the smile – intended for reassurance – was frightening. It was this sight that the boy was gazing at and screaming to. Eventually the mother lost patience. Adrift in the middle of the plaza with her protesting guide, she jerked the string and took a swipe at him with her staff. The little boy dodged. He was able, by long experience, to take advantage of his mother's blindness. She kept her son on a lead because she could not trust him to guide her. But he was too young for his responsibilities. Unable to strike the boy she tried instead to soothe the girl, who was becoming anxious. The horror of the scene lay in the fact that one sympathised with this mother who kept her son on a string. The Hondurans turned to watch, then strolled on. Nobody offered to help the blind woman. Maybe they did nothing because they saw nothing, just the usual woman in the usual place, making her way home to her hovel on the hillside, past the statue of General Morazán, the man who had wanted to unite Central America.

That had been in 1842. The attempt to impose unity led to war throughout the Isthmus. During one battle an old Guatemalan general, who had been born in a village famous for its wet-nurses, was losing. He sent for a wet-nurse from his village and retired to his tent for the night. In the morning, refreshed, he emerged and won the battle. The leaders of the individual states hated General Morazán for his liberalism and when they caught him, they shot him. Then they erected this statue.

12

The Act of Love

'State Coercion is an Act of Love.'

Comandante Tomás Borge, (on being asked to identify a Christian element in communism)

'And what does this mean, trade union freedom? Trade union freedom means the division of the working class.'

Comandante Tomás Borge, May Day 1982

'If I were the government I'd have all priests bled once a month . . . for the sake of law and order.'

Flaubert, *Madame Bovary*

If you stand on a rise in the centre of Managua, you can see the rain squalls crossing the lake like columns of smoke; the edge of the storm can be marked against the far shore. Another squall chases along a mile or so behind. On a clear day you can count twenty-one volcanoes on the opposite shore. After a good lunch you can count twenty-five.

Managua, the capital of Nicaragua, has suffered as much from acts of God as anywhere in America. The city was rased by an earthquake in March 1931, and severely damaged by fire in 1936. It was rased again in December 1972, in one of the most celebrated of modern earthquakes. The city centre, all of it, fell to the ground in the night. Then it was damaged by fighting in 1978 and 1979. On my first visit in 1982 there were calamitous floods; several slum districts were swept into the lake.

I walked through that part of the city where the earth moved. The road system still followed its neat rectangles and crescents but it ran nowhere, it divided not blocks of buildings but empty grass plots. Wherever you go in Central America you are haunted by the wreckage of earthquake. There is not a country which cannot recount its historical and continuing disasters. The entire Isthmus is a geological fault. The people who settled on this part of the earth were fated to develop a vivid imagination and a belief in a malign deity. When Spanish priests came to the Isthmus they replaced the blood-stained altars of the Mayan and Aztec religions with a religion of forgiveness and a God of love. They tried to replace fear with trust. The first saint of New Spain was not some swordsman-inquisitor but Rosa of Lima, famous for her care of the Indians and her skill as a doctor. Bartolomé de las Casas, 'the beloved apostle of the Indians', was among the first to reach Nicaragua, a country which was colonised not from Mexico City but from Panama. But the message of Rosa of Lima and Bartolomé de las Casas died. It could not make itself heard in the explosive fusion of Spaniard and Indian. Spanish spirituality was weaker than the Indian spirits. Spanish greed overcame the Indian dream and the God of love. The mines of Central America were soon exhausted, and the surplus wealth of agriculture and base metals was not abundant enough to pay for charity. The rapacity of those who preyed on the people they governed was not tempered by the bishops of New Spain. The rich refused to share their wealth and it eventually occurred to their subjects that they must be forced instead to surrender it. The Church, not wishing to become entirely superfluous, limps along in the wake of this new idea, but nothing it does can equal the grandeur it had when it represented an idea of its own.

I wanted to see the Cathedral of Managua, ruined by the earthquake of 1972. I took a taxi through the barren prairies of the city centre. The taxi-driver, not a Marxist-Leninist, was excited to hear news of Margaret Thatcher. 'Oho, *la Barbina*', he said. '*Muy BRAVA, muy forte.*' And he flexed his biceps and flashed his gold teeth. I left him in the plaza muttering about Mrs Thatcher's 'eggs' and picked my way up the steps of the former Cathedral.

In Cartagó, a town in Costa Rica, there is a church that was wrecked by earthquakes in 1841 and again in 1910. A notice outside says that it was totally destroyed in the earthquake of Saint Antolin and totally destroyed again in the earthquake of

Santa Monica. You have to have a certain familiarity with earthquakes before you start naming them. That church is now a carefully tended garden, the resort of courting couples. Such is not the case with the Cathedral of Managua.

Here the marble steps are cracked and trees spring up in the gaps. The roof has fallen in. You enter a church and find yourself in the nave, in a miniature jungle, the home of birds and rats. In the centre of the sanctuary the swollen grey body of a rat was crawling with ants and flies. There are fallen pillars and crumbled slabs of marble lying everywhere, though much of the devotional furniture remains. The statue of Our Lady of Perpetual Succour has gone, the lighthouse painted on the wall behind continues to shine. One side-altar still offers the inscription, '*In manus tuas Domine commendo spiritum meum*', spelt out on either side of some dead Cardinal's coat of arms. The standing pillars are tottering, weakened by jagged vertical cracks. The Cathedral has been in this state for twelve years, though they say that one day it will be rebuilt. Until then the stone dove, the Paraclete, flocks with living birds and on the back of the empty tabernacle an unknown hand has scrawled '*Cristo presente! J. Cristo viene pronto! Preparate!*' That is the only sign of a continuing love or interest in this building, once the centre of its country's religious life. Outside the entrance portico the Sandinista government has erected scaffolding, but it is not there to support the building. It displays a poster of A. C. Sandino in a cowboy hat, thirty feet high, which blocks out the front view of the Cathedral. It was in front of such posters that the Pope had to say mass while the Sandinista mobs jeered and chanted. Given the problems of the Church in Nicaragua today it seems rather unlikely that this Cathedral will ever be rebuilt.

The ideological battlelines in Nicaragua are drawn up on the border. In the customs hall they scooped up all the Central American newspapers I had collected so carefully and threw them on the floor. Confiscated. All foreign newspapers banned. Later I was told that if I had said I was a journalist they would have let me keep them. That made it worse; a typical totalitarian solution, the creation of a privileged class who owed the government a favour. Feeling rather irritated I started to read the slogans which were displayed all round the hall. 'Welcome!' they said. They mentioned 'struggle', 'progress', 'fraternity' and 'revolution', all in glowing terms. 'The Sandinista National Liberation Front is the indubitable ['*indiscutible*'] vanguard of our People.' This indubitable announcement is *chalked up*, twice, absolutely no *discutible* about it.

These slogans are one of the characteristic sights of Nicaragua. You might think that five years after a revolution the government would have organised a poster system; but that would not be romantic. Romance is very important to the Sandinistas, romance and an infant mythology. It is important for this government, the most determined and efficient the country has been subjected to, that it should appear to be still, in some sense, unofficial, amateur, part of the ordinary people, as it was when it first came to power. '*No pasaran*' is one of the most popular refrains, a phrase made famous by the beleaguered left in the Spanish Civil War. The two situations have little in common, but that's the sort of association they encourage. At first the slogans seem slightly over-insistent. Later they become suffocating. One longs for someone, a genuine graffiti-artist not a government one, to paint up something dangerously independent like 'put a sock in it'.

After I left the Cathedral I walked through the slogans of Managua, feeling depressed. I wanted normal life where there were usually more than two sides to a question. There was a girl on guard outside the house of the Defence Minister. She wore khaki and carried a sub-machine-gun, and her hair was braided and pinned up to frame her face. An older woman who resembled her was standing on the pavement outside the wire barricade. The older woman, in contrast to her daughter, was fashionably dressed. She was talking to the girl and making her laugh. The girl laughed easily, privately, perhaps at something a relative had said at some family meeting. This was an unofficial visit, a moment snatched from the strict timetable of military revolution. The mother stopped talking when I drew near and looked at me hard until I had passed on. She thought she might get her daughter into trouble by talking to her while she was on guard. The daughter felt nothing improper about her conversation. She was on guard duty and she was talking to her mother. So what?

Further down the street, under a large tree, in a small garden, a woman with grey hair sat back in an armchair she had carried out from the house. She had her feet up on a box. Behind her stood a small boy, equipped with a pair of tweezers, who picked the nits out of her hair and dropped them neatly into a steel bowl placed by his side. There seemed to be plenty of family life in this town. I walked on through Managua, and eventually found the Museum of the Revolution.

Nicaragua is one of those countries which a lot of people think they know about even though they have never been there. Others go there and find it is exactly as they expected, they might as well have stayed at home. The actress Julie Christie once returned to England from Nicaragua and wrote a letter to the *Observer* in which she suggested that there was more electoral freedom in Nicaragua than there was in Britain. It is for enthusiasts such as her that the Sandinistas have created the Museum of the Revolution. You know what you are in for here from the first exhibit, which is stacked outside the building. The placard reads, 'Barricade of paving stones, the essential trench of the urban struggle.' Opposite it loom the shattered brass hindquarters of the equestrian statue to Somoza's father which, during the period of his dictatorship, stood outside the national stadium and was illuminated every night. The human figure has disappeared but the horse's arse is on display. This is a People's museum.

The background to Nicaraguan politics, on cursory examination, seems concerned more with the rivalries of competing clans and families than with the world struggle between Marx and Capital. Augusto Cesar Sandino, the original Sandinista, was an Indian guerrilla who made his reputation ambushing U.S. marines in the 1930s. Although Sandino wanted land reform his ability to discomfort the gringos turned him into a national hero. Sandino's activities were brought to a triumphant climax by the election of Roosevelt in 1933. Roosevelt ordered the U.S. Marines home and Sandino was able to enter Managua. There he was warmly welcomed by the families who had ruled Nicaragua since it was founded. They were divided into conservative and liberal factions and it was the violence of their quarrels which had led to the intervention of U.S. Marines. Now at last they could unite – against land reform. Sandino was photographed with the leading dignitaries and kissed on both cheeks. It was a classical example of the *abrazo*, the Judas embrace. He was then invited to a banquet by the head of the National Guard, Anastasio Somoza, and murdered while he was eating. It was in that spectacular act of treachery that the 'Sandinista' movement was born. But it would be wrong to say that the Sandinista movement stands for 'No political murders during banquets'. Rather it stands for, 'Those who murder people while they are eating will also suffer indigestion'. In 1956, after twenty years of power, Anastasio Somoza attended a formal banquet held by the Liberal Party in León. There was an orchestra playing and he was gunned down during a noisy passage. Somoza was succeeded by the head of the National Guard, his son, also called Anastasio. Anastasio Jnr, who was overthrown by the Sandinistas, and many others, in 1979, died in Paraguay where he had placed himself under the protection of General Alfredo Stroessner. His armoured car was hit by a rocket. General Stroessner said that the assassination was carried out by Argentinian *monteñeros*. The Sandinistas said they did it. Some people suspected that General Stroessner did it because he wanted a quiet life: the rocket was just an unusually warm *abrazo*.

There is nothing about any of this in the Museum of the Revolution. Instead we have the familiar mythology of the Left, in embryonic form. It retells in pictures and documents and ancient guns the story of Pancho Villa, minus the accusations of banditry. Those involved in the early stages of the proletarian struggle, in 1914, pre-Sandino, are called 'the sons of sorrow'. Then we have the time in the hills, the period of reflection. A group of Sandino's followers are pictured 'deep in the Segovian mountains' in 1931; that is two years before the triumphant entry into Managua. But oddly enough the flag they have unfurled is not the hammer and sickle. It is the skull and crossbones. One wonders how much of Marx, A. C. Sandino read. The Museum makes its points in simple fashion. There are pictures of both Kennedy and Nixon with Somoza; there are pictures of fat bishops in full canonicals cutting up a Somoza cake. All the captured 'fascist' guns have pearl handles and silver chasing. The guns of the heroic revolutionaries tend to be stuck together with sellotape. There is a large armoured car in which the heroic Sandinistas of the western front engaged the Somocista National Guard in León. Then there is a much smaller tank, a '*ridiculo tanque*', which the fascist dictator Benito Mussolini presented to old man Somoza. Finally there is the centrepiece of the collection, the Somoza exhibit. They have pinned every medal he was given on to his uniform jacket, making it look like the costume of a pearly king. A stone head has been severed from one of his statues, his pyjamas are on display, so are the U.S. Marines' boy scout hat and the 'Our Leader' badge. There are two stone blocks with iron rings embedded in them, said to have been taken from the wall of his torture chamber. The exhibit is called 'Anastasio Somoza – the Last Marine' and is in itself memorable enough to justify a visit.

From their first day in power the Sandinistas have broken the promises they made to Nicaragua. Somoza was not overthrown by them alone. They had struggled unsuccessfully for years before a popular insurrection gave them the victory. But, with the National Guard defeated, the Sandinistas had all the guns. A democratic coalition was formed but it never had any power; that was always reserved for the Central Committee of the Sandinista Front and for the party's leaders or '*comandantes*'.

They first promised to pass a fundamental statute guaranteeing a plural society, a mixed economy and freedom of expression and religion. Comandante Daniel Ortega has since said that people might as well 'forget about the fundamental statute'. Instead there has been press censorship, political control of the judiciary, and a ban on opposition political activity and on independent trade unions. The Archbishop of Managua, who was one of their supporters before they won, but who has since become one of their most outspoken critics, has been humiliated and ridiculed, and divisions within the Catholic Church have been skilfully exploited.

Among those who supported the Archbishop was Father Bismark Carballo. One day, viewers of Sandinista television were surprised to see him parading naked in the streets of the town of Masaya with a naked woman of his acquaintance. The Sandinistas said that he had been caught in bed with her. He said that he had been visiting her house when armed men had broken in, forced them both to undress and told them to go outside where there happened to be a television crew waiting. Most Nicaraguans believed Father Bismark and thought he had been framed. In any event it did not do him great damage. Ever since he has been known as Father *Caballo*, or 'Father Stallion', in tribute to his most glamorous moment. Other priests who criticise the regime have been expelled or beaten up. The mobs have also been directed against their churches. Three Catholic college lecturers have been expelled and an auxiliary Bishop of Managua suffered head injuries after being attacked by a mob.

The Sandinistas do not bother to deny any of this. They justify it, and it is not difficult for them to do so, by reference to the state of emergency, and the 'political, economic and military aggression against Nicaragua' organised by the United States. That is the great triumph of U.S. foreign policy. It has acted as the indispensable midwife of an infant communist state, exactly the result which Washington has been most anxious to avoid.

The international supporters of the left in Nicaragua, who usually live in countries free of 'state coercion', find no trouble in accepting the Sandinistas' justifications. For Nicaraguans who hated Somoza, but who do not want to live in a communist state either, the future is a less exhilarating prospect. Pedro Chamorro is the editor of *La Prensa*, the biggest-selling paper in the country despite the censorship, and, with Archbishop Obando y Bravo, he is the chief spokesman of the unofficial opposition. He told me something of his life and of the life of everyone who works for a newspaper opposed to the Sandinistas. *La Prensa* is an evening paper so it is seen by the censor in the morning. Every page has to be passed in full. Spaces left blank are considered to be 'a provocation'. When an item is removed it has to be replaced. *La Prensa* used to sell all over Nicaragua on the day it was printed. The censor has put a stop to that by increasing the time taken to read the paper from two hours to five. The kind of material removed is sometimes politically significant, sometimes absurd. Military details are never printed, but the censorship is not only military, it is also political, it is also barmy. No implicit criticism of Russia or Cuba is ever allowed. Pictures of Mr Brezhnev have been removed, so was a picture of Sarah Miles, so was a picture of an elephant waterskiing in Florida. So was an article by Octavio Paz, one of Latin America's most distinguished writers. Sandinista informers have been planted in the office. The Sandinistas explain all this by claiming that, under Chamorro, *La Prensa* has become 'an instrument whose columns could be bought, with the purpose of destabilising the Government'.

There is also a more unpleasant and personal side to the story of *La Prensa*. Sandinista mobs have demonstrated outside the building. Filled with spontaneous anger over some critical news item they have tried to burn the office and have threatened the lives of the staff. Individual newsagents who sell the paper have also been threatened with arson and death and many have dropped *La Prensa* as a result. In one reference to the staff of *La Prensa*, Borge said that if the *contras* ever got to Managua they would find only dead bodies because the Sandinistas would kill all their enemies. 'We will skin them alive,' he added. And Comandante Humberto Ortega said on 10 October 1981 that 'the staff of *La Prensa* will be the first to be strung up along the highways'. Subsequently questioned about this promise by one of those he had referred to, Ortega dismissed it as 'a rhetorical flourish'.

I met a member of the government mob during a visit to the city graveyard. The graveyard was large and neatly kept. The black and red flag fluttered over several graves, beneath the flag the usual painted wooden cross. The flags marked the graves of the *hijos de la patria*, the children of the fatherland, those killed on the frontier in the patriotic war. Here, at least, there was no sense of a contradiction. Enrolled in a Marxist army, these soldiers lay in Christian graves. One, Daniel Arturo Teller Paz, member of F.S.L.N. Regional Committee VI, had died in April 1983, aged twenty-three, 'kidnapped, castrated, disembowelled'; the Spanish touch.

Just inside the entrance, a young man with long black hair was squatting, beaming contentedly at everyone who passed. He said that he was called Eduardo and that he was an exile from El Salvador. For work he dug graves. This was delightful: a Salvadoran in exile, so he became a gravedigger. He told me that he was also an agent for the D.G.S.E., the political police.

'Lend me fifty bucks,' was one of his first remarks; he spoke that much English. 'Gringo shit' followed shortly afterwards.

Eduardo Melgar Cardona imagined himself a future martyr to the revolution. That was what he wanted to be if he ever grew up. He walked with a limp and told me that he had been wounded fighting with the guerrillas in his country. He said that his brother had been killed three months earlier on the frontier. He showed me his brother's grave. I looked suitably solemn, then read on the gravestone a rather different name to his. 'I *love* to work here,' he said. 'This is my home now.'

Some mourners passed by. They were middle-aged men wearing multi-coloured baseball hats. 'Those people are *contras*,' said Eduardo glancing at them. 'I hate them. American shit.' We went on a tour of the graves. He offered to introduce me to his *jefe*. 'Pretend not to understand Spanish,' he said. 'I want to be an interpreter.' The *jefe* was having a snack in the shade of a tree. 'This man is a gringo shit,' said Eduardo, in Spanish. 'I am the interpreter. All gringos are shit. Ha ha ha.' I beamed in a friendly manner. The *jefe* had the grace to look thoroughly uncomfortable.

We inspected some of the new graves and Eduardo posed heroically in one, his pixie-bearded face peering out of the gaping hole, his arm brandishing a floral cross. He told me how much he hated 'Chamorro', but he couldn't remember which paper he edited. Nicaragua has three newspapers and they are all edited by members of the Chamorro family. There is Carlos Chamorro, the editor of *Barricada*, the *organo oficial del Frente Sandinista de Liberacion Nacional*. There is Ing. Xavier Chamorro, editor of the unaligned *El Nuevo Diario, un periodismo nuevo para el hombre nuevo*. Eduardo was of course thinking of Pedro Chamorro, brother of Carlos and Xavier, and editor of *La Prensa*. There was also a Señorita Chamorro, their sister, who worked in the government press office.

'That man, what's his name? Chamorro, bloody shit', said Eduardo. 'When he is dead I will drink a beer, and you will drink a beer in England.' He said he had been down to the office of the paper, 'What's it called?', and expressed his feelings. It was not difficult to imagine Eduardo at the head of a

Sandinista mob. He, a Salvadoran, was the kind of end-of-the-line idealist who would be used to frighten Pedro Chamorro out of the country.

Eduardo was by this time under the impression that he and I were to spend the rest of my visit together. He was planning a lucrative relationship. He was the most unpleasant man I had met for some time. To get rid of him I arranged a meeting on the following day, for an extended tour of the graveyard; an appointment I never intended to keep. 'Don't ask for soldiers' graves,' were his last words, shouted so that everyone could hear him. 'I hate that word "soldiers". Say *hijos de la patria*. No sweat. Cool.' I could just hear him chanting the party slogan, 'A Yanqui is an enemy of humanity.' No sweat.

The mobilisation of men like Eduardo Cardona is bitterly resented at *La Prensa*, for personal reasons. It has not been forgotten that when the Sandinistas were the guerrillas, *La Prensa* saved Tomás Borge's life. When Borge was seized in the street by Somoza's police he shouted to onlookers, 'I am Tomás Borge, tell *La Prensa*.' The paper immediately printed the news of his arrest, and Borge, rather to his own surprise, was imprisoned and tortured instead of being taken to certain death. The paper at that time was run by Pedro Chamorro's father, Pedro Joaquin Chamorro, who was a fierce opponent of Somoza. Because he was a member of one of the leading families in the country he was considered safe, and his murder in the streets of Managua on the 10 January 1978 so horrified people that it led to the popular insurrection which proved to be the dictator's downfall. Pedro Joaquin Chamorro is now proclaimed a 'Martyr of Civil Liberties'. It has become an obsession with his son, Pedro, to discover who was responsible for his father's death. The matter is being investigated by the Sandinista police and the man in charge of them is the minister of the interior, Tomás Borge. So far the enquiry has been inconclusive.

The official view is the generally accepted one, that Mr Chamorro was murdered by Somocista agents. It was that belief which sparked off the insurrection. It is now known that the actual murderer was a hired gunman, and that the man who hired him *was* a Somocista. But he was not nearly senior enough a figure to order the murder of a Chamorro. What is not yet known is, who ultimately arranged the killing? Since the Sandinistas have benefited so greatly from his father's death, and since they have proved so dilatory in investigating it, it is important for Pedro Chamorro that this question should be answered.

The Sandinista police are not always so ineffective. While I was in Nicaragua they cracked the 'Comrade Ana Maria' case. Despite everything said in Mexico City and La Palma, Ana Maria had been ice-picked to death not by the C.I.A. but by her own comrades in the Salvadoran revolution, by a dissident faction of the F.P.L. The facts, as unearthed by the police, did not emphasise the international importance of events in Central America. Instead the death of Comrade Ana Maria confirmed the essentially personal scale of political life in El Salvador and Nicaragua.

Comrade Ana Maria was christened Mélida Anaya Montes. Ana Maria was her *nom-de-guerre*. She first came to general notice in 1981. Describing herself as 'a leader of the F.M.L.N.', she announced that 'the Salvadoran revolutionary movement has entered into negotiations with the ruling junta'. This statement was promptly denied by both the F.M.L.N. and the F.D.R., the two leading umbrella organisations of the said movement. Comrade Ana Maria, they explained, had either been misquoted or 'was simply stating positions that do not correspond to the views currently held by the F.M.L.N. – F.D.R.'. Black mark for Comrade Ana Maria. Furthermore she was not 'a leader of the F.M.L.N.' – the Farabundo Martí Front for National Liberation – she was merely a second-in-command of the Farabundo Martí Popular Forces of Liberation, the F.P.L., one of the junior member groups of the F.M.L.N. Two black marks for Ana Maria.

Why was Comrade Ana Maria murdered, and who killed her? According to the Sandinista police, she was not killed because she favoured negotiations with 'the ruling junta' – because she did not favour such negotiations. She had favoured them in 1981. At the time of her death in 1983 she was one of the guerrilla faction most opposed to them. History had moved on. The analysis had changed. Was she murdered because she *opposed* negotiations with 'the ruling junta'? No, because she was murdered by fellow members of the minority in the F.P.L. who opposed negotiations even more strenuously than she did. Did she have any other significant disagreements with her fellow revolutionaries, with whom she was in such warm agreement on the issue of negotiations? Yes, she was in a minority of either one or two among the minority of her group which opposed negotiations, on the unrelated issue of whether or not there should be greater integration among the various Salvadoran guerrilla factions. Comrade Ana Maria wanted greater integration. Her fellow comrades in the minority on the issue of negotiations wanted no further integration. Her fellow comrades in the minority lived in Managua. Comrade Ana Maria lived in El Salvador. She made the mistake of spending three nights in Managua, the safe part of the Isthmus as far as she was concerned; and it was there that she was ice-picked while she slept. The Sandinista police knew all this because they raided the house of every resident Salvadoran guerrilla after she was murdered, in an authentic thirst for information. And so they discovered every detail of the plot; not just the ice-picks but the shop receipts for the ice-picks.

Why was she killed with an ice-pick? The police had nothing to say to that. Perhaps she was killed with the ice-pick because she considered herself a Trotskyist and her murderers considered themselves Stalinists. Or perhaps she was killed with an ice-pick because her murderers considered themselves Trotskyists and she had made some ill-advised crack about 'remember what happened to old Trotsky'. In Marxist-Leninist circles the ice-pick question amounts to social gossip, the left-wing equivalent of what little Amy Carter wore on her first day at school.

The murder of Comrade Ana Maria was followed by another sensation. The head of the F.P.L., Comrade Marcial, alias Salvador Cayetano Carpio, alias the celebrated grandfather of the Salvadoran guerrilla movement, committed suicide in Managua. It seemed he was heartbroken by the disintegration of his group. The Sandinista police had discovered that the murder of Ana Maria had been organised by one Rogelio Bazzaglio, a Stalinist member of the F.P.L. He had confessed to everything. Grandfather Carpio had protested to Tomás Borge about the rigour of the police investigation and Borge had replied by inviting him to the jail to verify that Bazzaglio had confessed freely. Bazzaglio not only confirmed this, he insisted he had been right. He said he had used ice-picks to make it look like the brutal work of the C.I.A. Mr Carpio, once a seminarian, like Stalin, had then gone home and shot himself.

Comandante Marcial was an important figure in the Salvadoran revolution. When a murderous struggle broke out between the F.M.L.N. and another group, the Armed Forces of Popular Resistance (F.A.R.N.), it was Carpio as head of the neutral F.P.L. who mediated between the two groups. What does Carpio's death teach us about the nature of the guerrilla movements of Central America? It shows that they are small-scale, personal, violent, clannish affairs, motivated by envy and individual hatred, prepared to use assassination like other political movements use committee meetings, driven by very private, almost family, compulsions. Carpio himself made a distinction between the Sandinistas and other guerrilla movements. The Sandinistas had one *indiscutible* advantage, he said; Somoza, a one-man band who was thoroughly hated. Somoza united them, and their progressive allies, into a formidable opposition. In El Salvador the revolution has no single enemy. The ruling junta is always changing, and its numerous members pop up several times on the same side as the guerrillas. The current president of El Salvador – the leader of the Christian Democrats, the darling of the United States, the moderate man of the centre, that is to say the most right-wing politician in El Salvador apart from *Arena* and Blowtorch Bob – is José Napoleon Duarte. In 1972 Duarte was the presidential candidate of the Salvadoran *Communist* Party. He may well be so again. Carpio once said, 'In El Salvador, the successive puppets have never been able to form a dynasty. They unseat each other, and in the brief period when it's their turn to kill and rob, they fatten till they burst.' Faced with this chimerical enemy, the Salvadoran guerrillas have also become chimerical. Somoza makes a much better enemy than the fourteen or the 244 families of El Salvador.

Only Marxism offers the politicians of Central America a way out of this maze of private interest and corruption, and in El Salvador not even Marxism can do it. Carpio's comments about the puppets of the junta could, in the light of his death, apply equally well to the Salvadoran revolutionaries. All that could certainly be said after the deaths of Carpio and Ana Maria was that the way to the top was from then on clearer for others. Guillermo Manuel Ungo, head of the F.D.R. and once communist vice-presidential partner to Duarte in 1972, is one of them. Ungo's predecessor as head of the F.D.R. was called Enrique Alvarez Cordoba. He too was assassinated. Before he was head of the F.D.R. he was a minister in the junta. Before that he was a member of one of El Salvador's fourteen families. The other man whose prospects improved was Joaquin Villalobos, aged thirty-two. Villalobos is the leader of Lucia's beloved E.R.P., the Maoists. In contrast to Carpio and Ana Maria, Villalobos is in favour of negotiations with the junta. Is he a moderate figure? Not exactly. He believes in, and *practises*, assassinations. Not assassinations of members of the fascist junta: assassinations of revolutionaries. Villalobos once signed a pact with the Military Youth movement, that is with those being trained to lead future military juntas. Then he shot Roque Dalton, a poet and revolutionary and rival, after denouncing him as a bourgeois and a C.I.A. agent – an action since described by Dalton's comrades in the F.A.R.N. as 'a serious misjudgment'. Sometimes the revolutionary leaders of El Salvador make Pancho Villa seem a warm-hearted fellow.

One evening I dined in a lobster restaurant. It was a very good restaurant. The lobster was delicious, the Chilean wine was excellent, as usual. There was even Italian white wine which had been a rarity in Mexico City. Nicaragua was short of rice, coffee, milk, shampoo, soap and many other goods, but this restaurant was well-stocked. It seemed equally popular with the wealthy survivors from the old days and with senior Sandinistas in uniform, and, no doubt, with Salvadoran guerrillas in exile. One of the Sandinistas kept his Fidel Castro cap on throughout the meal. Then, without warning, uproar in the kitchen. The door was open. Four young women could be seen in there and one rat. One woman was sitting on the range. The other three were chasing up and down a duckboard. One was armed with a broom, the two others were taking their chance in line astern. All four were either screaming or laughing. They pursued the rat to the end of the duckboard. When it turned they turned too and hurried back, the rat behind. Then they would turn and chase the rat. There was no calming them. The proprietor actually left her till and swept into the kitchen, but she was too young to rise to the occasion. She joined the hysterical, flat-footed quick march up and down the duckboard. Then somebody closed the kitchen door. The incident made everyone laugh, and the laughter was a relief. There is little fear in Nicaragua, but it is an oppressive place all the same.

After dinner I went to a film show attended by many of the 'internationalists', the serious young idealists who flock to Nicaragua and help the government to conquer illiteracy or censor the press. The film, which was made by an Austrian, purported to show the situation in the Indian Highlands of Guatemala. It was grotesque propaganda and enthusiastically received by this rather uncritical audience. I watched the film sitting beside a man who was not an internationalist; he was an edgy, aggressive man who kept trying to push me off my seat. At first I took him for a Nicaraguan. Later I discovered that he was Guatemalan and a notorious figure. He had once been secretary to President Lucas García of Guatemala, and had worked as liaison officer in the pistachio-coloured death house behind the presidential palace. In 1982 he fled to Panama and identified himself as an agent of the Guerrilla Army of the Poor. There was a feeling at the time that if he was an agent of the E.G.P. he had spent rather a long time with the death squads. There was a girl watching the film called Claudia, who worked for the Sandinista state publishing house. I noticed her because she was small and elegant and actually wore clothes that were coloured rather than khaki. I pointed out the undercover torturer to her and she gazed at his muscular, bespectacled figure with interest. She told me about her hopes of publishing Gabriel García Márquez and Octavio Paz. I decided not to ask her what she thought about Paz's article in *La Prensa* being censored. She probably wouldn't have believed me. Eventually she swept away on the arm of the head of Civil Aviation. It was cheering to be reminded that the world works much the same even after the Revolution.

Nicaragua is a country with very few maps. They have been restricted for reasons of national security. A further problem for travellers is that the names of many streets and some towns have been changed since the civil war. In 1982 I had visited León, the second city in Nicaragua, where some of the fiercest fighting took place. This time I wanted to visit the country's third city, Granada. León is an old city, it was founded in 1524, duly destroyed by earthquake, and moved twenty miles away from its original site under the volcano Momotombo. Its university was founded in 1804, it has the largest cathedral in Central America. It still has a considerable opinion of itself, its local paper is called *El Centroamericano*. In the nineteenth-century intellectual struggle between liberalism and conservatism, a struggle which was waged particularly fiercely in the Hispanic world, León was a centre of liberalism. Granada was the capital of conservative ideas. The liberals were anti-clerical, for freedom of thought and for the freedom of universities. The conservatives were the opposite. These two cities quarrelled so violently in this matter that the people of Nicaragua decided to bring them both down a peg, and founded a new capital, Managua, on the site of an Indian settlement whose only recommendation was that it was halfway between León and Granada.

The Chamorro family once dominated Granada. The Castellóns led León. Somoza, the fascist brute, was from liberal León. After three weeks in Nicaragua I met someone who had known Somoza. What was he like? 'He had a lot of charm. He acted the rogue. If he heard there was a foreign reporter in town he would ring his hotel and tell him to come up to the palace for a few drinks and a cigar.' Somoza was, by this description, teasing, intelligent and likeable. He was also like the Sandinistas in one thing, he censored the press. When people criticised his regime, I was told, 'he would say "Look. There's no hunger in Nicaragua". And if by Nicaragua you meant the cities and the Pacific coast and defined hunger in Honduran or Salvadoran terms, it was true. Unfortunately he had a weakness for massacres. He dropped 500lb bombs on León, his home-town, when there were only 150 Sandinistas there.' He also stole much of the best land in the country, tortured his opponents, exploited the poor and ruled by terror – backed to the very end by President Carter of the United States, the president who believed in human rights. People remember all that long after they have forgotten the charm.

Driving out to Granada I was soon lost. I found myself circling Lake Managua on the road that led back to Honduras. Eventually I came upon a fork and, in the absence of road signs, headed for the Santiago volcano. It has two craters, one awake, one asleep. I drove up to the summit and looked in. There was nothing to be seen, not even the flocks of green parakeets which are said to dive through the sulphur clouds. In Costa Rica I had ascended Irazú, which had last erupted fifteen years earlier; rubbery plants with swollen leaves had been growing directly out of the lava on its slopes. A few days later Irazú came to life and burped 137 times. Its neighbour, Arenal, long thought extinct, had just exploded with such force that it blew away its cone, as well as the campers who were sleeping on the floor of the crater. There is not much point in talking of 'live' and 'dead' volcanoes in Central America. Too many dead ones erupt.

It was a hot, sleepy day. When I reached Granada the city was locked up for the siesta. In a beautiful colonial colonnade, now become a school, two boys were playing an improvised game with bats and a ball, rather like fives or Real Tennis. In such forbidden midday occupations, in deserted cloisters, lie the origins of all games. This game required great judgment and skill, founded on a knowledge of the curve of this one roof and three walls. The game could not have been played anywhere else. On one wall a Sandinista notice-board had been erected. The notice urged the boys to be vigilant and to fight for the Sandinistas. Then there were prayers teaching hatred of Reagan and a love of the gun. This was a church school. The priest had probably put the notices up.

They were a strange assortment, these priests of Central America. In Panama City I had watched one, from New England, give a television show. For half an hour this pitiable wreck of a man pranced before an invited audience, dressed in a black suit and dog collar. 'Let's celebrate Life,' he howled over the noise of the piano; 'Get off your butt, get out of that rut.' All the while he wiggled his hips in a grotesque imitation of the Twist. 'I want you all to go home, look in the mirror and say "Hi, Gorgeous". That's what the Gospel's all about,' he said.

Then he became confidential: 'I used to belong to the old-fashioned Church. And we did you in. We thought we knew everything. But it turned out YOU knew everything. Why shouldn't I dance?' he yelped. 'David danced before the Ark of the Covenant.' On the charitable assumption that he had been brain-damaged at birth, one longed for someone to pull the plug out of his life-support system.

In San Salvador I had spoken to a Monsignore, a dignified and highly-intelligent man, who said that he did not consider a Marxist Government a danger to the country's religion and who denied that the Church should emphasise the ultimate importance of the spiritual over the temporal life. There had been another priest in El Salvador, a Jesuit who supported the guerrillas. Asked if he was aware of the fate of the Church in Cuba he dismissed the savage restrictions imposed there on the grounds that the Cuban Church had committed 'historical sins'. He also complained that in Poland the Pope had organised people 'against the Revolution'; he meant against Poland's Communist Government. And here in Nicaragua there was Father Fernando Cardenal, another Jesuit, and the Minister of Education. He had been prepared to see his own priesthood suspended rather than leave the Government, and had lamented this because Nicaragua was short of priests. Then he had stood silently by, while the government of which he was a member expelled ten priests who had demonstrated because a mass had been interrupted by a Sandinista mob. As Minister of Education his task was to carry out the Sandinista policy of dismantling the Church's influence in the schools. He defended his role on the grounds that he was 'maintaining a Christian presence in the Government'.

These priests were not representative of everyone. There had also been the Benedictines of Esquipulas whose work was to pray and sing the Divine Office, but who found time to organise an effective system of cheap credit for the peasants in their parish. They did this despite all the political problems of Guatemala; but they were not trying to rebuild the entire country, they were just trying to help the poor. And there had been the German priest in Antigua who remembered the Gospel and preached against violence, and who, despite his evident isolation, clung to the hope that there was a Man in the boat who could say to the storm 'Be still'. Such men were the best hope of their people; priests who still insisted on the promises of Christ, and the certainty of eternal life; men for whom the mass still meant more 'than a black cat crossing the path'. But they seemed to be in a minority. In most places the faith of the peasants had outlasted that of their priests.

Granada stands on the shores of Lake Nicaragua, which is connected to the Atlantic by the San Juan river. The lake is ninety miles long and thirty miles wide. Although it is a freshwater lake it is infested with sharks which swim up the river. English and French pirates also used to come up the river at night and sack the city. In 1855 a filibuster from New Orleans, William Walker, took the town and burnt it and nearly conquered Nicaragua. He was eventually repelled and one of those who died fighting him was Juan Santamaria, a boy from Costa Rica. When the Sandinistas came to power, the bones of Juan Santamaria were discovered and returned to Costa Rica in a gesture of international friendship. The reliquary was lodged in a Costa Rican museum. Then it was opened and the Costa Ricans discovered that the relics consisted largely of cattle bones. The Nicaraguans were outraged by this suggestion and demanded the return of the box. It was carried to the Nicaraguan official plane through crowds of Costa Ricans mooing like cows. Once back in Nicaragua it was reburied with full military honours. They honour history in this part of the world, even if the details of it, like the provenance of the bones, are sometimes a little unclear.

Since Granada was so quiet I went down to the beach. A vast iron launch was rusting inexplicably on the lake shore. It was 100 feet long. The machine, useless, abandoned, decomposing into minerals, was more reminiscent of Conrad's Africa than of a revolutionary future. They had tried to launch a little tourism here once, trips out to the Indian islands, that sort of thing, it had not caught on. I found a raffia awning and sat under it, and suffered the heat, and a boy brought me a bottle of warm Coke. A few scrawny cattle meandered into the water, making for a clump of distant reeds. A dog slept on the chair beside me, a monkey rattled its chains in a nearby tree. Some yards offshore a small animal, apparently a racoon, moved smoothly towards the beach, perched on the partly submerged shoulder of a man in a red shirt. A family bathing party, fleeing the heat, waded a good two hundred yards into the lake and bobbed up and down decorously among the sharks. But they weren't nervous. They lived here.

I sucked at the sticky drink and thought about the Sandinistas and decided that if I was a Nicaraguan I would be a reluctant supporter of theirs because they were nationalists; that is, I would support them for the 'wrong' reasons. The struggle between the United States and New Spain seems to me to be a historical quarrel rather than a political one. The people of North America have little idea of religion, but they have a strict public morality. The Latin people are without morality but they are highly religious. The two sides are attracted towards each other, but they also feel mutual contempt. What has failed in New Spain is a religious failure. Christianity could not make these cynical, quick-witted people moral. Marxism might; at least to the extent of providing honest government, something to release them from the greed and violence which have shaped the course of their lives for so long. One theory to explain the collapse of the Mayan civilisation holds that the people were shocked and disheartened by the theological errors of their priests. The Indian astronomers kept on getting it wrong. When the Mayans rose against the priesthood, their social system collapsed. These Spanish people have also been abandoned by their Gods; by liberalism, art, Christianity, just as the Mayans were. Now they are threatened by a country without a past. Faced with the United States they dread the same colonial status as they imposed on the Indians. They are riddled with history; they fear a historical fate.

That was the end of my adventure in Central America. By the lakeshore in Granada I decided to turn for home. I wondered what Cortés would have said if, when he set out in the wake of Columbus, he had foreseen the beach outside Granada. He knew in his bones of the glory to come, would he have known about its eclipse? A Church without the True Cross, unable to protect its buildings from earthquake or idolatry; the gold and silver mines exhausted; the children of the Conquest reduced to beggary, placing their trust in the redundant theories of a Victorian economist; the empire overwhelmed by its own pagan and monstrous child. What a fool time has made of Cortés and his pretensions. He should have turned back to Cuba, to his dice and his saints and his women, and left the Indians with the Gods they honour, against all the odds, to this day.

When I arrived back at London airport the baggage machinery broke down. There were no announcements. We stood there, waiting, for half an hour. The man next to me, an official of the United Nations, said, 'This country gets more Latin American every time I come here.' I looked at the grumpy and self-righteous porters, and at the two silent officials crouched behind a desk marked Information, urgently reading the bingo numbers in their newspapers, and I thought how wrong he was.